Forever Young

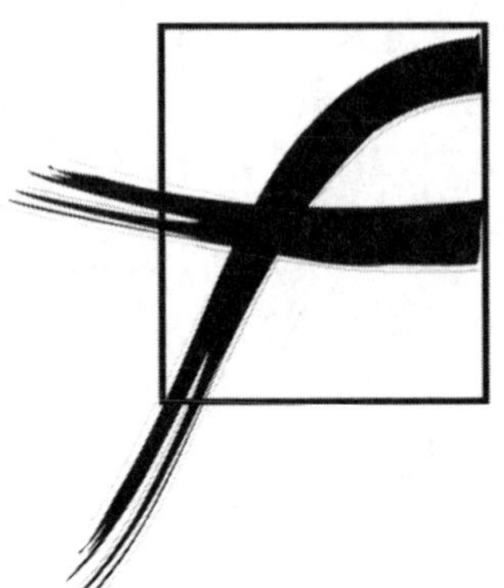

Intersections in Communications and Culture

Global Approaches and Transdisciplinary Perspectives

Cameron McCarthy and Angharad N. Valdivia
General Editors

Vol. 20

PETER LANG
New York • Washington, D.C./Baltimore • Bern
Frankfurt am Main • Berlin • Brussels • Vienna • Oxford

CHRIS RICHARDS

Forever Young

ESSAYS ON YOUNG ADULT FICTIONS

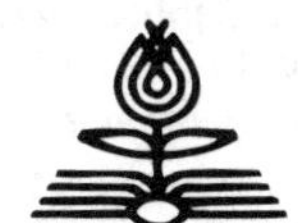

PETER LANG
New York • Washington, D.C./Baltimore • Bern
Frankfurt am Main • Berlin • Brussels • Vienna • Oxford

Library of Congress Cataloging-in-Publication Data

Richards, Chris.
Forever young: essays on young adult fictions / Chris Richards.
p. cm. — (Intersections in communications and culture; v. 20)
Includes bibliographical references and index.
1. Young adult fiction, American—History and criticism.
2. Young adult fiction, English—History and criticism. 3. Block, Francesca Lia—Criticism and interpretation. 4. Buffy, the vampire slayer (Television program)
5. Youth in literature. 6. Identity (Psychology) in literature. 7. Identity (Psychology) in youth. 8. Youth on television. 9. Mass media and youth. I. Title.
PS374.Y57.R53 823'.914099283—dc22 2008015049
ISBN 978-1-4331-0432-9 (hardcover)
ISBN 978-0-8204-9718-1 (paperback)
ISSN 1528-610X

Bibliographic information published by **Die Deutsche Bibliothek**.
Die Deutsche Bibliothek lists this publication in the "Deutsche Nationalbibliografie"; detailed bibliographic data is available on the Internet at http://dnb.ddb.de/.

Cover design by Joni Holst

The paper in this book meets the guidelines for permanence and durability of the Committee on Production Guidelines for Book Longevity of the Council of Library Resources.

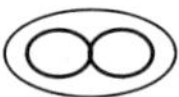

29 Broadway, 18th floor, New York, NY 10006
www.peterlang.com

Printed in the United States of America

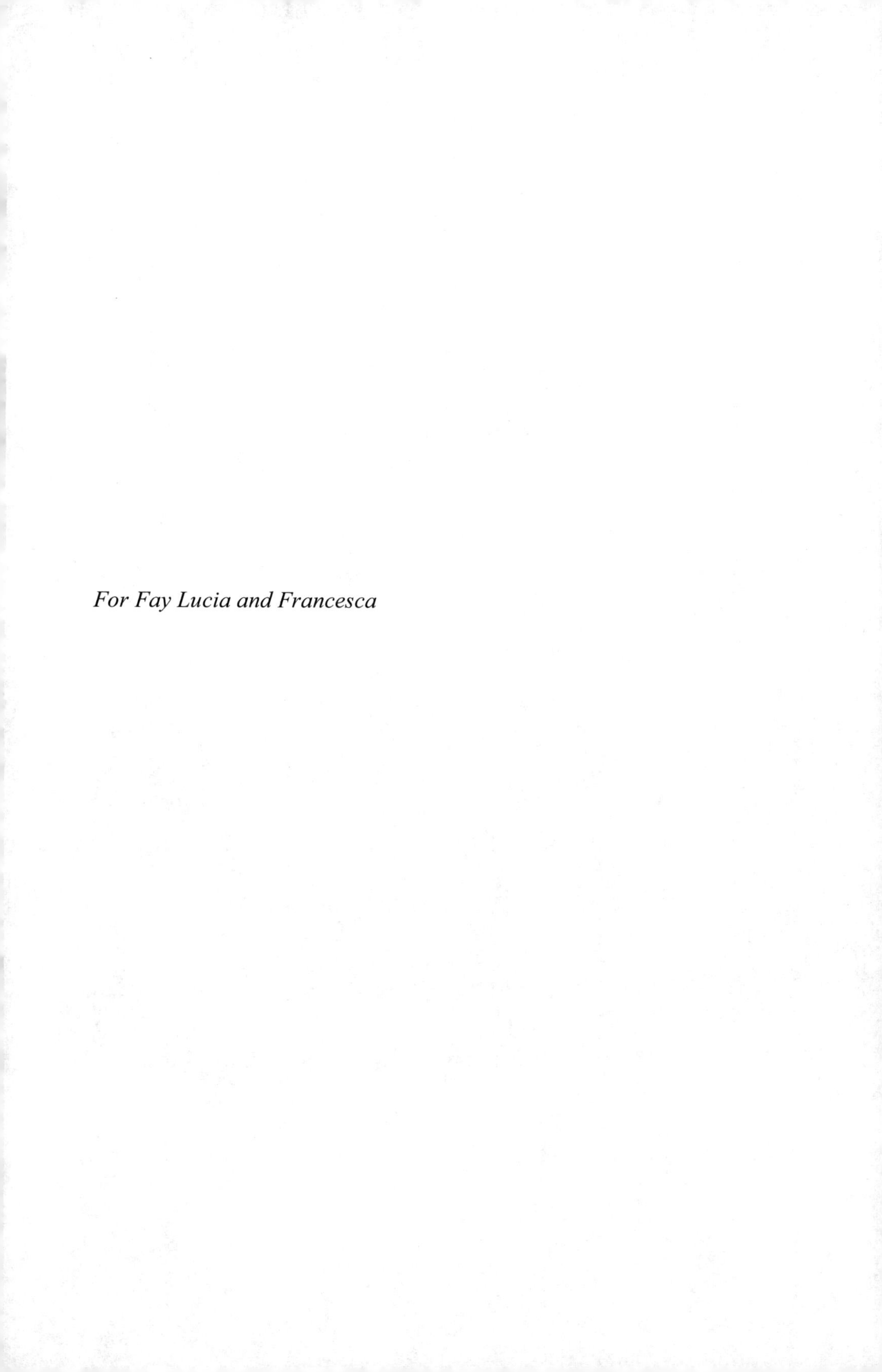

For Fay Lucia and Francesca

Contents

Acknowledgments

First of all, I want to thank Cameron McCarthy for suggesting that I put together a collection of essays for inclusion in this series. It was timely, as I was accumulating several interrelated studies otherwise likely to be published only in various disparate locations. Many of the chapters were first presented at Annual Meetings of the American Educational Research Association. Each one has been extensively revised for inclusion in this book. Chapter Two was presented at the AERA Annual Meeting April 12 2005 in Montreal, and Chapter Three at the AERA Annual Meeting April 11 2007 in Chicago. Chapter Four is an updated version of a paper presented at the AERA Annual Meeting April 1 2002 in New Orleans. An earlier version of this chapter was published as "What Are We? Adolescence, Sex and Intimacy in *Buffy the Vampire Slayer*" in *Continuum: Journal of Media and Cultural Studies* Vol 18 No 1, 121–137 (2004) and is reprinted here with the permission of the publisher, Taylor and Francis. *Continuum* can be located at http://www.informaworld.com. Chapter Five was presented at the AERA Annual Meeting April 11 2007 in Chicago as part of a panel session (Reading Girlhoods: Critical Examinations of Gender in Young-Adult Literature). I'd like to thank Beth Marshall (now of the Faculty of Education, Simon Fraser University, Vancouver, B.C.) for getting the panel together. Chapter Seven was presented at the AERA Annual Meeting in New York, March 25 2008.

An earlier version of Chapter One, "From Readers to Writers? Rethinking 'Young Adult' Fiction" was presented to the Beyond the Book: Contemporary Cultures of Reading conference August 31 2007, University of Birmingham, England. Some parts of Chapter Six were presented as "Dead White People: Sex and 'Race' in *Buffy the Vampire Slayer* and *Angel*" at Bring Your Own Subtext: Social Life, Human Experience and the Works of Joss Whedon – a conference at the University of Huddersfield, England (July 2005).

The time away from teaching to revise and complete these essays was supported by London Metropolitan University's Communication, Cultural and Media Studies Research Capability Fund. I would very much like to thank the Working Group for their positive response to my request. Thanks too to the Department of Education, for making space in the 2007–2008 session for me to complete the work.

I want to thank Debbie Blunden (www.yogatea.net) for introducing me to a dynamic alternative to sitting at the computer, David Blundell for taking over the running of the BA Education Studies programme, and David Buckingham at the Centre for the Study of Children, Youth, and Media for his encouragement.

Closer to home, thanks to Elizabeth Rouse, once again, for her continuing support, and for coming out to the Sierra Nevada to walk the John Muir Trail, despite the mountains and the food.

Last but not least I want to thank both those students whose writing I have quoted and those many others whose work has contributed to planning this book without, in the end, space for its inclusion.

The image on the front cover is reproduced from a monochrome photograph of Donatello's *David* on page 81 of L.R. Rogers (1969) *Sculpture: The Appreciation of the Arts/2,* London: Oxford University Press. The bronze statue of David (c. 1430–1432) by Donatello is normally exhibited in the Museo Nazionale del Bargello in Florence though, at the time of writing, the figure was prone, the object of sophisticated restoration. The image is reproduced here with the permission of the Ministero per i Beni e le Attivita Culturali. No further reproduction or duplication is allowed. The photograph of the author was taken by Sylvia Richards (1924–2008) in the 1960s.

Introduction:

Fictions of Youth

The title of this book – *Forever Young* – really poses a question. It is a familiar title, now a cliché, used repeatedly.[1] But its continuing resonance deserves consideration. Perhaps it is most often understood as unambiguously desirable, the state of being that is most regretted in its passing and to which an endless effort of recovery or preservation is directed (Osgerby, 2001, 2004). A DVD cover for *The Lost Boys* (1987/2004) proclaims: "Sleep all day. Party all night. It's fun to be a vampire." Such a hedonistic reworking of vampire mythology well illustrates the point: images of the immortally young, aging and decline denied, endlessly repeating the pleasures of youthful irresponsibility, have had a wide and persistent allure. More recently, Stephenie Meyer's novel *Twilight* (2005) introduced the god-like Edward Cullen who should have died of influenza in 1918 but lives on, in the twenty-first century, as a beautiful seventeen-year-old boy. But of course the vampire is nothing if not ambivalent and, as a metaphor for the preservation of youth, conveys a burden of suffering and despair. Though hedonistic representations of youth proliferate, the construction of youth and of "adolescence" in particular as also always painful and problematic persists, varying in the balance of excitement to distress from one genre to another.

The essays gathered here examine some recent fictional narratives of youth, sometimes addressed to a so-called "young adult" audience but also clearly a focus of interest for many who are far from young themselves. *Buffy the Vampire Slayer* (1997–2003) is an obvious and prominent example.[2] I also give some attention to the question of how young people represent themselves, mainly in writing, and in this respect the book sustains an interest in how young people participate in the production of stories about being young.[3]

Though there are overarching themes revisited throughout this book, it is important that readers engage with it as a collection of essays rather than the development of a single unified argument. Each chapter was originally written as a distinct case study. Nevertheless, in assembling them here, I have made sometimes quite extensive revisions and have highlighted interrelated themes wherever possible. Differences in focus and method across the various chapters remain and are reminders that this is not the outcome of one cohesive research project. To the contrary, they have been written in the midst of teaching mainly Education Studies undergraduates about children and television, young adult fiction and popular music.

Giving a "Voice"?

When possible and appropriate I have drawn upon some of my students' writing to extend, and to complicate, the arguments that I present. In the last chapter, student writing is the central focus. Giving attention to students' self-representations in this way could be traced through my own involvement with teaching young people, mainly in inner London schools, from the 1970s onwards.[4] But it is a part of a wider practice, within English teaching, of attending closely to what young people themselves write.[5] Indeed, the assumption that "young adult" fiction designates writing for young people by adult professionals alone was challenged in some versions of English teaching in the later 1960s, 1970s and 1980s (see, for example, Searle, 1977; Jones, 2003: 86).

English teaching in those decades saw value in giving a voice to those usually excluded from the domain of professional publishing. Young, and especially young working class, people were a particular focus of concern. In London, probably the best known example of this arose from the activities of the teacher Chris Searle, who published a collection of his young students' poetry as *Stepney Words* in 1971 and followed this with further publication of students' writing such as *The World in the Classroom* (1977). Also in London, in Hackney, the successful development of the café-bookshop *Centerprise* contributed significantly to the dissemination of published writing by non-professional writers.[6]

In 1975, I worked as a supplementary teacher for "West Indian" students in east London and lived just a few blocks from *Centerprise.* I taught at a high school in Leyton, but as I was hardly ever required to act as a teacher in any formal sense, I could "hang out" with a small group of fifteen and sixteen-year- old black boys unconstrained by school routines. I was keen to see student writing as much more than just a matter of assessment and of grading. Though not circulated beyond the school, I was involved in facilitating a black (Afro-Caribbean) students' magazine – *Uptight* (Richards, 1998a). The provision of resources, and a kind of background pedagogic support, for students' writing was certainly a productive challenge to the regime of school lessons, of homework and assessment. But it also, perhaps necessarily, entailed some degree of renunciation of the teacher's responsibility to engage critically with, or encourage self-critical evaluation of, students' writing.[7]

However, the political simplicities condensed in the rhetoric of "giving a voice" to the excluded and marginalized had to be confronted. According to Tom Woodin (2005), by 1980, the year I presented an account of school students writing an arguably "racist" story to the History Workshop conference in Brighton (Richards, 1981/82), the History Workshop group was already becoming "increasingly critical of experiential writing." Through the following years, the effort to develop a mode of teaching sufficiently subtle to allow both the production of young people's own writing and some further critical and recursive dialogue with its writers was considerable (Brooker and Humm, 1989; Moss, 1989; Buckingham, 1990; Jones, 1992; Buckingham and Sefton-Green, 1994; Buckingham, Grahame and Sefton-Green, 1995; Buckingham, 1998; Richards, 1998a, 1998b; Buckingham, 2003). And furthermore, as Gemma Moss (1989) argued, it was not possible to understand adequately what students wrote without a knowledge of the popular resources on which they drew.

Problems with Authenticity

The context of young people's self-representations, in whatever medium, is saturated with popular representations of youth. The "grassroots" publishing initiatives of the 1970s, continuing elements of 1960s counterculture, were perhaps unwilling to acknowledge such a context and were strongly located in a rhetoric of local and experiential authenticity. *Our Lives* (1979), *Jealousy* (1976 and 1978) and *Stepney Words* (1971), the latter cited by Woodin (2005) as containing "despondent" and "unhappy stuff," were all presented as giving a voice to young authors. Taken together, such publications implied that, where authorship is located in youth, the "authentic" voice of young people is somehow guaranteed by a proper degree of misery. Moreover, writing, at that time, was undoubtedly construed as a medium for truth, confession and testimony by contrast with the artifice of commercial media forms.

In the wider "professional" publication of "young adult" fiction, a related rhetoric of authenticity is evident. *The Outsiders* (S. E. Hinton, [1967] 1970), often identified with the emergence of contemporary young adult fiction, is repeatedly marketed as the "real thing." Susan Eloise Hinton is quoted on the inside front cover of the 1988 Lions Teen Tracks (London: Collins) edition thus:

> I never set out to be a ground breaker or to be controversial. I just wanted to tell the truth about teenage life and to tell it the way it really is. Most adults don't remember, or don't want to remember the emotional intensity and the idealism of being a teenager. That's what makes my work different. Mostly I just remember real well

> what it was like to be a teenager. Some of the problems change, but the feelings don't.

The distance implied by her self-positioning as an adult looking back is firmly countered with the line: "S. E. Hinton's first novel, THE OUTSIDERS, was published when she was seventeen." In a U.S. Penguin Classics edition (2006), Jodi Picoult claims in her introduction that *The Outsiders* "revolutionized the genre of young adult fiction, by giving voice to a generation that had not been allowed to speak for itself" (Picoult, in Hinton, 2006: p. viii). The back cover claims that "Defying convention, the groundbreaking novel became a touchstone of honesty and excellence in its genre." The Puffin Modern Classics edition (2003) has a brief introduction by Julia Eccleshare (Puffin Modern Classics series editor), making similar claims:

> Ponyboy's story, told in a direct, first-person voice, was written when S. E. Hinton was only seventeen herself. Maybe because of that, it is a miracle of honesty. Certainly, in the mid 1960s when it was first published, its ring of authenticity gave it great credibility and immediate appeal...Some things about adolescence remain unchanging. The struggle to find an identity and the feelings of alienation are things all teenagers must work through...S. E. Hinton knew the boys and the society she describes. She tells it straight. (Eccleshare in Hinton, 2003).

Picoult develops her commentary from Hinton's own observations about the failure of adult memory:

> Long ago, Carol Gilligan suggested that growing up involves forgetting the painful parts of adolescence – but at what cost? Could the careful examination of who we are and who we aren't that is endemic to adolescence somehow become a casualty during the transition to adulthood? ...Perhaps instead of expecting teens to just "grow up already," adults should be more willing to "grow down" – recalling what it felt like, as a teenager, to believe you could change the world... (Picoult in Hinton: 2006: p. xv)

Neither introduction, and despite the Puffin Modern Classics' self-description as "The Best Writing for Children," seems to address young people in particular. These are introductions primarily for adult readers. The value of the novel is constructed here in terms of its capacity to provide adult readers with a "reality" they can otherwise no longer access – and if the date of original publication risks any historical distancing of its portrayal of youth, thus undermining such a claim, then "adolescence" is characterized as reassuringly "unchanging," "timeless." Christine Griffin (1993) noted in a review of academic representations of youth that "adult society constructs [youth/adolescence] as simultaneously strange and familiar" and that it "remains the focus of adult fears and pity, of voyeurism and longing" (Griffin, 1993: 23). The logic of such an adult fascination with youth drives a persistent need for authenticity in its representation.

It is consistent with such a demand for authenticity that often first novels and autobiographies may be positioned in terms very similar to those employed in promoting "young adult" fiction as a "crossover" genre.[8] *This Boy's Life* (1990) and *The Basketball Diaries* (1978/1995), both also produced as films starring Leonardo Di Caprio, are prominent among many examples of the construction of youth as a matter of compelling interest to adults. The Harper Perennial edition of *This Boy's Life* (1990) claims that "In this unforgettable memoir of boyhood in the 1950s, we meet the young Toby Wolff" and that his "growing up is at once poignant and comical." Similarly, the cover copy for *The Basketball Diaries* (1995) invites readers into "a diary of unparalleled candor" in which Jim Carroll "conveys his alternately hilarious and terrifying teenage existence." Publishers' marketing discourse privileges writing that allows apparently unmediated access to experience, and to experience given most value when it is authentically intense and contradictory.

Two novels perhaps ambiguously located between "young adult" fiction and the first novel/autobiography category are worth noting here as further examples of the marketing emphasis on "authenticity." Shelley Stoehr's *Crosses* (1991) is presented as, even more immediately than S. E. Hinton, a "voicing" of teenage experience, written as the bleak trace of self-mutilation – "Shelley has been called 'one of the new young breed of truth-telling young adult writers' (Horn Book)." More recently, in the marketing of *Twelve* (2002), Nick McDonell is revered for his *insider's* sharp and satirical depiction of wealthy high school kids in Manhattan. Hunter S. Thompson is quoted on the cover of various editions: "Nick McDonell is the real thing, a powerful young writer with the look of a dangerous freak and very sharp teeth. The ratio of age to talent is horrifying. His trick is he writes the truth. I'm afraid he will do for his generation what I did for mine."

Though this rhetoric of "authenticity" may seem to favor, predominantly, accounts of male teenage life and genres of writing variously understood as realist, it is also evident, as a mark of value, in the reviewing of fantasy. For example, the sequel to Stephenie Meyer's *Twilight* (2005), *New Moon* (2007a) carries "Praise for *Twilight*" from *The Times*: "Her story, recounted in hypnotic, dreamy prose, encapsulates perfectly the teenage feeling of sexual tension and alienation." So even in this genre, amidst the supernatural, readers are assured of an encounter with the emotional reality of adolescence. The reputation of *Buffy the Vampire Slayer*, for adults, was also secured in part through its "insights" into the pain and trouble of youth (see Chapter Four).

However, in concluding this section, it needs to be reiterated that the notion of authenticity is problematic because it contributes to the separation of texts judged to be bearers of truth from those, implicitly "derivative," appearing to draw on popular precedents (Moss, 1989). But all narratives, including those reporting the "raw experience" of teenage life in supposedly more "straight," unmediated forms, need to be read as reworkings of available discourses (see Jenkins, 2006), as fictions of youth rather than the simple truth of their authors' experience.

Age Phases

To conclude this introduction, I want to turn now to the troubled question of "age phases," an issue also explored further in the next chapter. Though it has been argued that schooling is now somewhat marginal to young people's involvement in popular cultural consumption (Willis with Jones, Canaan, and Hurd, 1990), schools have a continuing significance in structuring the lives of young people. Most obviously the division of youth into age phases, integral to the arrangement of virtually all educational systems, also plays some part in structuring the wider market in commodities attracting young people. Participation in particular stages of schooling is partly constitutive of young people's lived cultural experience. The ordering of age phases may be unstable and the boundaries between them blurred, but some sequential "development" through childhood and youth towards maturity is widely embedded institutionally (Buchmann, 1989; Lesko, 2001). It is not surprising then that many of the popular cultural texts associated with youth also represent them in school settings.

However, there is no straightforward equivalence, and consistency, between the age phases constructed in discourses prominent in schooling and those employed elsewhere. For example, the age phase referent of "young adult" appears to shift significantly from one discourse to another. Where the context is primarily educational, it appears to refer to those between twelve and eighteen, though variations on that span do arise. In the wider commercial book market it may well refer to those between seventeen and thirty, but again some variation on this is common. It is a category circulating in reviews and publishers' promotions and is largely confined to exchanges between adult participants in the field of book selling and its associated activities. In this respect, "young adults" are not often directly addressed as such and the category serves more as a classificatory device, mapping correspondences between texts and age phases. In gateways to fiction such as school libraries, public libraries, bookstores and online booksellers, categories such as "children's literature" and "young adult fiction" serve as regulatory devices attempting to sustain distinctions likely to be given most attention by their adult users.

But such categories are not salient *between* young people in the way that, for example, film classifications have often been. The currency of such classifications in young people's experience has been indicative of struggles by young people to counter the power that adults exercise over them. Gaining access to films, and more recently videos and DVDs designated as adult has, to some extent, signaled a refusal to be positioned as a child (Buckingham, 1996). Certainly, young people no longer wishing to be addressed as children may avoid books classified as "for children" but there seems little evidence of, or need for, an active effort to access categories more associated with adult users. Occasionally, particular titles, genres or authors may generate such interest (Sarland, 1991). No doubt a more emphatic exercise of adult power over access to books would produce such a dynamic. But, comparatively, books, with the accumulated legitimacy of old media, are now usually regarded as more beneficial than visual and electronic media, and less "graphic" than music (hip hop, most obviously), films and computer games in their representation of violence and of sex, if not their use of language (Bragg, 2000, 2001, 2002; Barker and Petley, 2001). They rarely attract the kind of public debate associated with other media, though Melvin Burgess, in Britain, has briefly succeeded in achieving some notoriety with the publication of, for example, *Junk* (1996), *Lady: My Life as a Bitch* (2001) and *Doing It* (2003) (see Rosen, 1997; Fine, 2003).

In the USA, however, there is rather more evidence of some continuing contestation of access to a wide variety of fiction in educational settings (Jenkins, 2006: 192–205). For example, PABBIS – Parents Against Bad Books in Schools – maintains a quite elaborate website (http://www.pabbis.com) dedicated to exposing the provision of morally "offensive" writing, both new fiction and established "literary" works, in schools. Though not, on the whole, in Britain, the Harry Potter books have been especially subject to controversy (Jenkins, 2006). Even so, these controversies seem largely to be conducted between adults and to have little significance for young people.

Where films and videos are classified, the categories do not indicate the audience for whom these texts may have been made or even that to which they are marketed. The categories indicate, to the contrary, exclusions (no one below the age of…) or, with the most open category, everyone but not any audience in particular. The warning stickers on CDs indicate "explicit lyrics" but do not thus position them as appropriate for any particular audience. The "young adult" category has some continuing, if confused, meaning in book publishing, but in the wider field of popular media it is rare indeed. There are no "young adult" films and TV shows, but there are, of course, plenty of teen movies, and "teen TV" has had a substantial presence in the past twenty years. To categorize these products as "young adult" would imply a circumscription, and reduction, of the audience in accord with regulatory interests.

The commercial imperative in the production of popular teen media is to position them for both a "teen" and a "younger adult" market. So these texts offer youth as a site of adult fascination and, often in addition, as a representation of a lifestyle characterized as "youthful" but extending at least into what was once "early middle age." The production of these films and TV shows is largely an adult matter, though of course young people perform in them, enacting the attractions, if also the vicissitudes, of "youthfulness." The historical context of these adult preoccupations is outlined in Bill Osgerby's extension of the analysis offered by Bourdieu (1986):

> The rise of the "greying youth" market in both Europe and the US...could be seen as a facet of [a] new "ethic of fun" – notions of "youthful" hedonism coming to define the expressive, consumption-oriented lifestyles of an ascendant faction of the middle class. (Osgerby, 2004: 58)

An insistence on the pleasure of consumption and the obligation to have "fun," and thus to continue to appear to live a "youthful" lifestyle, can be traced through many of the most popular media texts of recent years. From television, *Friends* and *Sex and the City* are pre-eminent instances of a "younger adult" rather than "young adult" market, with some of the sexual and homosocial behavior attributed to "teenage" life now elaborated through characters in their twenties and thirties.

However, even among TV shows that might well be classed together as employing wit and humor and youthful performers, the "ethic of fun" is not quite as univocal as it may appear. *Buffy the Vampire Slayer,* for example, though often successful as comedy, also represented "youth" as profoundly troubled and painful, really not "fun" at all. This might suggest, consistent with Griffin's (1993) comment, that adult fascination with "youth" is poised between an envy of other people's pleasures and a displacement of trouble from "maturity." Together "fun" and "trouble," located in youth, sustain its currency as an image of an unsettled, irresponsible and exciting but also therefore emotionally risky lifestyle (Osgerby, 2004: 61). If there is "fun" in consumption, often what is consumed satisfies a more contradictory fascination with trouble and pleasure combined.

What Follows…

This collection is heterogeneous in its attention to various media forms. The argument for such variety is made rhetorically by juxtaposing chapters on television with others on novels and music, but can be stated more explicitly. Rather than assume a sequential displacement of old media forms, such as the novel, these forms are to some extent repositioned and perhaps "reworked" in the context of the electronic and new media. The proliferation of new media is a current and obvious concern (Sefton-Green, 1998; Buckingham, 2000; Livingstone, 2002), but the older print media have a continuing presence and, in combination with music, television, the Internet and film, figure in the emerging patterns of convergence identified in recent years (Jenkins, 2006). This is a book not only about "fiction," but about "fictions" across the media.

Chapter One focuses further on the meaning of the category "young adult" and the emergence of online writing by young people. The second and fifth chapters focus on the "young adult" author Francesca Lia Block: first of all exploring online fan, consumer review and censorship lobbying activities in relation to her work, then examining two of her novels in some detail, with particular attention to the themes of vulnerability, translucence and objectification. The third chapter examines the work of Melvin Burgess and Mark Haddon, two British writers associated with the youth market in fiction. Chapter Four and Chapter Six discuss the TV show *Buffy the Vampire Slayer,* first with a particular emphasis on sex and intimacy in the representation of "adolescence" and later, following some aspects of Richard Dyer's (1997) exploration of the association of whiteness with sterility and death, tracing the meanings of whiteness through several male characters. The final chapter returns to London to look at autobiographical writing by students asked to focus on the place of music in their experience – another source for "fictions of identity."

Chapter One

Young People Writing Online

Introduction

The idea of "young adulthood," if examined in close alliance with both the history of children's literature and the formation of a discourse of "adolescence," can be located at least as early as the later decades of the nineteenth century (see Graff, 1997; Lesko, 2001; Osgerby, 2001). To begin with, this chapter looks at the category "young adult," tracing its emergence initially in library and educational provision for young people. Second, it considers how the recent production of writing by young people online contributes to a redefinition of what "young adult" fiction means.

Nancy Lesko's (2001) book *Act Your Age!* focuses, in particular, on the late nineteenth and early twentieth centuries and locates adolescence in the context of colonial and racial ideologies. Adolescence, she argues, is constructed as a stage in a developmental theory of human growth inescapably tied to the belief that ontogeny repeats phylogeny – that individual progress to maturity replicates the progress of human societies to civilization or, indeed, their failure to achieve it. From this perspective, "adolescence" becomes the locus of anxieties around both young people and the society as a whole; to progress through and pass beyond "adolescence" is seen as crucial to the full maturity of individuals and the well-being of "advanced" societies, such as those of Britain and the United States. "Risk" in adolescence is thus emblematic of wider concerns about the maintenance and future of the social order (see also Rose, 1984; Buckingham, 2000). The work of "guiding" and "governing" those in "adolescence" – through schooling, the scouts and organized sport – is integral to the continued health of the "leading" nations of the world. In this there is some precedent for the emergence of a "literature" more finely graded than what "children's literature" alone allows – a literature constituted as that body of texts most appropriate in aiding those positioned as "struggling" to grow up, to move out of childhood to become adult. Given such an imperative, the constitution of such a category (whatever it might be called) and the selection and production of texts appropriate to it must remain firmly a matter for "responsible" and "informed" adults.

Informed by the discourse of "adolescence," young adult is a category unlikely to function independently of the powerfully naturalizing themes of growth, development, and maturation. Lesko argues,

> I suggest that a dominant aspect of the discourse on adolescence is its location within panoptical time, within a time framework that compels us – scholars, educators, parents, and teenagers – to attend to progress, precocity, arrest, or decline. Adolescence both makes and marks time. The developmental framework is simultaneously colonial (with privileged, invisible viewers and hypervisible, temporalized, and embodied others) and administrative (ranking, judging, making efficient and productive). (Lesko, 2001: 113)

Within the institutional domain of education, the persistence of the discourse of "adolescence" as a common sense about young people makes, as Lesko suggests, other ways of addressing them difficult to establish. If young people are routinely construed as other, often constructed as irrational, as biologically ensnared within bodies beyond their control, then whatever they may have to say is always already disqualified as "temporary," as hormonally tainted. Usually, at least on the basis of age alone, adults do not have to engage with any comparable presumption of the limited credibility of their utterances. "Adolescence" is an oppressive discourse, highlighted in Lesko's work through a series of sometimes unexpected parallels:

> Postcolonial scholarship offers broad, incisive, and useful critiques of Western knowledge, which help place the facts of adolescence into an unfamiliar perspective. If we take common attributes of adolescence – for example, they are emotional, confused, controlled by hormones, unstable – as a *set of relations* rather than as the natural qualities of people between the ages of 12 and 19, we begin to emphasize the processes of producing and consuming certain knowledge about the inferiority of youth. (Lesko, 2001: 124)

The discourse of "adolescence" circulates widely, but it is within particular institutional settings where it most powerfully informs relations between social actors, the social organization of space, and the actions and responsibilities of participants. Schools, in particular, are where "adolescence" is lived (in part "produced" and certainly sustained). Young people are variously positioned as "adolescent," as "teen/teenagers," as "kids," as "youth," as "pupils," "students," "young adults." Such subject positions are produced in various adult discourses about young people and are integral to the continuing struggle between "young" and "old." "Young adult" is most often encountered in those discourses closely allied with educational settings. Indeed, as I have suggested, it has very little currency in the wider context of popular media culture, where "teen" has been the main, and more commercial, category.

A further issue to note here is that the struggle between "youth" and "adulthood" is constructed differently in class terms (Buchmann, 1989). Bourdieu (1993) argues that:

> At the very least one ought to analyse the differences between different categories of "youth," or, to be brief, at least *two* types of "youth." For example, one could systematically compare the conditions of existence, the labour market, the time management, etc...., of "young people" who are already in work, and of adolescents of the same (biological) age who are students. (Bourdieu, 1993: 95)

There is a continuing need to differentiate "youth" in such terms, though, as Bourdieu also acknowledges, differences cannot be construed in simple polarities:

> In one case, you have a universe of adolescence...one of provisional irresponsibility: these "young people" are in a kind of social no man's land, they are adults for some things and children for others, they have it both ways...between these extreme positions – the bourgeois student at one end and, at the other, the young worker who does not even have an adolescence – one finds nowadays all the intermediate positions. (Bourdieu, 1993: 95–96)

"Young Adult" Fiction in Educational Discourse

According to the *Voice of Youth Advocates'* two-hundred-year chronology of developments in young adult library services provision "young people" or "children and young people" were the most widely used categories before the Second World War. For example, in 1930, the Young People's Reading Roundtable (YPRRT) was formed, and it is only in 1944 that "young adult" rather than "young people" appears, for example, in bibliographies published by the *Library Journal*. In 1948, "teenage" and "teen" also appear more frequently, though without displacing the recently established preference for "young adult." At the 1948 YPRRT program, 1,500 people came "to hear *Tops with Teens* columnist Sheila John Daly and marketing consultant Eugene Gilbert" (see Osgerby, 2001). Since then, the terms have coexisted, but "young adult" figures most often in exchanges *between* adult participants in educational and associated sites, and where young people themselves are addressed "teen" or some close variant of it is far more likely to be highlighted. "Young adult" is thus less a subject position which young people might actively "take up" and more a classificatory device, and where the intent is to draw the attention of young people, and perhaps also to sell to them, "teen" dominates.

In the United States, the American Library Association (ALA) has a considerable history of promoting, supporting, and sustaining young adult fiction as a distinctive field. It has a number of annual awards and events through which the category is made visible and, often, defended against critics mostly positioned as outside and to the political right of this liberal, progressive organization. The American Library Association represents itself as "the oldest and largest library association in the world." Since 1957 it has had a division "serving" young adults – originally the Young Adult Services Division (YASD), separating from the Children's Library Association, and renamed the Young Adult Library Services Association (YALSA) in 1992. However, the ALA's involvement with "young people" dates back somewhat earlier, with the Association's activities in this field including an emphasis on "fiction and reading for the young" at the Boston ALA conference in 1879 and, in 1896, links with the National Education Association (NEA), to which, in 1905, G. Stanley Hall spoke on "What Children Read and What They Ought to Read" (see *Voice of Youth Advocates*, 200 years of young adult library services history).[1]

The ALA sustains the category of "young adult fiction" through a variety of awards governed by quite finely differentiated criteria. The Michael L. Printz award was established to recognize books that exemplify "literary excellence in young adult literature." The Alex Awards "recognize that many teens enjoy and often prefer books written for adults, and...assist librarians in recommending adult books that appeal to teens." The award is named after Margaret Alexander Edwards, a "young adult specialist" who "firmly believed that adult books are as beneficial toward enhancing and enriching the minds of young adults as designated 'teen books'." In addition, the Margaret A. Edwards Award, introduced in 1988, "honors an author's lifetime achievement for writing books that have been popular over a period of time. It recognizes an author's work in helping adolescents become aware of themselves and addressing questions about their role and importance in relationships, society, and in the world."[2] In these brief descriptions there are elements of a discourse valuing texts primarily in terms of their "literariness," but, somewhat separately, there are those texts valued more through a kind of therapeutic discourse in which adolescence is a problematic time to which ameliorative resources are properly devoted. The production of fiction for young people, and its selection and provision, are integrally connected to the institutional ordering of youth in terms of age phases and their corresponding educational sites. Though more subdued, there are continuities with the moral discourse evident in G. Stanley Hall's concern with what the young "ought" to read. In addition to the activities of library associations, in the United States the National Council of Teachers of English has, within it, the Assembly on Literature for Adolescents of the NCTE. The assembly, abbreviated to ALAN, began in November 1973. It is described as "made up of teachers, authors, librarians, publishers, teacher-educators and their students, and others who are particularly interested in the area of young adult literature." The assembly bestows an award on those "who have made outstanding contributions to the field of adolescent literature. The recipient may be a publisher, author, librarian, scholar, editor, or servant to the organization."[3] Though in its title the slightly more clinical "adolescent" is retained, the contribution to the separation of "young adult" fiction both from children's literature and from general fiction is significant. In particular, it is worth restating the obvious – that the constitution of "adolescence" through education – the gathering together of young people in age phase cohorts – is itself crucial to the formation of the readership "young adult" fiction claims to address. Moreover, the articles published by the ALAN review imply, in common with the ALA awards, that "adolescence" is the site of trauma and difficulty and that either through realistic reflection of "problems" or through "literary" quality, reading can facilitate growth, development, and emotional progress. Implicitly, childhood is relatively calm and untroubled and adulthood typically settled and stable. Adults, thus removed from this zone of difficulty, can address those somewhat adrift within it, as precarious others to be led to safety.

The ALAN REVIEW's homepage defines its purpose as to publish:

> reviews of and articles on literature for adolescents and the teaching of that literature: research studies, papers presented at professional meetings, surveys of the literature, critiques of the literature, articles about authors, comparative studies across genre and/or cultures, articles on ways to teach the literature to adolescents, and interviews of authors.

It defines its audience as:

> classroom teachers of English in middle, junior, and senior high schools. Other readers include university faculty members in English and/or Education programs, researchers in the field of adolescent literature, librarians, authors, publishers, reading teachers and teachers of other related content areas.

Participation and agency in the arena defined by the ALAN REVIEW is restricted to adults, and primarily to those who hold professional status within educational settings.

In Britain the construction of the field of "young adult" fiction is similarly dominated by a discourse in which participation is legitimate for adult professionals. Claimed as the UK's first national conference on Young Adult Fiction in November 2004, *Turning Point* explicitly states its position: "Sorry, no under 18s: Turning Point is aimed at writers and people involved in promoting YAF, rather than its core readers."[4] The exclusion is also implicit in the conference location: at Nottingham Trent University's Clifton campus "10 minutes by car from junction 24 of the M1 and the same by taxi from Nottingham's main train and bus stations." Though the stance is not entirely unapologetic, this is a striking example of that discourse in which young people are neither expected to be producers nor significant participants in debates around the fiction that is supposedly written for them.

Such a discourse is not always monolithic and other inflections are evident. For example, in March 2004, some eight months before the Nottingham Trent conference, the Institute of Ideas in London (in association with Hodder's Children's books) held a one-day event, given a significantly "pop" inspired title *Teenage Kicks*,[5] in which young people participated and whose contributions are recorded in the conference report. In the United States, VOYA, though also defined through its adult professional action on behalf of young people, presents, in its April 2007 editorial, an account of the field placing far more emphasis on the permeability of the boundary between adult professionals and young people. Other initiatives making a comparable effort to shift "young adult" writing away from the exclusive dominance of its adult providers include Merlyn's Pen,[6] Pomegranate Words,[7] and The Write Stuff Club.[8]

The VOYA editorial is worth some more detailed attention. It is entitled *A Revolution Worth Celebrating* and claims that the journal *Voice of Youth Advocates* aims "not only to review teen materials but also to foster intellectual freedom and youth participation." The editor, Cathi Dunn MacRae, recounts her own experience as a YA librarian:

> Because I couldn't imagine doing my job without asking teens what they wanted in their library, I always started a Young Adult Advisory Board (YAAB).
>
> In the 1990s, devoted teen writers turned up every Saturday morning at the library for our writing group, advised by local professional writers...and each other...Yet beyond our booklet of their writings, school literary journals, or national contests, few venues for their work existed. (www.voya.com Accessed May 17 2007)

For nine years, VOYA has run a *Notes from the Teenage Underground* column and, though submissions were usually made through adult intermediaries, MacRae notes that now "teens who find VOYA on the Web send their own submissions, growing savvy about how to get published." She continues,

> This Celebration of Teen Writing [the theme of the April 2007 issue] is possible thanks to the Internet and Web 2.0, where young writers are visible blogging, making MySpace or Facebook pages and Web sites, creating original works from fanfiction to videos, and joining writing communities online. (www.voya.com Accessed May 17 2007)

Further initiatives associated with VOYA are cited:

> The nation is currently at perhaps only the beginning of a revolution in youth-produced media in print, online, and broadcast formats, says Anthony Bernier in his introduction to Youth Information-Seeking Behavior II[9]
>
> ...after finding VOYA on the Web, [Elisabeth Wilhelm] submitted her own top ten teen writing sites to *Notes from the Teenage Underground* (VOYA April 2005). As VOYA's Youth Correspondent, she attended the United Nations World Summit on the Information Society in Tunisia to accept an award for her online teen writing community, Absynthe Muse...(www.voya.com Accessed May 17 2007)

There are some tensions in this piece between a discourse in which young people are encouraged and supported by adult mentors and one recalling the language of 1960s countercultural activism – in this instance suggested by the idea of a "teenage underground," implicitly "out there" and just occasionally visible in VOYA itself or on the Web. Indeed, the "revolution" here appears to be one in which "authentic" youth productivity is given "expression" through online activity. More specifically, the implication may be that VOYA serves as a "cool hunter," locating and connecting teenage writers to publishers (Kenway and Bullen, 2001; Osgerby, 2004). Ultimately the editorial seeks to reconcile these differing emphases by positioning VOYA as a forum and facilitator for youthful "self-expression." Though this is, as I have suggested, a significant deviation from the somewhat closed professional discourse of "young adult" publishing in the *Turning Point* example, there is little evidence of any consistent argument with the terms of that discourse. Furthermore, "youth" remains undifferentiated and questions about what kind of young people might access these routes to publication are not posed. The VOYA editorial is substantially devoted to promoting the journal and other publications from Scarecrow Press and, in this respect, like the *Turning Point* (November 2004) conference[10] and the Hodder sponsored *Teenage Kicks* (March 2004), there is a commitment to the further market promotion of "young adult" fiction, a category, in book publishing, regarded as commercially "hot" in recent years (Quart, 2003).[11]

However, at the same time that "young adult" fiction has acquired a particular commercial impetus, the Internet has perhaps undermined the more regulatory function of the category of "young adult" fiction. The Internet facilitates access to, and the production of, texts only very loosely mapped into divisions of age phase appropriateness. The dissemination of texts from adults to young people within educationally framed relationships is marginal to the practices of Internet, "transmedia" promotion (Jenkins, 2006). The selling of texts follows the logic of marketing, not of educational regulation, and thus the educational location of fiction associated with the "young adult" category is now somewhat less evident in its promotion.

There is some evidence that, in the past ten years, some of what had previously been categorized as "young adult" fiction has been repositioned in a wider "youth-as-lifestyle" market (Richards, 2007) where, arguably, new identifications as "youthful" adults are in play (Pini, 2001: 168). Some authors, identified as writing for children and young people of school age, have also produced texts quite deliberately beyond the bounds of classroom use and in explicit competition, or collusion, with the wider field of popular media. In Britain, Melvin Burgess acknowledges and is enthusiastic about the new media context of young people's reading *and* asserts the importance of print fiction – and of his own novels – for teenage readers. His writing is discussed in Chapter Three.

Online Writing

To investigate young people's literacy practices with the expectation of uncovering an "underground" where new fiction is flourishing risks perpetuating assumptions deriving from 1960s counter-cultural activity. Rather than such an "underground," there is a far more fragmented and diverse array of activity, much of it strongly oriented to mainstream publishing. Certainly there is some evidence of extended prose constructed to sustain narratives across many pages, but such extended pieces of writing seem to proliferate mainly in the context of fan fiction. Indeed, Henry Jenkins, an energetic figure in the documentation of fan productivity, has provided evidence of young people, fans of *Harry Potter*, producing significant elaborations from the novels themselves:

> Flourish started reading *The X-Files* fan fiction when she was ten, wrote her first Harry Potter stories at twelve, and published her first online novel at fourteen. She quickly became a mentor for other emerging fan writers, including many who were twice her age or more. Most people assumed she was probably a college student. Interacting online allowed her to keep her age to herself until she had become so central to the fandom that nobody cared that she was in middle school. (Jenkins, 2006: 178)

Jenkins' case is that becoming a writer is no longer a process contained by the formal pedagogy of adult-to-child instruction. He continues:

> Many young authors began composing stories on their own as a spontaneous response to a popular culture. For these young writers, the next step was the discovery of fan fiction on the Internet, which provided alternative models for what it meant to

> be an author. At first, they might only read stories, but the fan community provides many incitements for readers to cross that last threshold into composing and submitting their stories. And once a fan submits, the feedback he or she receives inspires further and improved writing. (Jenkins, 2006: 178–179)

But as Jenkins himself also suggests, the practice he outlines may not be one in which forms such as the "novel" figure as the distinct works of individuals. It may be that, along with many other shorter forms, the substance of this practice is composed of traces of transactions between fans. In Jenkins' terms, this is more similar to a "traditional folk practice" (Jenkins: 2006: 179). It seems probable that, in a broad quantitative sense, most online "texts" are not "products" corresponding to those circulating in print publishing. The great majority of online production seems to involve the posting of relatively brief items (poems, short stories, personal anecdotes), and the embedding of such items in exchanges among participants in various sites.

The scale and variety of activity is so great that some means of classifying what is going on is desirable. In particular, it is necessary to consider whether Jenkins' vision of communities of practice in which exchanges among peers prevail is perhaps a little optimistic in its emphasis on the diminution of divisions between participants:

> Because the *Harry Potter* fandom involved both adults and children, it became a space where conversations could occur across generations. In talking about media pedagogies, then, we should no longer imagine this as a process where adults teach and children learn. Rather, we should see it as increasingly a space where children teach one another and where, if they would open their eyes, adults could learn a great deal. (Jenkins, 2006: 205)

The activity of online writing by young people needs to be conceptualized in more socially differentiated terms. Jenkins' examples of young people writing might thus be seen as characteristic of one mode of engagement in this online practice. This issue cannot be separated from constructions of professionalism and of amateurism. Clearly, the constitution of "young adult" fiction is dominated by the activities of publishers and of adult professional writers. To be an author in this context is to be the named producer of one or more complete volumes of prose narrative or poetry. Authorship, in this traditional and professionalized sense, is not achieved through various forms of online posting or even, fully, through self-publication in print. There are, occasionally, writers who achieve professional authorial status while still teenagers – S. E. Hinton in the late 1960s and Nick McDonell in this decade, both discussed in the introduction, are perhaps the best known examples. But these are exceptions. Looked at in these terms, "young adult" fiction is almost monolithically an adult business, and where teenage writers do appear, it is as early entrants to adult professional careers. Such well-known exceptions do not unsettle what is taken to be "young adult" fiction.

Turning to online production entails consideration of amateurism and of the logic of its various modes. The online writing activities of young people range across fan fiction, participation in writing communities, contributing to ezines, generating personal websites and also thematic websites (some specifically devoted to writing), participation in newsgroups associated with popular texts, participation in YouTube, MySpace, Facebook, emailing, and chatrooms.[12] The work of Robert A. Stebbins in the sociology of work and leisure offers some helpful ways of classifying these activities. Stebbins suggests three main categories of leisure activity – serious, casual, and project-based.

In Stebbins' terms, much of the writing produced online is probably "casual" ("immediately, intrinsically rewarding…relatively short-lived pleasurable core activity, requiring little or no special training to enjoy it," Stebbins, 2007: 5), thus mostly ephemeral and often embedded in particular exchanges (cf. Bernstein, 1996). Writing reviews, posting poetry and short stories, and developing relatively simple personal websites might be located in the intermediate project-based category ("short-term, reasonably complicated, one-off or occasional, though infrequent, creative undertaking (core activity) carried out in free time, or time free of disagreeable obligation," Stebbins, 2007: 5). Serious leisure involves the "systematic pursuit of an amateur, hobbyist, or volunteer core activity that people find so substantial, interesting, and fulfilling that…they launch themselves on a [leisure] career centered on acquiring and expressing a combination of its special skills, knowledge, and experience" (Stebbins, 2007: 5). This could be applied to more sustained contributions to fan fiction sites, to ezines, the more elaborate and protracted development of personal websites and of thematic websites. The domain of amateur production is thus somewhat fragmented and is characterized by tensions in part defined by a relationship to the professional domain. Serious leisure is most orientated to the professional domain and, in the context presented by "young adult" fiction, is where the most explicit challenges to the monopoly of professional production by adult subjects might become visible.

As examples of "serious leisure," I want to discuss two websites. One is a personal website developed by a sixteen-year-old girl:

> It indexes years of writing and poetry, and countless other things to browse through, if you're so inclined.

> I'm a sixteen-year-old aspiring writer; I'm very outspoken, consider myself creative, and have had websites since I was five. I inherited geek genes (my dad is a programmer; my mum, a web designer). I love words. I try to keep as unique an outlook on life as possible… (http://www.adriennewolter.com/ Accessed July 4 2007)

On her Writings page she begins:

> Welcome to my Writings page. I enjoy creative writing and poetry writing, so I decided to post a small sample of my stuff.
>
> I have several short stories here for now, but don't expect a novel or anything longer than 1–2 pages. ☺

Of her "original fiction" she notes, "I recently entered six of my stories into the 2005 Scholastic Writing Awards for Central PA…all six won something. The two golds went onto national competition, and both won one each of the 1200 writing awards." She also keeps an "IdeaBook":

> All writers should keep an "IdeaBook" of some kind, whether it be for fiction, poetry, or essays. It's basically a plain notebook with an explanation in the front, then ideas throughout the rest of the pages.
>
> …I write the date at the top and a brief description…The rest of the page is taken up by a plot outline, a conversation, a catchy summary (like you see on the back of books, heh… I write them in there a *lot*), or a timeline of sorts.
>
> (http://www.adriennewolter.com/stories/#pn. Accessed July 4 2007)

The self-positioning here is consistent with Stebbins' characterization of serious leisure and includes the elaboration of a trajectory strongly orientated to professional publication and underpinned by an existing, and sophisticated, knowledge of website design. But this is still located in the amateur domain and, as the efforts of a teenage girl is thus also implicitly "authentic," "originating" in youth, rather than constructing "youth" through professional writing practices from a distance. Ideas of "uniqueness" and "originality" figure in the girl's own self-representations, though it is striking that her accumulated writing is presented on a page listing an interrelated array of activities including a substantial involvement in fan fiction and in reviewing. "Writing" is not therefore placed as entirely separate from or superior to a wider participation in popular media culture. In this respect, such engagement contributes further to her authentification as a teenager – almost to a kind of ordinariness otherwise compromised by the fluency of her web design skills. Though this site is the product of sustained, systematic, and purposeful effort over a period of some years, it nevertheless produces the self as personal, distinctive, located, and exploratory. Through the deployment of particular kinds of cultural capital, she produces herself as an accomplishment-in-process. The majority of these sites are individual (not shared or collective) and, if not always at such a high level of skill, aspire to distinguish the author. Here, it might be argued, serious leisure is turned to the production of new middle class selves (Skeggs, 2004; Richards, 2005b).

A comparable example, but one involving a closer relationship to professional practice, is evident in the activities of Elisabeth Wilhelm, the originator of a thematic site called Absynthe Muse and, through those activities, the teenage correspondent for the *Voice of Youth Advocates* (cited in that role above). Wilhelm is the editor of the site, described as follows:

> Absynthe Muse, created in January 2005, is fast growing into a critically acclaimed and internationally recognized advocate and facilitator for young adult writers across the globe. That's fancy, bloated writing for "we're international, edgy, young, and fun," a website that is aimed at 13-year-olds all the way up through college-age students to 22.
>
> (http://www.absynthemuse.com/ Accessed July 4 2007).

On her personal website she records her "writing history":

> I started writing seriously after completing a homework assignment for US History which involved stained "old" paper and acrylic blood artistically spread across old style print…Talk of rape, identity issues, abuse, and historical accuracy was a pretty intense task for a 7th grader.
>
> Since then, I've been published over 120 times online and in print in a variety of publications and genres…
>
> I have also held editing positions including at *Kiwibox.com*…the *Open Directory Project… Moondance* ezine…
>
> I have extensive experience writing press releases, speeches, website copy, articles, creating conference materials, designing logos and press materials, creating grant letters, and product user guides…
>
> (http://community.livejournal.com/inkforblood Accessed July 7 2007)

In this case it is through leisure, but very closely associated with activity as a school student, that a career is formed, developed, and, at least initially, established. For Elisabeth Wilhelm, writing as a teenager, though still a matter of self-distinction, is also continuous with self-positioning as an international journalist, youth representative, and consultant. The language of both sites is somewhat more formal, and Absynthe Muse uses the category "young adult," rather than "teen," and thus allies itself with the educational and library service institutions addressing young people discussed earlier in this chapter. The Absynthe Muse site, despite its connotations of decadence and excess, also makes explicit that it does not "condone underage drinking or use of illicit substances." Wilhelm's distance from those discourses in which "authenticity" might be perceived is perhaps moderated by her maintenance of a live journal and by the "subjective" and self-referential elements in some of her journalism (e.g. "Saving the World, One Mouseclick at a Time," www.voya.com). This is an extract from her live journal for June 28 2007:

> I just got back from Brussels, Belgium, where I visited my Uncle Tom who works for NATO. On Friday, we got up at the buttcrack of dawn to take a bus down to Paris to see the Paris Air Show...
>
> Over a three-course meal and mint mousse for desert, with a bunch of drooling Air Force and Navy pilots surrounding me, I had a nice conversation with one of the most senior guys at Raytheon.
>
> Interesting people. Interesting business. Excellent wine. But you can't help but leave the temp building feeling totally creeped out. Those are merchents of death, but hey, somebody's gotta build the bombs and hate planes that drop them. (http://iremos.livejournal.com/ Accessed July 11 2007)

The career path of this very "well connected" young woman is well assured, but, as an advocate of young adult writing by young people themselves, the kind of pacy, impressionistic, and slightly careless presentation of her live journal entries perhaps helps to sustain a sense of youthful amateurism. This is a kind of compromise formation – in which the "characteristics of youth" (inexperience, uncertainty, assertion) are held in tension with the ethos of professionalism (efficiency, accountability, productivity). Wilhelm, in Stebbins' terms, is a shifting subject, self-positioned as amateur but caught up in a variety of identifications and refusals in relation to the domain of professional fiction and journalism. Kearney's (2006) comments on riot grrrl zines are apposite here:

> Though the Dadaists and Situationists celebrated amateurism, punks alone seem to have connected this aesthetic specifically to *youth*, as the label they use to identify themselves suggests. In doing so, they call attention to, while also rejecting, the adultism inherent in the standards of professionalism that structure dominant society and commercial culture. By dismissing the conventional standards for artistic expression and success, and repeatedly invoking the DIY mantra, punk culture has motivated many young people without formal training or talent to become actively involved in media production. (Kearney, 2006: 159)

Clearly, in these terms, Wilhelm's strategies are ultimately orientated to a resolution in favor of adult professionalism. [13]

Casual amateurism is by definition somewhat more difficult to identify and illustrate. Some of what participants present in MySpace or Facebook might be looked at in these terms. But with respect to the field of young adult fiction in particular, it might also be appropriate to survey the variety of sites that are very much adult owned and managed but which encourage and facilitate occasional, brief, and perhaps quite ephemeral postings of pieces of writing by young people. Examples of such sites include The Diary Project ("a non-profit organization…a global multimedia resource that encourages teens to write about their day-to-day experiences growing up"), gURL, HarlemLive,[14] TeenInk ("published by the Young Authors Foundation Inc., Newton, Massachusetts…written by teens for teens") and YO![15] Looked at as locations for the sustained production of fiction, they are mostly relatively slight. But if autobiographical writing and some journalistic activity are taken together with short story writing and poetry, several can be seen as hosting numerous if perhaps intermittent contributions by young people.

gURL, for example, started in 1996 as a site managed from the Interactive Telecommunications Program at New York University (now operated by iVillage Inc.), but offers participation in these terms:

> meet new people from all over the world in our shout boards
> become a gURL advice buddy (or find one)
> create your own polls for other gURL members to take in the shout out boards
> get creative on our boards – you can post pictures and change fonts and colors in your posts!
> give and get advice from other gURLS in our advice gURL panel or on our shout out boards
> create your own room on gURL
> get your comics and stories published
> voice your views about everything and anything on our boards, in our dig or dis feature, or in clips about clips
> (http://www.gurl.com/ Accessed July 11 2007)

This is an informative and well-designed site. However, it is not one where participants are encouraged to position themselves as "creative writers" or "authors." A variety of poetry is included. Quite a lengthy list of stories is also available, but these are written as accounts of personal experience in a confessional or informational mode, rather than as fiction. The basis of exchange here is primarily that of making available knowledge and experience arising from everyday experience as teenage girls. "Writing" is thus not construed as a skilled practice to which participants might be consciously orientated. Nor are their contributions valued in these formal terms. The content, in most cases reported personal experience, is given priority. These young "writers" are not, unlike the "serious leisure" examples discussed above, launching themselves into careers as "authors."

Conclusion

Though there is undoubtedly a great deal of writing being produced on line by young people, the field of production is structured by the division between amateur and professional practice. Mostly, what young people produce remains within the category of amateur production and though it may circulate among various online participants, securing a sense of identity as a writer for some (and by contrast with Jenkins' examples) still seems anchored in a systematic and determined effort to achieve publication in print. Such a focused pursuit of authorial status entails negotiation of the contradiction between the distance and disengagement implied by professionalism and the claims to authenticity allowed by a youthful amateurism. Indeed, others may reject such aspirations to professionalism and persist in self-positioning as both young and amateur (see Kearney, 2006). In doing so, they enact "their age" in apparent defiance of the obligation to aspire.

Chapter Two

Online: Reading, Rating, and Rejecting Francesca Lia Block

Introduction

Francesca Lia Block's (born 1962) career as a published author began in 1989 when she was just past her mid-twenties. Though she claims not to have intended a career as a "young adult" author, her novels and short stories have been located in the "young adult" and "crossover" market (see Smith, 2005). In 1998, the republication in one volume of five interrelated novels, *Dangerous Angels,* marked a decisive move to position her writing for a readership defined by a "young adult" lifestyle but not confined to the "young adult" age phase (Richards, 2007). Her novels and short stories have been the focus for disputes over the boundaries between children's, "young adult" and adult fiction. The variety of responses to her work is apparent across American Library Association reviews and awards, reviews in literary journals and in the press, and online reviews on such websites as Amazon.com and various online exchanges among her readers. In addition, some pressure groups concerned to regulate reading in schools and school libraries have also named and commented on her novels. Two groups, Parents Against Bad Books in Schools and Mission America, have challenged her work.

The World of Shangri-L.A.

Henry Jenkins remarks that "storytelling has become the art of world building" (Jenkins, 2006: 114), and, though not on the scale of the major media franchises of interest to Jenkins (*Star Wars*, *Star Trek*, *The Matrix*), Block's work as a whole can be read as constructing Los Angeles as a fictional "world." Mike Davis, in *City of Quartz* (1990), refers to Southern California's "unsure boundary between reality and science fiction" (Davis, 1990: 41), and in *Dangerous Angels* and its late sequel *Necklace of Kisses* (2005) Los Angeles is both a named and mapped place and a setting for the re-enactment of myth and fairy tale, "Shangri-L.A," recalling *Lost Horizon* (1937). As in *Buffy the Vampire Slayer* (1997–2003) and *Angel* (1999–2004), Southern California is both recognizable and extraordinary. Block's writing similarly occupies a hybrid space between genres (teen fiction and fairy tale).

Dangerous Angels is central: together, the five novels construct a post-counterculture enclave and constitute a moral world where matters of sexual uncertainty and identity are negotiated and resolved, provisionally, both in talk and in magic. Other novels, such as *The Hanged Man* (1994), though not developing the same characters, are constructed in similar terms and include episodes that can be read as either or both psychological realism and fantasy (see Chapter Five). *Nymph* (2000) was placed, in its publication, beyond the boundary of Block's Shangri-L.A., not least because it includes relatively explicit sexual descriptions. But it is nevertheless consistent with the "world" of Shangri-L.A. and sustains its core preoccupation with the construction of intimacy.

The reception of Block's work, the main concern of this chapter, varies widely. Her novels have been welcomed and endorsed by pro-gay/lesbian groups (for example, by the Gay and Lesbian Educators of British Columbia – Vancouver, B.C. – http://www.galebc.org/main.htm) but also by the American Library Association.[1] *Necklace of Kisses* (2005) has a back cover endorsement from John Cameron Mitchell, director of *Hedwig and the Angry Inch* (2001) and *Shortbus* (2006). Several of her novels have also won awards from the ALA, and in 2005 she won the ALA's Margaret A. Edwards Award.[2] Her work has also been reviewed favorably, if also with some reservations, by the Assembly on Literature for Adolescents at the National Council of Teachers of English in the ALAN REVIEW (Reid and Hutchinson, 1994; http://scholar.lib.vt.edu/ejournals/ALAN/).

However, there are also significant criticisms, even from those who appear to be enthusiastic about her writing. In particular, it has been argued that her representation of Los Angeles is virtually exclusively white and "bohemian" middle class. For example, Jan Susina argues that Block's world is "a consumeristic paradise and [her characters] rarely look beyond the confines of their own richly-appointed magic kingdom of wealthy white upper-class privilege" (Susina, 2002: 198). The question of whiteness and its "others" will be examined in Chapter Five but here I want to address Susina's critical observation on class.

Los Angeles is already saturated in decades of popular representation (Davis, 1990) and is increasingly portrayed as a global or "post-modern" city (Harvey, 1989: 299-300; Susina, 2002). California, but especially Los Angeles, has also long had a currency in popular discourse as the antithesis of tradition, a place where the future happens first (*Blade Runner,* 1982, for example). Block is strongly identified with Los Angeles. The reiteration of Block's place of residence on every book cover, however understated, implies a degree of correspondence between her writing and the city. But as Susina suggests, Block's fictional world is extremely circumscribed, with a core ensemble of mainly white characters living without the need to work in any routine way and always very much preoccupied with style and consumption. Though "located" in Los Angeles through repeated reference to named places, these are not social novels documenting the late twentieth-century social composition of the city.

However, Block's writing is concerned with something other than representational authenticity. In terms of named locations, her writing locates its scene of action as "in" Los Angeles. But the apparently solid cityscape is in fact being demolished or otherwise remade and often the buildings described are recalled as having-been-there – a Hollywood that Weetzie, her first heroine, remembers. The Weetzie Bat books project a way of life beyond the constraints of the "real." For example, drawing on magical realist precedents, Block constructs dialogues between characters across generations: the living talk with the dead. The sense of "belonging," of continuity and of "family" here is not always constrained by the boundary between life and death, nor by biological paternity, heterosexuality, or, arguably, monoculturalism. Across *Dangerous Angels*, the overarching construction of the loosely assembled but inclusive "family" is the moral core of a way of life elaborated in implicit defiance of new right politics and Christian fundamentalism (see Hedges, 2007). The market strategy pursued by the publishers in collecting the five novels together as *Dangerous Angels* has contributed to their status as a cohesive "world," where these issues are explored, if with shifting focalizations, through a sustained narrative (Richards, 2007). Even in the apparently "narcissistic" preoccupation with the interrelated matters of style and consumption, there is also a concern with identity and a speculative "life-politics" (Giddens, 1991; Kenway and Bullen, 2001: 159). As Kenway and Bullen suggest,

> style can also be understood as providing tools for "constructing personhood," as a statement about who one is and wishes to be. Style allows people to imagine themselves differently; it provides an opportunity to define and redefine themselves; it can be an expression of fantasy – to quote Barthes (1983 [*The Fashion System*]) "a dream of identity," and even a "dream of wholeness," in an age of fragmentation and alienation. (Kenway and Bullen, 2001: 19)

Online Fans: Witchbaby

Media audience research, mainly focused on television, has produced significant studies of the media in people's everyday lives (Livingstone, 1998; Gray, 1992; Morley, 1992, 2000; Gillespie, 1995; Gauntlett and Hill, 1999), often emphasizing how embedded in domestic life engagement may be. One striking piece of research, into readers of women's magazines, concluded that they were "popular" because they were "easy to put down" (Hermes, 1995). By contrast, studies of fans, and of "cult" texts, focus more on what arrests people's attention and perhaps sustains interest over many years. Some writers on fan fiction report lifelong and apparently "self-forming" preoccupations. In media research, Matt Hills' (2002) discussion of *Dr Who* is illuminating, both as an instance of his own long-term fandom and as a commentary on the relationship between the "self" as fan and as "scholar." Both *Buffy the Vampire Slayer* and the Harry Potter novels and films have generated substantial fan followings, and, as with *Dr Who,* some fans simultaneously construct their academic identities through their, occasionally reverential, textual analyses (Wilcox, 2005). However, the contributors to Witchbaby (a 'group' hosted by Yahoo!), though posting their comments in the online public domain, are not so obviously negotiating such enduring identity careers. Kenway and Bullen's comments above provide some basis for considering how participants in the Witchbaby fan network, formed in the aftermath of the publication of *Dangerous Angels* (1998), negotiate a sense of "self."

Named after a key figure in the *Dangerous Angels* novels, the Witchbaby list was very active for several years, but is now defunct. The majority of the posts that I discuss come from late in 2003 and from occasional bursts of activity through 2004. The most frequent contributors to Witchbaby in the period that I monitored appeared to be girls, though one participant identified himself as male. There was no explicit exclusion of boys and men and, in the responses to his contributions, there was little to suggest that his emails were regarded as intrusive. He was sometimes referred to as "hyper" and implicitly perhaps "excessive," but the responses were characterized more by amusement than irritation. References to boyfriends, though not central or insistent, were frequent in many of the contributors' emails. In the period I examined, the primary object of the Witchbaby exchanges was the "self," rather than Block's writing as explicitly and consistently matter for interpretation and debate. Indeed, the self is constituted in the exchanges often without any direct or overt reference to Block at all. However, her writing informs the conduct of the exchanges to the extent that the self-as-negotiable is legitimated in the "world" that Block constructs.

The sexual politics of the list are broadly inclusive. For example, an actively sexual self, exploratory, certainly heterosexual but also bisexual, lesbian, and gay is securely within the scope of the exchanges. In this post, a girl reflects on her response to the end of a relationship with another girl in a personal and highly self-reflective mode:

> Apparently, having a relationship is stressing her out so much that she would like to end ours. Somehow, I myself am not stressful, according to her, but our dating is. She wants to remain close friends. I'm not sure if I can do that right now, but maybe later.
>
> I sound far more composed writing that than I should, as I've spent the majority of the evening crying and cursing my poor romantic luck. She has conveyed to me how guilty and terrible she feels for breaking up with me, especially considering the rather pleasant nature of our relationship. I feel bad, therefore, about making my upset feelings known, because I hate for her to feel bad, but at the same time, a small, evil part of me wants her to fully know how her actions have affected me, for good or for bad. I told her that I loved her and had been struggling with how to tell her. I told her she was beautiful, had made my life wonderful, and had made me able to write again. She told me that made her feel even worse for dumping me. I don't understand, then, why she persisted in doing so.
>
> I'm bothered for many reasons. First, naturally, I was madly in love with her, and still am. Second, I am sick and tired of starting the school year off single. It makes me feel desperate. Third, I have the sex drive of an eighteen-year-old boy, and am thus sexually frustrated. I try to be patient in relationships and not hurry things, but the relationships never last more than a few months, and such a quandary is taking its toll on me sexually. Right now, I'm posting myself back onto personal sites and trying not to think about her. Have to go, perhaps will post replies and such tomorrow.

This wry and articulate commentary is significant in that the "same-sex" status of the relationship is not itself made an explicit issue.

Consumption is also warranted and thus, from time to time, participants exchange lists of what they have most recently bought, or eaten or what they currently listen to and what they read. Self-construction through consumption is an explicit concern:

> Recent reading: James Frazer, The Golden Bough; Georges Perec, 53 Days (finished, though the novel's unfinished); John Bannville, Eclipse; Shakespeare, Hamlet (finished. WHY have I never read this until now? I may read it again straightaway; it's certainly my favorite Shakespeare play); Thomas Pynchon, V. (decent, but I can't get over the idiotic names he gives his characters).
>
> Recent listening: X, Beyond & Back (the second disc; the recording quality on the first is too poor for me to enjoy so much); The Pixies, Surfer Rosa (I LOVE this album! I've listened to it at least once a day since I checked it out from the library); Pavement, Wowee Zowee (I love this one too, surprisingly as I'm not usually much for what they call indie rock these days).

Though such listings of books and music are frequent, they are not overtly competitive and seem to serve more as ways of situating the "self" and of inviting a continuing dialogue. This could be called "consumerism" but the negative connotation is problematic (see Slater, 1997: 83–99). These exchanges, in the somewhat anonymous "space" of an online medium, use "what is to hand" to construct commonality between participants. For "Witchbabies," the "self" is often not so simply objectified as lists of commodities suggest, and is sometimes a matter for more explicit reflection. The sense of energy and engagement displayed by contributors might be admired as an instance of creativity in ordinary life, a "change and transformation of persons, the development of the expressive self and its greater use value as a dynamic symbolic force" (Willis, 2000: 71). Dreams, with hesitation and circumscription, are sometimes reported, and the "self" is thus acknowledged to be elusive, beyond reliable self-knowledge:

> ok i've been having this dream that's been really bothering me lately. its not always exactly the same, but this is pretty much the gist of it. I'm at the summer camp where my mom has been working at since I was 10. There's this building that no one will go near and everyone wants me to go and see what is in it. I get really scared because everyone says it is haunted by some sort of spirit or ghost. When I enter the building everything turns black and all I see is this elderly woman's face. She just stares at me and blinks and then I wake up, scared shitless for no apparent reason. I have never seen this woman in my life but her features are very vivid. Its really weird because you know how in most dreams the faces are vague and unimportant, (at least they are in mine) well her features were so vivid to me that if i was any good at art and drawing I could probably draw a sketch of her. For some reason this dream really bothers me and I'm not completely sure why.

Above all, the self here is a reflexive project, open to eclectic construction and reconstruction – and thus religious prescription and especially traditional forms of Christianity are rejected. Religious thinking, including pagan religions, is made a resource from which to borrow rather than within which to be fixed:

> my parents raised me catholic, and i remember so much of my life spent looking at the floor in shame for things. Maybe it's not the church's fault, but i think if i had been raised without religion, or maybe in one with less guilt attached to it, i wouldn't be like i am now. apologizing for everything i say and all of that. it's pathetic...

> Witchies – Hello my dears. How are you all?...I myself am feeling kind of lonely. See, I have been thinking about my dear old friend, Miss. See, we fell apart a little while ago. The whole story is that she and I were Pagan together, then she met this boy. They became very close and he convinced her back to Christianity. I am so fine with this...But he also convinced her that I was worshipping the devil pretty much

> and that she should try to save me. It tore us apart. She told the whole school I was a Satanist.

The argument that, in post-traditional societies, the self has become a "reflexive project" (Giddens, 1991) is an issue crucial to the discussion of Block's reception. Beverley Skeggs (2004) has argued, for example, that "the self as a reflexive project" is a distinctively middle-class phenomenon, and that mobility of the self is claimed against, always by contrast with, the "fixity" of others. Her critique of the denial of class in much recent sociology provides an important background to any discussion of how Block's readers position themselves in their exchanges with each other. It is not possible to know very much about any of the Witchbaby contributors, but in reading their exchanges, the intention is not to "trace" individuals, but to show that identities are constructed in this publicly accessible, but not highly publicized domain, as "flexible" and "unfixed."

So, attributing data from such exchanges to individuals of whom one has little reliable knowledge (about age, gender, "race," or class, for example) is indefinitely problematic. Occasionally, participants do identify themselves explicitly, also sometimes posting photographs, or photographs claimed as images of themselves. But these "self-identifications" are best read as rhetorical characteristics of this domain of discursive exchange and as indicative of its implicit rules of participation. Bakhtin's discussion of speech genres is helpful here:

> An essential (constitutive) marker of the utterance is its quality of being directed to someone, its *addressivity*. As distinct from the signifying units of a language – words and sentences – that are impersonal, belonging to nobody and addressed to nobody, the utterance has both an author...and an addressee…Both the composition and, particularly, the style of the utterance depend on those to whom the utterance is addressed, how the speaker (or writer) senses and imagines his addressees, and the force of their effect on the utterance. Each speech genre in each area of speech communication has its own typical conception of the addressee, and this defines it as a genre. (Bakhtin, 1994: 95)

The social relations of Witchbaby exchanges are produced and sustained through the form of the email "utterance": typically the mode of address suggests informal, nonhierarchical relations between peers.

Particular contributors do employ distinctive vocabularies, modes of greeting and response – and thus construct online personas – but these are within boundaries. Moreover the boundaries are sometimes very actively constructed – by, for example, inviting responses in which contributors name the music they are currently listening to, their favorite Block books and other favorite authors, or their most recent purchases. Of course such invitations could produce a sense of divergence, noncongruence, and even misunderstanding, but in practice the participants seem to offer repertoires which overlap and thus establish a sense of commonality. For example, there are frequent references to Tori Amos, the TV show *My So-Called Life* (1994–95), 1960s music, and various current indie bands. Those few choices that do stand out as "different" or "idiosyncratic" are thus allowed to function as markers of collective tolerance and eclecticism.

Most exchanges are overtly supportive and sometimes celebratory – responses are thus strongly inclusive, and disagreement, dispute, and conflict, at least in the months I monitored, appeared to be unacceptable. Indeed there is some sensitivity to this so that even a potentially slight criticism is both apologized for and explained. The principle appears to be that this is not a domain into which people enter with the expectation that they may be putting themselves at risk of ridicule, mockery, or challenge:

> I'm coming out of a pretty dark spell just now. Fortunately these things are brief. It occurred to me a few days ago that there is a fundamental sense in which I do not exist. Since I was small and can remember, my life has been one role after another – I'm not trying to go on about the oppressions of society, they were all self-induced. (Who have I supposed is watching? God? Posterity?) Just layers upon layers, and always the abiding sense that I am no more than a host of characters in my own fiction. (A variant, perhaps, of the "Sophie's World" experiences you mentioned, [V], if indeed you're still around.) If you peeled one away there'd always be another. I was trying to figure out what if anything could lay at the core just before you get down to mechanics. The neurotic habits I have: biting my nails, compiling lists of imaginary names and maps of imaginary towns? Context defines me, even if inversely. Maybe there is no one thing that is the personality; perhaps this is the common experience and people generally just don't think about it overmuch.

Presumably when participants do have critical comments to make, they simply remain silent. This is not a forum for debate, argument, and counterargument. Participants co-construct "trust" and thus from time to time they exchange their own poetry – writing typically constructed as especially personal and intimate.[3] The exchanges are "personal," idiosyncratic and experiential within the limits of the version of "tolerance" mapped out in *Dangerous Angels*.

Though email is now a well established medium of exchange, the email "utterances" in this list are very much a hybrid form drawing from, with varying degrees of emphasis, relatively traditional letter forms, personal diaries, speech (especially catchphrases), texting, and, also, the distinctive vocabulary used in some of Francesca Lia Block's novels – especially the Weetzie Bat books. Though borrowing from genres in which intimacy and interiority can be produced, these "utterances" are not addressed to a single other or even to a reliably known other – on the contrary they address numerous, indeterminate, and unknown others as if indeed belonging to the Witchbaby group reliably distinguishes those who participate from those who do not belong or may not be competent to participate. In addition, though informal, the writing is also sometimes very controlled and somewhat literary. To participate in these exchanges requires a competence in this mix of genres and thus particular kinds of cultural capital – some informal but others more usually associated with high levels of achievement in formal education. This example, though typically informal, also explicitly characterizes the network in terms of educational capital:

> Hey Witchbabies. Sorry for the lack of participation since "In Love With My Guitarist" post. What I forgot to tell you all is... I'M HIS BOSS TOO!...But it's turning out okay. He's on vacation for one more week, then I'm on vacation (sitting at home on my ass and going to fairs) for a week. So, I won't see a lot of him and it will go away. At least I hope so. We've been e-mailing back and forth. He's quite witty.
>
> Anyway, I've just been super busy. The three people who work under me took vacations at the same time, so I was stuck doing a lot of extra work. It was really frustrating and I didn't want to end up dumping it on you all. But, while I shelved today, I got to thinking about how much I miss you guys. I call you all my educated women. I have a distinct lack of them around here. I have my mum and my best friend. But they don't really hang around much right now.

Very occasionally, disruptions, or “incompetent” posts appear. For example:

> Hi my name is Victoria and I am 20 year old college student. Right now I am running my own Avon business. Avon is cheap, affordable, and worth it. Now easier to get then ever. You can now order your favorite Avon products online. Let me be your E-representative. Contact me if you would also like to sell?

This commercial, reductively consumerist, intrusion very obviously disrupts the modes of address appropriate to this domain. Witchbaby is not a public forum where any contribution is legitimate but, in this case, the contribution makes apparent how public and vulnerable the network actually may be.

The Boundaries of Cool

I want to examine further the question of Witchbaby’s implicit politics. I have suggested that Block’s writing itself informs the boundaries of the list’s “world.” Though not overtly informed by feminist separatism, there are also some similarities to the riot grrrl phenomenon, with which Block is sometimes also loosely associated (see Block and Carlip, 1998). Kearney characterizes riot grrrls, by contrast with working-class young women, as:

> privileged with more education, greater access to the means of cultural production and advanced forms of communication…and a longer transitional stage between adolescence and adulthood…more time to experiment with new subject positions, social identifications, relationships, and forms of work… (Kearney, 1998: 163–164)

Though it is not possible to know either reliably or in detail, the cumulative evidence from the Witchbaby exchanges suggests that these contributors have access to exactly the resources outlined in Kearney's comments.

Following Skeggs' (2004) recovery of class analysis, it is important to reiterate that there are limits to the relative optimism of Willis (2000) or of Kenway and Bullen (2001). The mobile construction of the self is, in Skeggs' view, enacted in social relations where "others" are defined as immobile, not open to reflexive self-construction. For readers of Francesca Lia Block, there must presumably be people who are "unhip" or "uncool" (Danesi, 1994). Certainly, whatever the composition of Block's audience, the contributors to Witchbaby position themselves as distant from, and largely uninterested in engaging with, the lives of people who are not middle class, "my educated women." Kearney, again, points to this problem in riot grrrl culture, arguing that:

> too few riot grrrls have critically interrogated how their privileging of a white, middle-class, punk identity over other possible identifications tends to reproduce the dominant understanding of riot grrrl as a movement for only white, middle-class youth. (Kearney, 1998: 175)

In the fifth novel in the *Dangerous Angels* series, *Baby Be-Bop,* some of this is evident in the way "uncool" others are invoked as threats to the young gay character Dirk. Here, Dirk is talking in his bedroom to Pup Lambert, a boy with whom he is falling in love:

> On the wall was a chalk drawing Dirk had made of Jimi Hendrix.
>
> "My mom went out with this gross trucker guy once," Pup told him. "He saw the Jimi poster in my room and goes, 'That nigger looks like he's got a mouth full of cum'. I wanted to kill him. I told my mom I would if she didn't stop seeing him."
> "Did she?"
> "Yeah. But I don't think that's why. Her next boyfriend saw my Bowie poster and started calling him a fag. My mom said if I ever dressed like that she'd kick me out of the house." (Block, 1995: 15–16)

Narratively, this functions as a displaced acknowledgment of the legitimacy of gay identities between two boys otherwise unable to move beyond friendship and into a sexual relationship with each other. But this is achieved, in this passage, by attributing homophobia to a broadly emblematic working-class figure, "this gross trucker guy," an almost entirely absent "other" to the middle-class bohemian world of Weetzie Bat, her friends and family. Perhaps the first particular appearance of such "uncool" figures is that of Chuck, Duck's mother's new partner in *Witch Baby.* He too is the bearer of homophobic "attitudes." Duck refers to him as a "greaseburger" and he does not figure in the subsequent reunion and reconciliation between Duck and his family.

This construction of a class boundary within the text is, according to Susina (2002), reflected in her readership. However, he makes this case by citing Zipes (2001) to whom he attributes the view that Block's audience is confined to "white, middle class children, their parents, teachers, university students, and professionals in the field" (Zipes, 2001: 35, cited in Susina 2002: 198). But Zipcs actually argues not that Block is unusual in this respect but that this is a wider pattern in the reading of children's and young adult fiction:

> Though there is a striking number of gifted and concerned writers who write about the conditions that produce the Mindy Turners of our society – I am thinking of Robert Cormier, Virginia Hamilton, Rosa Guy, Norma Fox Mazier, Brock Cole, Bruce Brooks, Francesca Block, Jerry Spinelli, Chris Crutcher, Anne Fine, and Michael Rosen – their books are rarely read by the young people depicted in them. Certainly, the major readers, or should I say consumers, of children's literature and so-called young adult literature, are white, middle-class children, their parents, teachers, university students, and professionals in the field, even when the books are multicultural and diverse – and this is not to argue that other ethnic groups are not reading. (Zipes, 2001: 35)

To the extent that the Witchbaby network provides evidence of Block's readership, it seems to confirm that it is composed predominantly of girls and young women who may well also be white and middle class. An article in the *Los Angeles Times* in 1999 also represents her readers as young, presumably white, girls:

> They face each other from across a card table, Francesca Lia Block and a jury of her protagonist's peers. The girls, all 12 to 15 years old, sit in folding chairs in the back room of the Midnight Special Bookstore in Santa Monica, paperbacks in hand. Everyone looks shy. They've come across town on a school night. (Hotaling, 1999)

Given the particularity of her audience, it might be argued then that Block's writing does not, despite its awards in the ALA category of "reluctant young adult readers," address potential readers for whom the "unreality" of the settings, events, and characters may be experienced as meaningless and exclusive. Their "crossover" appeal may thus be largely across age phases within a predominantly white, middle-class, female readership.

Rating Block: Amazon Reviews

In this section, I want to examine Amazon customer reviews as, potentially, evidence of a more diverse readership. Though, as with Witchbaby, it is unwise to assume that the identities of participants can be determined reliably, there is some scope for a broad assessment of the proportional composition of online reviewers. Out of 122 reviews posted in relation to *Dangerous Angels* (in April 2005), though many reviewers do not specify their age or gender, it is possible to identify some seventy or eighty reviews as probably contributed by teenage girls or women in their twenties. There are perhaps a dozen from young men, several of whom identify themselves as gay. Those positioning themselves as outsiders to the young adult audience and thus as either "adult" or a "kid" number perhaps eight and two, respectively.

The reviews entered on the Amazon website (see www.amazon.com) in relation to Francesca Lia Block, though rarely engaging specifically with each other, include some strongly disputing the value, credibility, and "appropriateness" of her novels and short stories. Of those reviews posted in relation to *Dangerous Angels*, 98 award five stars, 9 four stars, 1 three stars, 4 two stars, and 9 one star. Though overall the reviews are thus substantially favorable, the disjunction between the large majority of positive reviews and the most strongly adverse comments is worth some attention.

Participants here do not enter as "members," and though some contributors self-identify as fans, many write as "consumers," recording their satisfaction or dissatisfaction at having bought one or more books by her. Some give their ages (thirteen appears to be the youngest); others locate themselves as teachers, librarians, parents, or as students. Here, between these intersecting social interests, a sense of controversy both about what constitutes young adult fiction and about what it is that Francesca Lia Block writes emerges in terms excluded from Witchbaby. Though it must be emphasized that even here, the participants are self-selected in that they have (mostly) bought at least one book by her and have (mostly) actually read one, or attempted to do so.

There are several interrelated points of contention introduced in these reviews. First of all there is that of "quality" – of what is taken to constitute good writing. Second, there is the issue of realism, with reference to character, plot, and setting. Third is the question of for whom the novels are written – children, young adults, adults. Fourth, some reviews complain of being misled by the cover, by the book's description, and by other reviewers. The fifth issue is that of how differences in readers' responses and in their tastes are construed between the various reviewers. Those aspects of Block's writing regarded as belonging to "childhood" are taken to be indicative of a lack of both quality and realism: "storybook happy ending," "the written fantasies of a pre-teen," "Block writes in short sentences, and jumps around a lot. i would NOT recommend this book if you are used to more sophisticated styles of writing," "as even my daughter noticed, it is poorly written. Kids deserve examples of fine writing, there is no need to dumb down vocabulary and grammar for them," "this author writes as if words of more than one syllable don't exist – unless they're pretentiously cute inventions such as 'slinkster'."

Block does borrow extensively from fairy tales. She also adopts a rhythm, and habits of repetition and listing, and of word play, that seem derived from stories for young children. But the characters, and the scenes they inhabit, belong mostly to late adolescence. Many readers appear to be disorientated by the effects of blending elements of genres associated with children's literature with themes understood to be of most concern to those entering adult life.

Such a generic hybrid calls on readers to learn, in the process of reading itself, just how the text constructs a coherent social world. But those who have given up – and write the most negative reviews – are clearly too uncomfortable with being addressed as children, and perhaps particularly as girls. Sometimes Block writes as if reading to a child:

> And so, Witch Baby stayed on in the house, and took turns terrorizing Cherokee and being terrorized by Cherokee, and eating up all of Duck's Fig Newtons, and using Dirk's Aqua Net, and insisting on being in My Secret Agent Lover man's movies, and dressing up in Weetzie's clothes, and pulling heads off Barbie dolls and sticking them on the TV antenna and ruining the reception.
>
> But that's how witch babies are. (Block, 1989: 64–65)

Thus positioned some reviewers reject the text. The listing and description of clothing – of dressing up – and of foods seems to provoke similar unease, perhaps especially from those who, naming themselves, appear to be male. One comments that *Dangerous Angels* is "shallow and pointless" and that it is by far the worst story that he has read. In particular, he complains that the plot is "odd and twisted" and that it has "long, tedious paragraphs jampacked with metaphors and simlies (sic)." Another, if not so dismissive, records an intense disappointment, close to physical distaste. Heading his review "Unrealistic, childish," he comments that it left him with "a very very sour taste" in his mouth. He also complains that there is a lot of "unnecessary detail" and, perhaps confirming most clearly the masculine standpoint of his review, he writes, with apparent exasperation, that "we don't need, nor want, to know the specifics of what Wheetzie (sic) ate for lunch, nor do we need a documentary of her wardrobe." A third example of this kind of response again highlights a sense of disappointment: "I picked this book up hoping for something big. And I guess I got it – a big disappointment!!!" He is offended by Block's "pretentiously cute" style and concludes with a withering condemnation: "this mess of hippy-dippy, shallow dithering left me feeling cheated." For these reviewers, Block's writing appears to lack the muscularity and action of more male orientated genres of fantasy adventure. Faced with such writing they seem to want to publicly disown their encounter with it and thus to cancel the endorsement implicit in having bought the book. Paradoxically, of course, they put on record the fact that they have done so.

There are other similarly negative reviews that, though making comparable criticisms, are also very explicitly inscribed as from adult, parental, and pedagogic positions and thus claim the right to judge on behalf of young readers. They seek to intervene, invoking standards of morality and quality they see as salient in the fields of children's and young adult fiction. There is, for example, "A Mom's Point of View," a fairly thoughtful review avoiding simplistic condemnation. The reviewer acknowledges the importance of "contemporary issues" in young adult fiction but is disconcerted by the disjunction between the cover and the "very mature content" of *Dangerous Angels* (cf. Richards, 2007). She remarks that the edition she read does not give any advance warning, to "the reader or parent," of what the text offers, and argues that there should a suggested age range for potential readers and a warning to parents. For her, the novels are insufficiently didactic, and she comments in particular that though "AIDS is given some serious regard, behaviors associated with AIDS are made out to be natural and readily acceptable." This rather evasive reference to sexual, and especially homosexual, promiscuity is followed by a slightly pompous final judgment: "Block exhibits talent in character development and humor, but both need redirection." Others similarly construct their reviews through discourse of both moral and aesthetic quality. One begins "My daughter brought this book home" as if it must be made clear that the reviewer was not responsible for this unwelcome intrusion into the familial scene. The review continues, somewhat patronizing the girl in question: "I can see why many young girls like it, but as even my daughter noticed, it is poorly written," adding that "Kids deserve examples of fine writing." Another review entitled "Where's the magic?" judges the writing to be "disappointingly impoverished." Shifting into moral discourse, the review then records some indignation: "alluding to these stories as 'fairy tales' and acceptable reading material for children and young teens is outrageous" and concludes that the "characters live dissolute lives, and there are many offbeat sexual situations. It simply is not suitable for those under 18." A final example of these adverse commentaries succinctly conveys deep moral contempt. With the title "Fallen Angels is more like it," the reviewer accuses Block of glorifying "social dysfunction and Hollywood glamour." He ends with "I read about half before I put it down for good. Don't bother, unless you're a druggie wannabe." Though this reviewer does not disclose his position within his review of Block, he identifies himself as male and as a parent in strongly endorsing Jim Trelease's *The Read-Aloud Handbook.* He recalls that this book introduced him and his children "to a wonderful world of excellent literature," using it as "a guide as I read to my children every evening." He adds, "a grandparent's delight." In sharp contrast to all of these examples, there are also instances of parents supporting the choices made by their daughters. One, exclaiming, "I loved the book!!!" reports that her thirteen year old daughter brought the book home from school, though in this case this was a far from unwelcome crossing of that boundary: "The book took me on a journey, which a month later, still moves me. I loved all the characters and wished I was still among them. It was inspirational and made me nostalgic for something I don't have."

Many other reviewers contest these various condemnations, and also position themselves in ways that imply other, and various, grounds for judgment. Some identify themselves as academics with Ph.D.s, others as "kids" or as young teenagers or as having read Block as teenagers, and some as gay or lesbian or at least not solely heterosexual. Perhaps the most direct challenge to other reviewers is made by a "literature Ph.D." who construes the negative responses in terms of intelligence, or the lack of it. With the title "Intelligence Required" and the comment that the book is not for stupid people, this is one of the more confrontational reviews advocating Block's writing. The reviewer asserts that *Dangerous Angels* is "not a children's book," explaining that "at 22 I had to re-read the first page to understand the book." The recommendation also stipulates what qualities a reader will need - it is for anyone "who possesses the imagination and perseverance to plunge in!"

Several others, though similarly positioning themselves as academic readers, are less explicitly disdainful but do, to varying degrees, imply that negative reviewers' comments are misunderstandings arising from a lack of maturity and experience in reading. There are three further examples worth citing here:

> This book is gorgeous, inspiring, heartbreaking, and heart-mending. This is one of my very favorite books. And I'm not a teen. I'm in my 30s and I have a Ph.D. in literature.

> ...to those who have read her series and dismissed it as "trite" or "too simplistic" I would merely like to encourage that they reconsider the series in a critical sense, and realize its incredible potential for even the most academic reader...So if you are fifteen, or fifty...open the book, open your mind, and perhaps you will be pleasantly surprised.

> Francesca Lia Block achieves in a few pages a depth of characterization some authors can't get across in an entire book. She does so with a stylized way of writing some have criticized as too simple. I couldn't disagree more. Her short, snappy sentence structure I found reminiscent of beat poetry, highlights of the environment that are the small, important details in these characters' lives.

What these reviewers do not entirely acknowledge is that their own readings of Block's prose require a particular cultural capital mostly associated with those who are at ease with "literary" studies in high school and beyond. They thus assert the value of Block's writing without conceding the particularity of their own cultural competence in doing so. In particular, as the language of poetry has a relatively marginal place in the popular domain, it is perhaps not surprising that when the negative reviewers are not unsettled by being addressed as children, they find the use of metaphor, for example, arty and obscure.

Other reviewers, not claiming to be experienced academic readers, lay claim to Block's writing as personal devotees, emphasizing the emotional strength of their response and the intensity of their reading experience – often by stressing how *rapidly* they read all five novels. Emotional intensity and authenticity are especially prominent. The following five examples illustrate the responses of reviewers identifying themselves as teenage, or possibly younger, readers. The first, aged thirteen, says quite simply: "I loved this book. My grandmother bought it for me on the 16th and I was done reading it on the 17th. I read the entire book in two sit down sessions." The second offers a similarly unequivocal and enthusiastic endorsement: "I started reading Francesca Lia Block at the age of 11, and now at 14 I can say I know every line, and word. I love these books. They rock!!!" Rather more sharply, and in direct criticism of adult reviewers, the third titles the review "Not an overprotective parent, but a bookworm teen" and addresses parents explicitly: "WE KNOW ABOUT THESE SUBJECTS! Sex, drugs, homosexuality, aren't they all common conversation ground for teenagers? Isn't it possible that we don't need any more shielding from the world?" The fourth example here again emphasizes the speed and intensity of the reading encounter with *Dangerous Angels*: "I struggle to read any book longer than 200 pages, and I flew through this collection of 5 stories in less than a week. Francesca Lia Block's words touched my heart and made sense to me in a way I didn't even know books could do." Finally, and again with a degree of surprise, and pride, in having read such a lengthy collection: "This book was great! I loved it. This book was the biggest book I have read but worth it…I couldn't put it down I was hooked on it." Whatever misgivings there may be about the designation of Block's writing as addressing "reluctant" young adult readers, there is at least some, tentative, evidence here that her novels do engage some young readers usually unaccustomed to reading in any sustained way. Customer reviews do not constitute data that can be properly quantified or discussed as if it represents a form of systematic enquiry into reception. But it at least makes visible some of the responses of readers who are not, perhaps, participants in the more sustained fan sites.

If a large majority of the very favorable reviews come from girls and young women, among those positive reviews I assume to be contributed by men, these identify themselves specifically as gay. The first seems defensive, a little dismayed by the very negative reviews posted by disgruntled Amazon customers. He begins "admittedly this might not be the best written book ever. or the most plausible story. That's not the point." He goes on to situate his reading of *Dangerous Angels* autobiographically, locating it in high school, when he was fifteen and "the only gay kid I knew of." He was given the first of the *Weetzie Bat* novels by a female friend and followed that by getting the rest from the library. He identifies these novels as offering reassurance because they represented "people who loved each other beyond the conventional perceptions of what family is." He concludes his review: "this book didn't 'save my life' but it certainly gave me something to look forward to." The second example is much more assertive, defying critics on both aesthetic and moral grounds. He claims that Block writes "in a world entirely of her own," "the prose equivalent of an early Joni Mitchell album." Referring to the last of the five novels in *Dangerous Angels*, *Baby Be-Bop*, he argues that it "successfully takes on every other YA book about coming out, and leaves them in the dust." Like the previous reviewer, but at a later age, he identifies the novels as significant contributions to his life and his sense of legitimacy as a gay man: "If I saw Block, I would give her a huge hug…I was in tears by the end of Be-Bop, because, after 28 years, I finally heard that it's perfectly fine to be who I am. Thank you Francesca."

Whatever the actual age and gender of these contributors, their self-identifications, and the presentation of features of their reading experience they judge salient in the context of the Amazon site, are rhetorical strategies through which they position themselves in the field of debate constituted around the novels. Furthermore, features of their contributions, such as volume, sentence structure, punctuation, and wider literary and cultural reference, contribute to the power they claim to contest other reviews and assert the credibility of their own. Read in this way, it might be argued that those who review *Dangerous Angels* negatively are marginalized as variously naïve, incompetent, and foolish by the number and prevailing fluency of the favorable reviews. Those who write in order to denounce Block's writing as inappropriate for young people also appear as a prudish minority failing to exercise the control they seek. It could be argued that, as Amazon.com is a commercial website, such an outcome underpins further sales – and that this tendency is intrinsic to the process of customer reviewing. In effect, it is those who have already bought the product, and in that literal sense have invested in it, who mostly participate in publicly defining its value. It is appropriate then to turn now to those websites where the case for censorship and proscription is made, not in competition with readers on a commercial website or with fans in an online network, but univocally in the furtherance of a systematic campaign.

Rejecting Block

In 2000, Block published a collection of erotic short stories entitled *Nymph.* Though they were published by a specialist in the genre (Circlet Press) and not in a Young Adult imprint, the title appears along with all her others in any routine search of a commercial website such as Amazon.com. One reviewer, contributing to the Amazon.com site, implicitly denounces the lack of clearly regulated categories:

> As a Young Adult Librarian, I enjoy…Francesca Lia Block... however, this is not a book worthy of place in anyone's collection. The vocabulary is vulgar, insulting, and the stories are not for the age group…she intends. If I were a parent, and my Young Adult brought home this book, I would be shocked, angry, and demand why anyone would purchase such a collection of vividly sexual short stories, and make them available for anyone to read! As an adult, I found the stories appalling and merely written as, for lack of better terms, super-market smut. I am very disappointed with this book and would expect better from such a notable writer.

The first story in the collection, about a surfer and mermaid (who moves on land in a wheelchair), is perhaps illustrative of what, for the librarian, is a shocking disjunction between her expectation and the text. As I suggested in the previous chapter, "Young adult" in the context of library provision refers to an age phase identified with school, to people still living with their parents, not sexually active twenty-somethings:

> Mer stays with Tom MacDougal in the little beach house with the wisteria vine and the glass porch. No on knows what goes on in there, only that Mac has started surfing again...that his mysterious young girlfriend in the wheelchair sits on the sand and watches him, that when he returns from the sea he plunges to his knees before her and kisses her as if she contains the breath he had lost that time he almost drowned. Maybe she does. People speculate as to how they fuck, what is under the narrow spangled sheath she always wears over her lower body. Some think she is crazy, playing out a fantasy so he can't get inside her. Maybe she'd been molested as a child or raped as a teenager travelling along the coast and that is why she invented the wheelchair thing and the costume. Others think it is real. But Mac and Mer don't care. His mouth on her tender, swollen, glossy breasts making her come when he caresses her nipples; her mouth sliding down the shaft of his thick cock, they rescue each other from land and from the sea again and again. (Block, 2000a: 21–22)

As I have argued, with the rapid expansion of online bookselling, the containment of texts within categories, such as children's literature or young adult fiction, is virtually impossible. Within such commercial sites, extensive cross-referencing is promoted both within the internal search processes and through customers' own listings. Of course access to computers and to the credit-based means of buying online do limit the use of sites such as Amazon.com to those with the necessary financial means. But there is no way of confining readers to products deemed to be appropriate to the age category to which they belong. In this context, therefore, the campaigns to proscribe Block's writing in schools seem curiously selective in their concern with the provision of books only in educational settings. Given the ready availability of Block – and much else besides – in the bookselling market, it seems thus that these campaigns are more concerned with establishing claims to control the curriculum, the school library, and the activities of teachers than with actually making particular texts unavailable to young readers.

However "conservative" the Young Adult librarian cited above may appear, where the main concern seems to be that of keeping texts in their allotted categories, PABBIS and Mission America are considerably more authoritarian in their intentions. In representing the Christian right, they directly challenge the notion of the "self as a reflexive project." The "life-politics" of *Dangerous Angels* is condemned as un-Christian by Linda P. Harvey in an article, "Heresy in the Hood: Teen Witchcraft in America (1)," posted on the Mission America website. She argues that "teen fiction today" is:

> an ungodly witches' brew of street values, sorcery and sexuality…[*Dangerous Angels* is]…a nightmare of children raising themselves in a Christ-less world devoid of standards and devoted to partying…a teen girl…shares her home with two homosexual guys and her live-in lover. She deliberately gets impregnated by one of the two homosexuals in a group sex encounter... (http://www.missionamerica.com/)

The Mission America website pursues campaigns against "tolerance" in education – that is, tolerance of groups seen as incompatible with a Christian way of life (see Hedges, 2007). Much of the website appears to be devoted to identifying and challenging educational initiatives supportive of gay students (see, for example, Fighting the Gay Agenda – Tolerance Lessons in Schools: Anti-Christian Bigotry in Disguise? – http://www.missionamerica.com/).

PABBIS is similar to Mission America in its politics but more exclusively focused on fiction in schools. The following is a general statement from their website (2002), explaining their aims:

> 1. To inform people about the issue of controversial books in schools
> 2. To let people know exactly what material is in the books
> 3. To let people know what they can do about it
> (http://www.pabbis.com)

Elsewhere on the site they argue that they are not concerned to deny anyone the right to read whatever they wish, noting that "controversial" books are available in bookstores and public libraries. Their focus, very explicitly, is on schools and they make clear their intention to prevent them from endorsing "age-inappropriate, vulgar, indecent and violent reading material in their libraries and classrooms" where such material conflicts with "individual family values" (http://www.pabbis.com). They regard the educational provision of books with "extreme controversial content" as indicating to school students that their families' values and standards of morality are unimportant (http://www.pabbis.com). However, in these statements, there is never any acknowledgment of children and young people as actively selecting and engaging with what they read and watch. Children, in the terms favored by PABBIS, should be under the control of parents and, in the matter of their education, it is the parents alone who have the right to make decisions about how they should be educated (for an alternative view, see Lindley, 1989). The "organization" thus favors an unequivocal reassertion of parental authority over children. Children are, implicitly, possessions and, in relation to schools, it is their parents who are defined as "clients." Parents are constructed as the primary "consumers" of education and thus entitled to know exactly how their taxes are being spent. There is no interest in how children themselves experience their childhood and youth. For PABBIS, childhood appears to be a distinct, fixed, and subordinate condition. There is sustained antipathy to teachers and to librarians, especially those seen to represent the ALA. Education, for PABBIS, appears to be a mainly instrumental matter, and the curriculum is defined in terms of instruction in and the attainment of skills though their intent is to enforce moral closure.

Their approach to texts is quite crudely quantitative. Books may be judged offensive because of the number of instances of, for example, particular words or particular kinds of events. The meanings given to such words and events in their narrative context are largely ignored. Sometimes, therefore, even a single instance of something judged to be offensive is taken as a sufficient basis to proscribe the text. Indeed, the effect of selecting out material deemed to be offensive – and assembled on the PABBIS website – is to produce another kind of text where all the offending utterances and events are arbitrarily juxtaposed and, effectively, condensed. How in practice the various novels and short stories they cite may be read is thus ignored in their textual substitutions. For PABBIS, Block is most consistently unacceptable because she represents gay characters in, as they put it, "100% positive" terms.

Henry Giroux has argued that "learning in the postmodern age" is located increasingly in:

> popular spheres that shape…identities through forms of knowledge and desire that appear absent from what is taught in schools. The literacies of the postmodern age are electronic, aural, and image based; and it is precisely within the diverse terrain of popular culture that pedagogical practices must be established as part of a broader politics of public life – practices that will aggressively subject dominant power to criticism, analysis, and transformation as part of a progressive reconstruction of democratic society. (Giroux, 1998: 49)

In some respects, PABBIS might be seen as "aggressively subject[ing] dominant power to criticism," but, with the "progressive reconstruction of democratic society" as his goal, it is unlikely that their critique is one he would support. In his discussion of the "Harry Potter wars," Henry Jenkins (2006) is concerned to explain the context of even the more fundamentalist Christian groups' activities. In particular, he stresses the sense of "threat" experienced in encountering the "immersive worlds" generated in "convergence culture":

> If educational reformers such as James Gee hope to break the stranglehold formal education has on children's learning and to expand the opportunities for children to practice literacy outside the classroom, these voices are more cautious, trying to reassert traditional values and structures in a world they can no longer fully control…Where some see a world more free from gatekeepers, they see a world where the floodgates have opened and no one can control the flow of "raw sewage" into

> their homes. Such groups want to assert a collective response to problems individual parents feel unable to confront on their own. (Jenkins, 2006: 198)

Given the expanded "transmedia" context in which fiction can be accessed, the concern with schools may seem to be beside the point. However, PABBIS contests the *legitimacy* bestowed by schools on the texts they make available. Clearly, their intention is quite strictly to circumscribe the school curriculum in accord with conservative interests. However, rather than respond to these arguments with a reiteration of a "libertarian" position on censorship, it is important to note the disparities in the classification of books alongside other media. The visual media (films for theatrical screening, videos, DVDs) are now routinely classified and described in terms of their content and, very broadly, in terms of what might be an appropriate audience. Buckingham (1996) has argued that there is some value in a system of classification, allowing viewers to judge in advance what they may be about to see. Following that argument, it seems inconsistent that books carry no comparable guide to their contents. Indeed, it could be argued that to exempt books alone from such a requirement perpetuates a notion of the "literary" as of value beyond that achieved by supposedly more "commercial" media. In a school context, such labeling, perhaps a matter of self-regulation by publishers, would allow teachers and librarians to assess, and place, books accordingly (see NCTE, 1994). But, as I have suggested in discussing the category "young adult," book classifications are likely to be of use to adults and of relatively little interest to young people. How young people themselves would respond to the elaboration of a more descriptive set of classifications is a complex and unpredictable matter.

PABBIS wants more than classification and description. For example, without regard for children as agents in their own learning, they argue that it is only directly to parents, not school students, that information about controversial books should be provided. Moreover, they demand that such information should be delivered into the hands of parents rather than being made available for consultation and that it should be detailed, comprehensive and include evidence of all that is "potentially objectionable" by "type, frequency, vividness/graphicness" (http://www.pabbis.com). The focus maintained by PABBIS is very consistently upon teachers and librarians – and on their website they specifically name those of whom they are critical. In their recommendation, they attempt to position teachers and librarians as subservient to parental interests, laboring to satisfy the conditions dictated to them. Excluding any consideration of children's agency furthers their strategy to construct the issue in terms of a contest between parents and teachers.[4] In some respects, this conflict is one between teachers as agents of a new middle class and various, religiously framed, ideals of traditional family life.

Conclusion

In conclusion, it is important to emphasize how differently Francesca Lia Block's work is read. For Witchbaby participants, her writing is one among many sources for a process of self-production, reflection, and reconstruction. As the Witchbaby group appears to have ceased some years ago, the often intense activity of exchange among its contributors is not now recoverable. Indeed, repeated online searches produce relatively little evidence of its former life. There are, however, many other online fan groups devoted to Francesca Lia Block. Some make direct reference to the Witchbaby group and represent it somewhat differently from the way I have described it in this chapter. "Peachypie" (Yahoo! Groups), for example, announces: "As much as I like the Witchbaby list, it does tend to get pretty intolerant. I'm making this list as an open, more tolerant alternative for Witchbaby members and non-members alike." Another, "SlinksterCool" (Yahoo! Groups), similarly distances itself from the Witchbaby group: "I set up this group to be a more open and positive alternative to the witchbaby egroup. Call me crazy, but I think if you set up or join a group devoted to Francesca Lia Block, you should actually like Francesca's writing." There is considerably more scope to investigate these sometimes elusive, and relatively ephemeral, online groups. But here, clearly, there is some evidence that, even among self-identified fans of Block's writing, there is no stable consensus and, perhaps, some significant rivalry.

For those who contribute, as customers, to Amazon.com, Block's work is always visibly contested. Discourses of consumer satisfaction, rather than fan following, prevail in what is a relatively public site. Nevertheless, and despite the fact that her writing is most often admired, reviewers contribute, from a relatively wide variety of standpoints, to a continuing debate around the moral and aesthetic status of her work. For PABBIS, her novels and short stories are bad objects and, in their edited highlighting of what they consider "inappropriate" passages, they are reconstituted as gratuitously offensive. PABBIS is hostile to the agency of children, seeks to fix them in place under parental authority, and denies any sense of the self as open to dialogue, reflection, and remaking.

Cutting across, but in the background of, these various sites of reception is a tension between different class inflected models of the "self" and of its formation in childhood and youth. Though socially circumscribed, the "world" constructed in Block's work is nevertheless one where sexual identities and relationships are matters for reflection and negotiation by children and young people themselves. The "traditional" authority of families is relinquished and the moral superiority of adults is rendered uncertain, tenuous, and negotiable. Faced with such a "world," reviewers, readers and fans, socially located in quite widely varying class cultures, position and reposition themselves, often strongly asserting their beliefs about what constitutes legitimate sexuality and the wider moral conduct of the self. I will return to Block's work in Chapter Five to consider, through more detailed attention to two novels, *The Hanged Man* and *Missing Angel Juan*, how these matters are explored through the imagery of whiteness.

Chapter Three

Writing for Young Adults: Melvin Burgess and Mark Haddon

Introduction

This chapter examines just two novels by two British novelists. But it illustrates aspects of a wider debate. The conceptualization of a "young adult" audience by those who apparently write for it is central. Though published in the same year, and both as "crossover" fiction marketed simultaneously for both young adult and adult readers, *Doing It* by Melvin Burgess (2003) and *The Curious Incident of the Dog in the Night-Time* by Mark Haddon (2003) provide sharply contrasting cases.

In this chapter, I also want to include some evidence of how students read the texts presented to them in class, in the "Young Adult Fictions" module that I teach at London Metropolitan University. On the whole, the students represented here are not those for whom literature occupies a central place, either in their leisure or in their studies. A majority of the students are women, from a wide array of ethnic and religious backgrounds, and often with few of the high school qualifications associated with traditional routes to university education.

The novels are particularly salient examples of the production of fiction for "young adult readers" in a "new media" context dominated by talk of "convergence," unregulated access, and, in education, the disturbance of hierarchical relations of authority between teacher and learner (Livingstone, 2002; Snyder, 2002; Kress, 2003). Most studies of new media literacies focus on the distinctively new forms that have emerged in recent years, with print fiction often seen as marginal to the new media culture of young people (Kress, 2003). However, as I have suggested in earlier chapters, existing forms of communication are not replaced by new media in any absolute sense. Rather, they are repositioned and in some respects "remade." Even old forms such as the novel are not simply abandoned by audiences but are variously taken up in conjunction with other media forms. The "young adult" audience, in particular, is now often characterized as strongly orientated to visual and new media and, as I have argued, also less confined to reading practices regulated by school (Richards, 2007). Changes in the marketing, design, and textual organization of "young adult" novels contribute further to the process of repositioning an old form. This is a strategy pursued by publishers, but it is also a response to changes in the formation of "readership" networks (Witchbaby, for example) and a concomitant intensification of "transmedia" connections (see Jenkins, 2006). Such "networks" are both less dependent on school-based dissemination and are more attentive to popular commercial (and online) modes of publicity and exchange. In many respects, this suggests a further shift in the relationship between schooled literacy and wider informal literacies, but in this case print surfaces where visual media are believed to be entirely dominant.

Doing It

It is useful to consider, first of all, the discourses that may inform current discussions of children and young people as media audiences. These are usefully outlined in Buckingham, Davies, Jones, and Kelley's (1999) discussion of how those involved in producing television for children characterize their audience. They suggest that there are four main discourses evident in the talk about children documented in interviews with their respondents:

> we can identify four broad subcategories of producer discourse about the child audience. The first of these centres on the idea of the "vulnerable child" – the child threatened by the bad effects of television or seductively interpellated by consumer culture, and for both reasons in need of protection. The second is a "child-centred" discourse, in which ideas about children's essential nature, the stages of children's development and their consequent needs and wants are used to justify particular kinds of scheduling and programme-making. The third and fourth types of discourse involve an assumption that children are articulate "social actors." They are similar in that they stress the primacy of children's preferences and draw attention to children's social capabilities. They differ in so far as they inflect this socially active child in conceptually distinct – though in practice overlapping – ways: the child is understood here either as a *consumer* or as a potential *citizen*. (Buckingham et al., 1999: 149)

Melvin Burgess well illustrates one way that writers tactically self-position themselves in relation to the field of young adult fiction and the broader context of popular media consumption. For example, he has argued that books for "young adults" are just beginning to "catch up" with the popular media that he now also claims define the context for his own writing:

> Teenage fiction is an area that has developed out of recognition…I can't recall any books written specifically for me when I was that age...The film industry, the music industry, computer games, magazines, comics – they all know very well about the

youth market. There is an age group of about fourteen to twenty five that is extremely profitable for everyone.

(Burgess, 2000a – http://web.onetel.net.uk/~melvinburgess/)

Burgess draws on aspects of a child-centered discourse but thoroughly re-inflected by that of the child as consumer. Vulnerability and protectionism have no place. The older genre of "young adult" fiction, against which Burgess defines his own writing, is implicitly defined, rather monolithically, by what it excludes – sex, drugs, swearing.[1] In some respects, Burgess's case is persuasive. There are many novels apparently addressing teenagers but which arguably make a priority of satisfying those who actively select and mediate books for young readers – teachers, librarians, bookstore managers (Zipes, 2001). Such writing is positioned as "safe" for adults, especially those working with young people, to give to them because it does not make available knowledge of sex or drugs, for example. Books are assumed to be located in "pedagogically" regulated relations between adults and young people unlike texts circulating in the popular media. Indeed it is as if books are seen as implying a more immediate face-to-face encounter between generations. And unlike teen magazines, television or the Internet, they retain their status as "in the gift" of adults. The activities of PABBIS, discussed in the previous chapter, focus on exactly this positioning of print fiction in relations between adults and young people.

Though historically Burgess (born 1954) is not entirely right – there were books written specifically for teenagers in the late 1960s and early 1970s – his self-orientation to an audience no longer defined by high school attendance and to a market he regards as highly "profitable" combines a claim to give young people what they need with an imperative to do so on a career sustaining scale. Central to his writing career is an offer of authenticity, especially in relation to the representation of drug use and teenage sexual activity. Such "authenticity" or "honesty" is the basis of his claim to meet the needs of young adult readers and the primary means of marketing and selling significant quantities of his titles. The credibility of his claim depends, in his view, on the achievement of an authenticity defined through comparison with representations available in the popular media. Controversy, with the publication of *Junk* (1996), *Lady: My Life as a Bitch* (2001), and, more recently, *Doing It* (2003) is perhaps welcome as both evidence of the strength of his challenge to the allegedly "insulated" and "backward" book market and a further heightening of "profitability." The production of controversial titles is, if spasmodically, one effective way of restoring print's position alongside other media.

However, recalling Lesko (2001), to specify a "young adult" age phase does contribute to the perpetuation of "adolescence." To call for more writing for this audience, as Burgess does, may be intended to reassure publishers that such a market exists, but it also contributes to a classification of readers in terms of a normative and developmental trajectory. Whatever Burgess's intent, the "young adult" designation warns adults (teachers, parents, librarians) that the book thus labeled is not "children's literature" and protects publishers from the allegation that their marketing irresponsibly intrudes into childhood and bypasses parents in so doing. But Burgess often implies that his own writing engages teenage readers almost despite adult gatekeepers. In various reviews, interviews, and articles assembled on his own website, Burgess positions himself as knowing, and being honest in representing, what young people's lives are like:

> If you are aged sixteen or seventeen and you want to read fiction that talks about your life – your recreation, your sex life, your feelings and emotions – you're either stuck with stuff about twenty-somethings, or…soft stuff that seems to be written for younger readers, or…some polite, carefully edited stuff that doesn't dare talk about reality. (On *Junk* - see http://web.onetel.net.uk/~melvinburgess/)

His claim is, centrally, to write for young people otherwise left to fiction not specifically written "for" them, though here the characterization of such fiction as "soft" and "polite" hints at a preference for the "masculinity" explored in *Doing It*.

Yet Burgess, apparently so confident in seeking to engage young people directly, does also acknowledge the significance of schools in the formation of a market for his writing. There is an evident tension in his position between writing those texts which will be endorsed by schools, thus sustaining his continuing success as a professional writer, and writing that more directly aligns itself with popular cultural entertainment and thus, he argues, more directly engages his intended audience:

> Teenagers as a group consume…narrative entertainment – by the barrel load…. Who can blame them? It's so rich – sexy, loud, violent, ironic and cruel, but also beautiful, dreamy and intense. Schools have an obvious problem with this kind of thing…one reason why books for teenagers have been so slow to take on the experience of other media. (Burgess, 2000b – http://web.onetel.net.uk/~melvinburgess/)

Because Burgess has a continuing relationship with schools and positions himself as a "young adult" author, he is compelled to negotiate his writing with some regard for the power of educational gatekeepers. Though ambivalent, he remains a writer for young people of school age. So though *Doing It*

(2003) might be judged "explicit" in its sexual descriptions and in the spoken language of its characters, it is not sexually explicit in the deliberately erotic mode of, for example, Francesca Lia Block's *Nymph* (2000). *Doing It* may not be written to be read in class, but it still anchors its authenticity in a claim to represent the emotional realities of teenage boys' lives and, to that extent, also addresses teachers and other adults likely to work with and have responsibility to young people.

As Henry Jenkins suggests, some advocates of media education persist in seeing the media as "threats" (Jenkins, 2006: 259). Perhaps Henry Giroux, among them, might argue that if Burgess has succeeded in "re-enchanting" (Kenway and Bullen, 2001) the book for a generation of young readers, he has done so by emulating aspects of the popular media that should be objects of criticism. It could be argued that if Burgess and Giroux share a recognition of the importance of "electronic, aural, and image based" media (Giroux, 1998: 49), Burgess addresses young people more as consumers than citizens, advocating engagement in the popular domain without any concern for "teacherly" intervention. One critic has suggested that, in effect, Burgess has abused his position as a "young adult" author, by extending oppressive aspects of media culture into writing for children and young people. Anne Fine (author of *The Tulip Touch*) in her review of *Doing It* (*The Guardian*, March 29 2003) comments:

> What are three separate children's publishers thinking of, peddling this grubby book, which demeans both young women and young men? It will prove as effective a form of sexual bullying as any hardcore porno mag passed round...No girl or young woman should ever have to read these vile, disgusting musings about themselves.

In the following section, I want to introduce some of the responses to *Doing It* from a class composed predominantly of young women. Fine's uncompromisingly protectionist stance, and that of other critics, is subject to some thoughtful consideration from an audience including the kind of young women she wishes to defend.

Teaching *Doing It*

The students that I quote here are institutionally removed from youth as defined in the school context, but in terms of age some are still relatively close to the upper end of school age. As second year undergraduates, they read *Doing It* as not directly addressing them but a readership to which they feel some proximity. They also take up a mediating stance in the dispute between Burgess and Fine. To some extent, their responses can be read in terms of current discourses on childhood and youth discussed above (Buckingham et al., 1999). Though the comments discussed here come from students rather than media professionals, these discourses circulate in everyday "common sense" about young people. The first example I want to cite comes from a paper written in response to the question "To what extent do novels written for 'young adults' offer moral advice?" Bertha was a student in her late twenties (born 1977), originally from a village in northern Ghana but mostly educated in south London. She positions herself in her writing as looking back to her own youth and, significantly, articulating a degree of moral censure both from the distance, and from the religious stance, to which she lays claim:

> In today's society adolescents are far more advanced in their sexuality because of the media portrayal of sex through our television screens and teenage magazines. It is arguable that the explicit exploration of sex using such mediums is corrupting the minds of the young people therefore destroying their sense of innocence.
>
> Such teaching is not morally correct because they are impressionable young people who are trusting and the Christian belief is that sex should not take place outside of marriage. This is not a means to repress teenagers in their desire to have sex, or their curiosity to explore this issue but it is for benefit of protection from all the negative consequences it can bring.
>
> I remember reading *Forever*, some 16 years ago and thinking that the content was extremely graphic in its choice of language...As a teenager I would be uncomfortable about reading such material in the company of my mother, but through recommendations of friends I read them and found that I preferred books that were softer in tone. Novels such as *Sweet Valley High* and *The Last Battle* written by C.S. Lewis. I believe problem novels take away young people's "innocence" at times by providing them with adult material before their time, endorsing the experimentation with sex, which results in teenage pregnancies or increased drugs use both negative consequences on the shoulders of young people.

There is an insistent strand of protectionism in this, though it is combined with recognition of the pervasive presence of sex in the experience of young people as media consumers. On Melvin Burgess, she comments:

> Problem books are written with the assumption that adolescent readers are only interested in such topics...but I think it serves two purposes and that is [to] advertise and promote the writer. Anything of a graphic nature will cause controversy and that in itself is publicity for the author. Having fun does not have to involve sex, drugs or violence because such material is not morally conducive to society.

Youth is understood here in terms of stages in maturation from innocence to adult responsibility. Her articulation of a moral conservatism identified with

Christianity is also justified more pragmatically as preventing the damage that young people may do to themselves. In this account, television and teenage magazines, and the young adult novels introduced to her by her friends sixteen years ago, and again in class, disrupt the order of growth and development and threaten social order. Moreover, to the extent that print fiction attempts to emulate the visual media, it too is assimilated to the "effects" discourse through which drug taking and teenage pregnancy become consequences of exposure to the wrong kind of texts. Though this is a familiar discourse, well embedded in the popular domain, its emergence in her writing carries a lingering emotional weight. Here, and in a more extensive autobiographical piece to be discussed in Chapter Seven, she records the uneasy experience of disjunction between the moral world of the family ("reading such material in the company of my mother") and that of her south London friends. Despite the intentions of the course – to question and debate notions of moral guidance and of adult authority in print fiction addressing young people – and the educational capital to be gained by responding to those intentions, she returns to and reasserts the difficulty of negotiating the disjunction in her own personal history of reading. In many respects a confident and articulate student with a strong sense of educational aspiration, she nevertheless declines to engage in the forms of tentative, dispassionate and more impersonally "argued" discourse to which a high value is attached in academic essay writing.

Though other students tended to strongly support Burgess's writing, they also declined to be dispassionate, favoring a more personalized and experiential justification for their views. The following comments were made in an essay by a nineteen-year-old white woman (born 1985) from Pennsylvania, studying at the university for one semester:

> Having read the book I didn't find it overly demeaning to women at all. It was a mere two years ago that I was the same age as the characters in the book. I'm not sure if I am just simply used to the idea of being treated that way or if it really is a commonality now but I could relate to each and every one of the characters, even the boys. It takes a long time to figure out how to be a man and these boys are not unlike all of the boys before them…As far as I'm concerned, Melvin Burgess does nothing but speak the truth about young people and how they discover their sexuality. How can it be offensive or sexist when we've all gone through it and we know that every generation has had their share of these moments growing up?

In this case, the student positions herself as in alliance with Burgess on the grounds of the text's authenticity for her and for "everyone" ("we've all gone through it"). She represents it as offering recognition, as corresponding to her own, and again to everyone's, experience of male sexuality. This is perhaps the most common mode of engagement I have encountered in discussing the novel with groups of women from late teens through to thirties. They repeatedly affirm the accuracy of the representation of behavior and language with reference to their own real world experience. They do not situate the text in relation to other representations either within the field of print fiction, or more broadly, in relation to visual media. The discourse in which they articulate their reading relation to the text privileges a referential, "real world," interpretation. In their "common-sense" reading of the text they are seemingly confirming the power of normalization, specifically of the male gaze to which as young women they are subject. However, their endorsement of the text's "authenticity" does not preclude an engagement with moral questions located in their social world. The text is read as fully referential, representing the world as they know it. Questions of textual construction (of narrative, genre, character) are, for them, somewhat beside the point. They take the novel as a starting point for consideration of relational issues in the real social world, not as an object for critical analysis.

Bourdieu comments on this type of engagement by contrasting it with forms of "distancing":

> [The] popular reaction is the very opposite of the detachment of the aesthete, who, as is seen whenever he appropriates one of the objects of popular taste (e.g. Westerns or strip cartoons), introduces a distance, a gap – the measure of his distant distinction – vis-à-vis "first-degree" perception, by displacing the interest from the "content," characters, plot etc., to the form, to the specifically artistic effects which are only appreciated relationally, through a comparison with other works which is incompatible with immersion in the singularity of the work immediately given. Detachment, disinterestedness, indifference – aesthetic theory has so often presented these as the only way to recognize the work of art for what it is, autonomous, *selbstandig,* that one ends up forgetting that they really mean disinvestment, detachment, indifference, in other words, the refusal to invest oneself and take things seriously. (Bourdieu, 1986: 34)

These students appear to occupy the position of "popular realism," attributed, in *Distinction*, to the working class:

> The popular realism which inclines working people to reduce practices to the reality of their function, to do what they do, and be what they are ("That's the way I am"), without "kidding themselves" ("That's the way it is")...[is] the near-perfect antithesis of the aesthetic disavowal which, by a sort of essential hypocrisy (seen, for example, in the opposition between pornography and eroticism) masks the interest in function by the primacy given to form, so that what people do, they do as if they were not doing it. (Bourdieu, 1986: 200)

However, it may be that such a position is also articulated as a kind of resistance to the authority of educational demands that they "reclassify" their own reading experience and, further, do so in response to the "distancing strategies" of their teacher, a male academic. Though there is little direct comment in students' writing on their experience of being addressed in these academic terms, it is worth noting that in one twenty-two-year-old (born 1983) black woman's essay, she comments specifically on the strategies of "disinvestment" adopted by the male contributors to a BBC TV discussion of the novel between Mark Lawson (writer, panel chair), Mark Kermode (film critic), Will Self (writer), and Rosie Boycott (journalist). The following extract from the discussion illustrates her "case":

> Rosie Boycott: You always heard…that boys do think a lot about this stuff, and it's clear from this book just how much boys do think about it. But I liked the fact very much that there is also a kind of responsibility in there…. There was a kind of adulthood in them…
>
> Will Self: I think he has a bit of a problem – I don't think he got the age register quite right. For me, this was the sensibility, the sort of puerile smutty talk about sex was what I remember from being around 14 or 15, and these are meant to be 17-year-old lads. What he also can't get is the cultural reference. Adolescence is absolutely preoccupied by the minutiae of pop music, film, clothing, style…I would suspect teenagers feel quite preached to by this kind of literature. It's about responsibility and behaving yourself.
>
> Mark Kermode: I was a teenage boy and I don't recognise myself in this at all. My problem with it, I agree with Will, is that it doesn't read to me like the words of a 17-year-old. It reads like the words of a 40-year-old attempting to do an impression of a 17-year-old.... His motives are honourable, but at the end of it I felt rather creepy.

The student comments:

> The difference of opinion could be seen as gendered…the female thought that the book answered questions that she always wanted to know, an insight in to how men at that time thought, but the men on the other hand gave the impression that it was an invasion of privacy, they were both very defensive and were adamant not to associate themselves with characters in the book, the sense of them being invaded, even insulted that a fellow male would write about such insecurities…for all to see, but women found it to be intriguing and fascinating because finally the male species now made sense.[2]

Again the text is taken here to be a disclosure of the real rather than – as I would argue in teaching the novel – a comic representation constructing a particular version of male adolescent sexuality from precedents in the wider field of popular media discourse. If all my attempts to make the text a matter for analysis are rendered evasive, refusing the truth revealed in the book, then clearly teaching needs to engage explicitly with, and further reflection on, the positions from which people read. Both gender and class complicate such positions, but neither Kermode nor Self acknowledge this in distancing themselves from Burgess's account of adolescence.

A white working-class male student in his late thirties (born 1965) comments directly on Anne Fine's review in class terms suggesting that her "critique …missed its mark, by aiming fears at the text, which were perhaps based on middle class presumptions of feminine sensibilities from a time past." But again I would also not want to accept that the process of teaching – calling for reflection on modes of representation, for example – can be collapsed into Bourdieu's account of the distancing strategies of aesthetic discourse. In teaching *Doing It*, it is possible both to address questions about heterosexual relationships *and* to question the particular representation of them privileged in Burgess's novel. To do so, there is every reason to pursue a teaching strategy that concentrates effort on locating and comparing the novel in the wider context of media representation of young people's sexual relationships.[3]

The Curious Incident of the Dog in the Night-Time

Like Burgess, Mark Haddon has been identified for some years with writing for children. *The Curious Incident of the Dog in the Night-Time* (2003), his first novel, was "published twice over, like a double helping of good news, as a crossover book for adults (Jonathan Cape) and for teenagers (David Fickling)" (Kellaway, *The Observer* Review 27 April 27 2003). But the position taken by Haddon as a novelist differs considerably from that of Burgess. Though known as a writer for children, he has not made any claim to write for a "young adult" audience and does not therefore engage in the debate about the needs of such an audience or, like Block, take any responsibility for whether or not his writing is "appropriate" for those who read it. Claiming that he wrote the novel for himself, he emphasizes the fluidity of its position in the book market:

> Much was made of the "crossover" appeal of the novel, something that Haddon himself dismissed as being nothing more than a marketing and media construct…. In response to those who believed that it was primarily a children's book Haddon said, "like most writers, I wrote for myself and as a 41-year-old I saw it as an adult book."(http://www.contemporarywriters.com/authors)

Thus, unlike *Doing It, The Curious Incident of the Dog in the Night-Time* does not take its place amidst explicit claims to attract a "young adult" readership by offering a version of teenage life as "authentic" or as constituted by sex, drugs, and music. But its publication for a "young adult" audience – and its evident success with relatively young readers – does suggest interesting questions about how it engages them.

The narrator, Christopher, is a fifteen-year-old boy, still at school, and suffering the estrangement of his parents. The novel deals with a crisis, condensed in the mystery of a neighbor's dog impaled on a fork, and pursues its consequences through various ordeals to a more settled conclusion. Christopher has survived without adults and is more experienced and more "self-possessed." In these respects it is like many other novels classified as "young adult."[4] But there are features of the text that suggest an interest in rethinking how print fiction should address its readers amidst the proliferation of visual and new media. Like Burgess, Haddon writes as an already established author for children and with a comparable awareness of the wider media context, but he produces a significantly different "solution" to the implicit question of what a "novel" should be. The form of the novel, with its varied and "self-conscious" emphasis on typography, on layout, and on visual components, suggests a concern with the design of the page consistent with developments in electronic media. Together the specific concern with visual design and with typography, *and* the supposedly "autistic" and "non-literary" disposition of its narrator make this novel look especially appropriate to an audience with a more visual orientation to texts (Kress, 2003). Haddon's novel provides an illustration of an approach to the form of the novel emphasizing "design," and thus engaging readers more routinely accustomed to negotiating screens rather than page after page of print. In addition to writing for children, Haddon is also a cartoonist and illustrator and his website (http://www.markhaddon.com/) further exemplifies a concern with visual design, and, in addition, color. Here, the "re-enchantment" of print takes a different direction from that pursued by Burgess.

Teaching *The Curious Incident of the Dog in the Night-Time*

Readings of *The Curious Incident of the Dog in the Night-Time* are framed by its position in the market and the publishers' "packaging." Where the novel is categorized as "young adult," readings are cued perhaps most strongly as privileging the character of Christopher as offering an insight into autism. This is a reading that is, in part, invited by the publishers, despite comments from the author to the effect that Christopher's "voice" preceded the decision to develop the character as autistic (Kellaway, 2003). Positioning the novel as "about autism" implies a kind of transparency, with the text providing a way into the kind of mind that is usually understood to be closed and inaccessible. Such a reading is encouraged by the quotations used on the book covers of both the "young adult" and the "crossover" editions. Framed as a realist portrait of an autistic adolescent boy, other ways of engaging this text are implicitly marginalized. Perhaps a majority of commentators on Haddon's novel have discussed it in terms of the authenticity of its portrayal of Asperger's syndrome. Germaine Greer is certainly among those who interpret the novel in this way:

> His world makes sense. It's just not the same world as the world of other people...when he comes up against other people, they seem insane, and he seems sane. Their behaviour is outrageous, cruel, stupid, vulgar, because this child is so intelligent, so focused, so orderly. He is involved, like any subject people, in this attempt to make himself understood to other people.... [5]

But, in her commentary, what also emerges is some further acknowledgment of the consequences of seeing other people from Christopher's standpoint.

In teaching this novel, I do acknowledge the reading that engages with "Christopher" as an insight into the mind of an autistic boy but I also attempt to introduce a perspective derived from debates in "formalist" literary theory. In particular, I have introduced the concept of defamiliarization (Jameson, 1974: 55-59; Bennett, 1979) as a way of describing the effect of reading such a curious first person narrative in which the mundane world and ordinary events within it are rendered strange, puzzling, and troublesome. In this respect I have wanted to emphasize the novel's critical and satirical representation of the ordinary social world. Both for its use of defamiliarization techniques, and of drawings, I have encouraged students to compare the novel with passages from Kurt Vonnegut's (1973) *Breakfast of Champions.* To some extent, this approach could be justified by referring back to Mark Haddon's comments on his own interest in developing the novel. In a telephone interview with Powell's Books (Portland, Oregon) he comments:

> For me, disability is a way of getting some extremity...that throws an interesting light on people. But it's also something that's terribly, terribly ordinary. There are these extreme situations, but they're happening somewhere in your street at this very moment. And that's important to me, to find the extraordinary inside the ordinary. (http://www.powells.com/authors/haddon.html Accessed January 2 2008).

Though he does not draw in any way explicitly on the concept of defamiliarization, the reference to "finding the extraordinary inside the ordinary" hints at the strategy of making strange routine and taken-for-granted behavior.

At least in writing, students taking the Young Adult Fictions course have not responded to this proposed reading. As I have suggested, it is insufficiently cued by its market context. But read as a "young adult" novel (in a course on YA fiction), its defamiliarizing techniques are perhaps even more difficult to acknowledge because this is not what either children's or young adult fiction is expected to do. As with other "young adult" fiction, the expectation is that it will portray adolescent life rather than that of adults. Read as a psychology of autism, *The Curious Incident of the Dog in the Night-Time*'s most powerfully satirical passages might well be undermined and reduced to a quirky outlook associated with an individual pathology. The intricate hypocrisies of adult life, the semiotic clutter of Paddington station, or the curiosities of religious belief, sharply illuminated in the novel, may thus be read as "odd" only because of Christopher's "inadequacies."

Though there are significant problems in seeking to position the novel as "literary," it is worth exploring briefly what might be gained in doing so. For most of the students taking the course I have described, textual analysis is not a familiar practice. Like most people, they have no experience in reading literary theory. To read the novel as I have suggested it might be does not obviously "make sense." The particular cultural capital they bring into play in reading the novel includes their knowledge of its settings (specific and typical), of young people, and of social and educational practices; on the whole, it does not include textual theory. For example, consideration of how the embedding of a variety of everyday language in the novel makes it an object of curiosity rather than routine functionality is not, for them, of particular concern. For Haddon, writing *The Curious Incident of the Dog in the Night-Time* was intended to be a move from children's fiction to "literature" (http://www.powells.com/authors/haddon.html Accessed January 2 2008). However, if such categories as "young adult" and even general "fiction" are constructed both as separate from and as unconcerned with the processes thus, in a complementary movement, sequestered as "literary" and "specialist," Haddon's satirical purposes may be unrecognized.

Conclusion

This chapter has suggested how new print fiction, especially marketed toward a "young adult" and "younger adult" audience, has responded to the intensification and expansion of electronic media. These are tentative arguments but, as these forms mutate, are offered as notes on a rapidly shifting process of repositioning and innovation. *Doing It* and *The Curious Incident of the Dog in the Night-Time* will be joined by many other examples (see, for example, Cabot, 2002). To make any sense of print fiction without reference to the wider media is somewhat futile, even for those instances where the text is claimed as "literary." Moreover, if young people are broadly familiar with a wide array of "communicative modes" and have variously well-developed competences and reading orientations across the various media available to them, then the play with text and image in *The Curious Incident of the Dog in the Night-Time* may well be much more familiar and more enjoyable than for those more accustomed to a more "straightforwardly" referential text. In teaching these texts, it is essential to situate print more rigorously alongside other media *and* to draw on precedents in social semiotics to articulate, and explore, more explicitly how meanings are produced by texts and negotiated by their readers (Burn and Parker, 2003; Richards, 2005a).

Chapter Four

What Are We? Adolescence, Sex, and Intimacy in *Buffy the Vampire Slayer*

Introduction

In this chapter, I discuss *Buffy the Vampire Slayer,* a TV show that has attracted sustained adult attention. It presents youth both as troubled and as excitingly in touch with danger.[1] I look back to those episodes of *Buffy the Vampire Slayer* where the characters encounter questions of sex and intimacy for the first time as teenagers.[2] In doing so I want to consider why the mythology of vampirism has become such a successful resource in exploring such issues. In particular, I want to argue that the show is distinctive and powerful because it addresses a key question – what is it like to encounter sex, to begin to engage in intimate relationships, for young people in the "post-AIDS" era? There are now many studies of *Buffy the Vampire Slayer*, ample evidence, to which I am adding, of the enduring fascination it has elicited from a wide array of academics (Kaveney, 2001; Wilcox and Lavery, 2002; Burr, 2003a,b; Jowett, 2005; Wilcox, 2005; Williamson, 2005). The emphasis of this contribution to the archive is on the need to approach sex and intimacy as historically formed (Weeks, 1995). Rather than construe *Buffy the Vampire Slayer* as a story about "adolescence" or "sex" as natural and unchanging hurdles in the process of growing up, I argue that its core themes are animated by more historically recent uncertainties encountered in the process of "becoming sexual."

Questions of identity in adolescence arise throughout the first three seasons of *Buffy the Vampire Slayer* and return with some force in the fifth, with the introduction of Dawn, Buffy's sister. But in this fictive world, issues of identity become almost ontological questions – and hence my title, not "who are we?" but "what are we?" The show frequently poses the question of what kind of being (human, vampire, demon, witch, robot, hybrid) each character may be. Moreover, reading others – identifying them, and making judgments about what kinds of being they are – is made problematic. There is an insistent concern with how reliable a correspondence there might be between the surface exterior of the body and what might (or might not) be its bloody and emotional interior. This complicates sex – with what, exactly, is it possible, or safe, to have sex? And can intimacy figure in relations between different kinds of being?

Buffy the Vampire Slayer has been widely admired for its mixing together of seemingly disparate genres (Kaveney, 2001; Wilcox and Lavery, 2002; South, 2003). Yet the importance of melodrama has been neglected – surprisingly because so often its self-referential poise of lightly ironic comedy veers into the bleak and uncomfortable logic of this "other," sometimes disparaged, genre.[3] Steve Neale (1986: 12) has argued that

> Melodramas tend to deal in terms of subject matter with desire and its vicissitudes... and in particular the blockages to its fulfilment...Blockages, barriers and bars to the fulfilment of desire are constantly introduced as events change course.

Understood in these terms, melodrama is a crucial resource for a show preoccupied with intimacy and sexual relations as problematic and precarious. In *Buffy the Vampire Slayer,* melodrama characterizes those narrative strands where characters' relations with each other, both sexual and familial – or quasi-familial – are blocked in part by their differing states of being, rather than by differences in social position. Most prominently, in the first three seasons, Angel/Angelus and Buffy contend with desire caught in the radical differences between them – living and undead, slayer and vampire, young and old, mortal and immortal.

Among studies of vampire mythology attentive to its sexual meanings, Franco Moretti's essay "Dialectic of Fear" (Moretti, 1988) has served here to open up a reading of *Buffy the Vampire Slayer* as exploring anxieties about intimacy and sex but which the show itself cannot name. For example, pursuing a psychoanalytic argument, Moretti suggests that the vampire is invented to serve an emotional purpose: to appear as an external menace where the source of anxiety and dread is inside us. Moretti's case is that the "literary formalization, the rhetorical figure...has a double function: it *expresses* the unconscious content and at the same time *hides* it" (Moretti, 1988: 103). Thus,

> ...the function of this literature [is] to take up within itself determinate fears in order to present them *in a form different from their real one*: to transform them into *other* fears, so that readers do not have to face up to what might really frighten them. (Moretti, 1988: 105)

Following Moretti, it might be argued that the show provides a kind of reassurance that what is really frightening comes only out of Hellmouth, not out of the teenagers' actions and relationships themselves. In this light each episode secures "mystification" by providing narrative, and emotional, closure with the routine destruction through formulaic violence of these "more threatening" figures.

If the concept of "disavowal" is applied to the construction of the fictive world of *Buffy the Vampire Slayer,* it could be argued, though necessarily with only the most oblique evidence, that it "re-presents" anxieties integral to teenage life but often denied in popular culture. So, following the logic of a psychoanalytic reading, the vampire mythology allows, precisely, a disavowal of HIV/AIDS in representing contemporary sex. The imagery of biting, sucking, and drinking blood allies sex with violence, risk, and possible death. But, to the extent that sex is refracted through vampire mythology in *Buffy the Vampire Slayer,* anxieties about sexual activity and its consequences are displaced into the realm of the supernatural. In this argument HIV/AIDS, *as such*, might never appear.

There are indeed few explicit references to HIV/AIDS in *Buffy the Vampire Slayer*, though *Anne* (3001)[4] does offer a scenario implying its existence: Buffy discovers that teenagers adrift on the streets go missing but reappear, soon after, many decades older. In her investigations, she visits a blood bank where teenagers sell their blood. Behind her there is an AIDS poster. No reference is made to it – though the plot turns in part around a distinction between "healthy" and "unhealthy" teenagers. Otherwise, references are slight and ambiguous. But as Weeks insists:

> If sex and the health, fitness and well-being of the body are principal elements of personal identity in the modern world, and if modern identity is in part at least based on an avoidance of death, then inevitably an epidemic which associates sexual activity (heterosexual as well as homosexual) with death is likely to have a profound existential impact. (Weeks, 1995: 169)

The key point is that to the extent that the wider cultural construction of sex and sexuality has been unsettled by the emergence of HIV/AIDS in the past twenty-five years, the show engages *not* with AIDS but with sex as redefined by this recent and continuing history.

The characters, then, grow up in peculiar and dangerous circumstances. They get older, they move on, leave school, go to college, and, as they do so, they encounter death and loss, pain and frustration. Much of their talk is about dealing with traumatic events and their consequences. Specific threats are eliminated but there always have to be more – thus the form of the show confers a kind of embattled gravity, spiked with humor, on the central ensemble. Caught up in the process of "becoming" adult, there is a shared self-consciousness about what the outcome might be, literally what they could become, beyond the liminal phase of adolescence. If, in popular discourse, adolescence is seen as a "hormonal storm," and in the adult world sex appears to have become tortuous and potentially dangerous, it is thus more difficult to foresee how the adolescent "storm" might end (see Griffin, 1993; Richards, 1998b). Indeed, as the various characters age from fifteen to twenty, and into adulthood, their uncertainties about both what it means to be human – or otherwise – and with whom intimacy can be secured are not given any simple or reassuring resolution.

The following sections of this chapter explore these themes through three interrelated discussions. The first section "Being the Slayer" examines Buffy as a participant in teenage life – as a teenage girl caught up in, amongst other things, "becoming sexual." She is very much embedded in "adolescent" life and is, as the contrast with Kendra her "replacement" slayer makes clear, in no way a detached "Olympian" superhero. The second section, "Object Choices," pursues the question of intimacy primarily in relation to Buffy's struggle to secure her relationship with Angel, but also in terms of the broader question of what kinds of being characters fall in love with, what motivates their choice, and what risks intimacy entails. The last section looks at one episode, *Blood Ties* (5013), where the issues of identity in adolescence and of intimacy are explored in terms of relations between "sisters" rather than between lovers. Here, beyond the despair of her struggles to secure sexual intimacy, Buffy lays claim, against the odds, to a human relationship with "Dawn."

Being the Slayer

Buffy the Vampire Slayer constructs a rhetoric of identity with some consistency across all of its seasons. How do we know what we are? By looking in a mirror perhaps: something human beings can do, and vampires cannot. Or by looking back at photographs of ourselves. To some extent we assume that our bodily surface confirms both our being human and our being a particular, individual human. Furthermore, adolescence has been relentlessly constructed as a period of intense self-scrutiny, of minute attention to the skin and to the elimination of blemishes and threats to the perfection of its surface. Hair and eyes and other facial features demand further monitoring. Clothes command a comparable attention to self-display. Perhaps more than in other "phases," in adolescence we are supposed to know ourselves by what we are on the outside. In market terms, of course, such a version of "youth" sustains a whole array of aids to surface maintenance. Such anxious surface perfection suggests a disavowal of all that lies beneath. After all, adolescence is also constructed as awash with "raging hormones," as the time when bodies go out of control and emotions swing relentlessly to extremes. Blood, semen, sweat, and pus are taken as symptomatic of change deep within bodies precariously poised between the glowing perfection of sexual maturity and its monstrous underbelly. The smell of bodies, their fluids, and their hairiness are both routinely invoked and efficiently suppressed in the array of advertising, magazine and television imagery representing and addressing "teenagers." Addressed as such, young people – girls especially (Holland, Ramazanoglu, Sharpe, and Thomson, 1998) – may take on the work of sustaining that embodiment and in precisely those years when their bodies seem most unsettled. To repeat, desire, for oneself and for others, is located on the surface, in the sheen of the smooth, unblemished, and hairless skin. Horror lies beneath, in the flesh: pus, blood, fat, and hair threaten to erupt from below, disrupting that surface and the desire it elicits. In *Buffy the Vampire Slayer*, this "disavowal" is both sustained and undermined.

Buffy and her friends, in common with characters in most Hollywood productions featuring young people, are unexceptional in that as teenagers and twenty-somethings their bodies are portrayed as the locus of sexual desire. In this respect, rather than freedom and irresponsibility, there is a considerable burden in being young. Buffy, the blond, blue-eyed slayer carries it all. Her own body is an object of discipline, of training, kept in place by her Watcher, Giles, and, implicitly, by the watchers, an audience of millions. She must watch herself, keep herself on form, in order to fulfill her destiny – she is, but must also work at, being the slayer. Her task, to eliminate vampires and demons, is thus to repel and destroy transgressive and monstrous bodies endlessly invading the nocturnal world – a world teenagers to some extent share with these monstrous others (both are marginal to the ordinary adult world). Following Moretti, this might be read as a disavowal of what is inside and thus an internal conflict is staged as a weekly battle to eliminate an external threat. Moretti (1988: 102) comments,

> The literature of terror is studded with passages where the protagonists brush against the awareness – described by Freud – that the perturbing element is *within them*: that it is they themselves that produce the monsters they fear.

In these terms, the anxiety of transformation in adolescence is thus enacted, and "managed," as a struggle against supernatural forces.

The "post-AIDS" context might be further understood as defining the scale and gravity of Buffy's burden. Weeks (1995) argues that since "the early 1980s AIDS, HIV disease, has haunted the sexual imaginary embodying the danger and fear that trails in the wake of the body and its pleasures"

(Weeks, 1995: 15). Against the "terror of disease" there has been "a fetishization of fitness" and, he argues, in common with others, that "fitness and health have become a new focus for a sense of self and a harnessing of the resilience of the body" (1995: 21–22). There is the possible implication here that Buffy's task is to eliminate the diseased, and such a reading might thus construe the show as a highly illiberal fantasy of purification.[5] But this would entail tying the show down as an allegory, as if each element could be made to stand for a social category in the real world – most obviously, in these terms, the undead, the vampires, could "stand for" people with AIDS or who are HIV positive. But the show does not propose such a neat assurance of the visible differences between the "healthy" and the "unhealthy." Dyer argues that

> the habit of looking for knowledge persists in ever more troubled forms. The routinised charity poster of starving children, the "is this the face of a killer?" coverage of serial killers, the centrality in the coverage of AIDS, an invisible malady, of giant enlargements of the virus and the display of KS lesions – we go on looking even while we know we are not going to learn. (Dyer, 1997: 106)

Indeed, as Dyer suggests, "looking," to see inside, persists but, in *Buffy the Vampire Slayer,* looking is often also explicitly frustrated. As Scott says to Buffy at the end of *Beauty and the Beasts* (3004), "You never really know what's going on inside somebody, do you?"

So rather than an allegorical battle with the bearers of disease, I want to emphasize that her struggle is not against a particular category of beings but with what it means to become a sexual being when sex itself has been contaminated with death. As a kind of superhero, though she has to work at it, among her perhaps impossible, and emotionally contradictory, tasks is that of disconnecting sex from death, to disentangle sexual pleasure and intimacy from mortal danger. In popular discourses, adolescence is not when people choose to be sexual: sex is construed as there within, waiting to surface from inside (see Donald, 1992: 111). Such a construction of sex in adolescence makes it a potentially monstrous eruption from the interior and therefore somewhat beyond rational agency. Coupled with its potential for the transmission of disease – and consequent death – sex is thus encountered as both insistently desirable and self-endangering.

In the wider currency of sexual exchange, it could be argued that unprotected sex can be made a signifier of intimacy. But between Buffy and Angel, the too literal question of whether they have sex with a condom simply cannot arise because in the most fundamental sense her entire relationship with him is "unsafe." It would be uninteresting if it was otherwise: the peculiarly fraught and dangerous character of their relationship displays sex-in-uncertainty (Weeks, 1995; Burr, 2003a; 2003b). The point lies in her struggle to achieve intimacy with him despite and because he is a vampire. Buffy's risky quest is to retrieve sex as intimacy and to stay alive and self-possessed in so doing. As I note below, with reference to her "rival" slayers, Kendra doesn't do sex; Faith doesn't do intimacy. Buffy tries to do both.

But what kind of rescue can Buffy achieve? Moretti argues that the "literature of terror is born precisely *out of the terror of a split society,* and out of the desire to heal it" (1988: 83) and that "whoever dares to fight the monster automatically becomes the representative of the species, of the whole of society" (1988: 84). *Buffy the Vampire Slayer* sustains elements of this rhetoric in its frequent staging of major battles "to save the world." Giles frequently reasserts Buffy's duty in such apocalyptic terms. Faced with this, in *Prophecy Girl* (1012) for example, Buffy protests at her responsibility, "Giles, I'm sixteen years old – I don't want to die."

However, though "the world" is invoked, it is never convincingly represented by Sunnydale or Sunnydale High. At least in the earlier seasons, the split in this society is between adults and teenagers, and among teenagers themselves (high school cliques, jocks, and nerds). Buffy's burden is announced to her and monitored by adults. But *her* world intersects with that of the vampires: after dark, where adults are not, and teenagers are. Teenagers and vampires (undead but also forever young) inhabit overlapping zones. Moreover, Willow and Tara pursue witchcraft, Oz is a werewolf, Anya a demon and so on. And, consistent with Stoker's *Dracula*, it is as young people that Angel, Drusilla, and Spike became vampires. Unlike Riley and his military outfit (in season 4), who are remarkably distant from all of this, Buffy belongs to those spaces where teenagers hang out – especially the parks and streets at night. Buffy is less "the representative of the species" and more a figure particular to the social world of teenagers, and anxious to define herself as belonging to that world. In *Gingerbread* (3011) this division is made explicit when even Buffy's mother turns against her, forming MOO (Mothers Opposed to the Occult) and counter-posing the town's "grown-ups" to monsters, witches, and slayers (categories that thus include Oz, Willow, and Buffy among the enemy). Ironically, of course, it is the "grown-ups" with the most authority, the school principal and the mayor, who are ultimately the most monstrous.

Several interrelated episodes in season 2 confirm the gravity of Buffy's responsibility as the slayer. Together, *What's My Line? Part 1 and Part 2* (2009, 2010) require some comment. There are several narrative strands. First of all it is the school's careers fair and students are completing aptitude assessment questionnaires, thus somewhat heightening Buffy's resistance to being "the slayer." As she remarks to Willow: "Do the words 'sealed in fate' ring any bells for you, Willow? Why go there? I'd say my future is pretty much a non-issue" (*What's My Line? Part 1,* 2009). Meanwhile, Spike is seeking to restore Drusilla to full vampire health, by means of a ritual requiring, and certain to kill, her "sire" Angel. To eliminate Buffy he has called upon an ancient order of assassins to pursue her. Coincidentally, because Buffy briefly died in an earlier episode (*Prophecy Girl,* 1012), a new slayer, Kendra, has been sent to Sunnydale.

In a brief confrontation with Giles, before Kendra's appearance, Buffy slides from anger to despair:

> If you don't like the way I'm doing my job, why don't you find someone else…Oh that's right there can only be one, as long as I'm alive there can be no one else. Well there you go, I don't have to be the slayer, I could be dead…It wouldn't be much of a change, either way I'm bored, constricted, I never get to shop and my hair and finger nails still continue to grow, so really when you think about it, what's the diff?

A little later, as Buffy rushes to the task ahead of Giles, he accuses her of "behaving remarkably immaturely," and she replies, "You know what, I am immature, I'm a teen, I get to mature" (2009). Explicitly in these assertions, but also in her fast and witty "youth" speak, in her dress and in her insistence on the pursuit of a relationship with Angel, she identifies herself as belonging to "teen culture." With the arrival of Kendra, Buffy's identity and interests become even more sharply delineated.

Kendra is a slayer entirely devoted to the work of killing vampires. Kendra demonstrates an austere commitment. She was given to her Watcher in infancy, expects to act in secret, does not attend school, has no friends, and is "not permitted to speak with boys" (Kendra, in 2010). There is considerable comedy in the revelation of her singular commitment to slaying and her ignorance of what it means to be young. But she is also scholarly, within the confines of the arcane study of the supernatural, and is thus greeted with some enthusiasm by Giles. Buffy, by contrast, is portrayed as much more of an ordinary high school kid, getting by but not that studious: "With Buffy some flexibility is required" (Giles, in 2010). Buffy's scope for retaliation is limited: Kendra, who is black, is also dressed with a comparable concern for sexual display and is thus far from being a bookish nerd. So Buffy turns to wondering "if it would be so bad being replaced" and speculates that "maybe after the thing with Spike and the assassins is over, I can say 'Kendra, you stay, I'm going to Disneyland'…maybe I could even have a normal life" (2010). And, later, "When this is over I'm thinking pineapple pizza and teen movie video fest, possibly something from the Ringwald oeuvre" (2010). These fantasies of escape strengthen Buffy's identification with other teenagers and distance her from Kendra's belief that she is saving "the world" from vampires. A crucial exchange between Buffy and Kendra occurs when, together, they go in pursuit of Spike, who has succeeded in capturing Angel for the fatal ritual:

> Kendra: "Is that all you're worried about, your boyfriend?"
> Buffy: "No but it's enough"
> Kendra: "He's a vampire, he should die, why am I the only person who sees it – are you that big a fool?"

The difference between Kendra and Buffy is clear. Buffy aims to recover a sexual relationship with a hopelessly paradoxical figure: both dead and immortal, torturing and tortured, a vampire with a conscience. By the slayer code, as Kendra knows, she should just kill him. But Kendra has no stake in sex and is (almost) immune to his allure. Buffy's way of being the slayer is much riskier because for her the boundary between human and vampire, human and demon, is itself to be contested. Kendra accuses Buffy of talking "about slaying as if it's a job, it's not, it's who you are" (2010) but what these two episodes suggest is that in Buffy "slayer" and "teen" eventually, though far from finally, coalesce and *together* shape the logic of her actions.

Fate, destiny, and duty are repeatedly impressed upon Buffy, most often by adult male figures, especially her Watcher, Giles. And what she encounters again and again in the power and strength of her own body is its apparent confirmation of the "destiny" announced to her. She is thus simultaneously "powerful" and "disempowered": positioned by men who tell her what she is and what her "duty" will be. But, by contrast with Kendra, who is efficient but deferential, or with Faith (the disturbed and obsessive slayer introduced in season 3), Buffy struggles to exceed her ascribed identity, remaking her self among friends, hanging out as neither Kendra nor Faith can. Buffy is then a distinctively teenage figure and, as both ordinary and heroic, most sharply defines the relational dilemmas encountered in the social world to which she belongs.

Object Choices

Among such "relational dilemmas" the issue of "object choice" is central. As I have argued, the question "what are we?" is a pervasive issue in the show. And if there are doubts about one's own ontology, a related and recurrent problem, in choosing with whom to be intimate, is that of how to know what the object of one's desire really is and what risks are taken in "falling" in love with "it" (see *Teacher's Pet,* 1004; *Inca Mummy Girl* 2004; *Reptile Boy* 2005). A further concern is that of how, if at all, elements of the contradictory "other" can be disentangled and "saved." Reading the surfaces of others' bodies to determine what they are proves to be a much more complex matter than any simple division between, and visualization of, "us" (humans) and "them" (vampires, demons, robots, witches, gods, werewolves) might suggest. Both the stability of this boundary and the guarantee apparently offered by surface "perfection" are repeatedly thrown into question. Buffy falls in love with Angel, Willow with Oz. But as both of them transform into grotesque figures, their neat features, smooth skins, and enviable haircuts turn out to be both unstable and unreliable. On the other hand, some demons turn out not to be so irrevocably demonic (Anya in seasons 4 and 5, Doyle in season 1 of *Angel*) and some "ordinary people" turn out to be manipulative and damaging (Krzywinska, 2002). Thus, after Angel, when Buffy attempts to confine her "object choices" to human beings, her "one night stand" with Parker in *The Harsh Light of Day* (4003) is as troublesome as her companions' encounters with demons, mummies, and robots.

Buffy, burdened with being the slayer, also has to work most insistently at determining what kind of beings others are. Though vampires are mostly unambiguous and are routinely staked, many other demons take longer to identify, generating scenes of frantic library research to determine just what kind of threat has emerged, yet again, at "Hellmouth." However, Buffy's difficulty is not primarily who to "kill" – though her violent confrontation with a possible stepfather does also raise that issue (*Ted,* 2011). The problem is more that of who to be intimate with. In this respect, in season 5, the problem of what others are inside is given an alarming twist when it becomes apparent, too late, that Ben, to whom Buffy is attracted, is her main adversary, Glory, a malevolent god appearing in both male and female form. She has made a sustained misreading, leading eventually to her own death.

Looking back to the earlier seasons, Buffy's problem is, in one sense, practical. How does a superhero who patrols the streets, parks, and cemeteries at night have a "social life?" The implications for her are developed in several early episodes. Consistent with the resistance to her role discussed above, Buffy's powers are also shown to conflict with her wish to be a "normal" girl. The discourse of heterosexual romance powerfully maps out those positions in which girls "should" locate themselves, and as Valerie Hey comments, in her study of teenage girls' friendships, girls themselves take up and display "a common investment in proposing the desired place as 'normal' and the despised and feared place of the other as 'abnormal'" (Hey,

1997: 135). *Never Kill a Boy on the First Date* (1005) explores Buffy's desire to have a boyfriend and thus to be an "ordinary" teenage girl and hence her particular fury as she dispenses with her adversary by propelling him into a furnace – "You killed my date!" Buffy's peculiar problem is that her nightlife, unlike that of other girls, is shown to be far too dangerous to allow her unwitting boyfriend to accompany her. So how can she have the kind of relationship that might "qualify" her as "normal" within the terms of heterosexual romance? What kind of boy might enable her to achieve that? The paradoxical and dangerous answer is that the "boy" must belong to the nocturnal world of Sunnydale and must have powers comparable to her own.

Though he is present as a background figure from the beginning, it is only in the seventh episode of season 1 that her particular, and enduring, object choice is made decisively apparent. In a sense, in *Angel* (1007), Buffy's predicament is apparently eased. Through a potentially sexual relationship with Angel, a powerful outsider to the daytime world of Sunnydale High, she is able to claim the kind of prestige carried by securing a relationship with an older, more experienced figure. He is absolutely not "boyish." But of course the choice of Angel also initiates the protracted melodrama continuing through the second and into the third season and makes this question central – Just what kind of being has Buffy fallen in love with?

If Angel is only one of many figures positioned as a problematic object of desire for one or other of the core ensemble, he is by far the most central and most complex. Though transformed into a vampire more than two hundred years before, he has since become, due to a gypsy curse, a vampire with a soul and a conscience. He is dark and tall and dresses in black. He is also muscular, often silent and unsmiling. Like Darcy, in *Pride and Prejudice*, and many other heroes of romantic fiction, he is "hard to read."[6] Angel is conventionally masculine, both by comparison with the "visualization" of heroes in romantic fiction (Radway, 1984; Dyer, 1997) and with the bodily display of male models in much recent advertising. In all these respects, he seems no more than the ideal figure for a romantic melodrama. However, as I have suggested, Buffy's problem is with whom she can be intimate, and in Angel, many of the emotional uncertainties and physical risks of sexual intimacy are condensed.

For Buffy, disappointment in what others turn out to be is persistent and becomes an enduring theme. Though sometimes dispelled by dispassionately witty lines, on the whole this strand is constructed at a level of gravity in marked contrast to the comedy of her companions' earlier encounters.[7] In season 2 she meets Billy Ford, her "giant fifth grade crush" (*Lie to Me,* 2007) and is dismayed to find that in fact he wants to trade her, with Spike, for the immortality of becoming a vampire. Once exposed, he tells her: "I've got six months left and what they bury won't even look like me. I'll be bald and shrivelled and smell bad…does the nest of tumours liquefying my brain spoil the fun?" (2007). In the final scene of the episode, beside his grave, she tells Giles, "Nothing's ever simple any more. I'm constantly trying to work it out, who to love, who to hate, who to trust. It's just like the more I know, the more confused I get."

Even Angel's disclosures about his own murderous past do not enable her to "simplify" her relationship with him. Her desire is almost unimpeded. In this discourse of heterosexual romance, sexual desire is thus implicitly something other than a rational choice – knowing the other is problematic but so too is the relationship between knowledge of, and desire for, the other. The attempt to have a sexual relationship with Angel is a central melodramatic narrative in the first three seasons. The interrelationship of sex, happiness, and human ontology is denied to Angel. In him, sex and death have become negatively entwined: to have sexual contentment deprives him of his "soul" and returns him to the world of the vampires, reducing him to a murderous and insatiable need to maintain the outward appearance of life by sucking the blood of the living. In *Becoming Part 2* (2022) in the final moments, Angel recovers his soul and becomes human again. But rather than collude in what now appears an inescapable repetition of the passage from sex to death and vampirism, Buffy, telling Angel she loves him and asking him gently to close his eyes, thrusts her sword through him. Certainly she does what she has to do and "saves the world" (see Krimmer and Raval, 2002). But is she only doing what Kendra insisted that, as a vampire slayer, she must do?

The more compelling logic of her action here seems to lie in the need to eliminate him as the locus of her desire and thus to save herself. This is not a matter of revenge for the abuse she has been subjected to by Angel(us). However, to pursue sexual intimacy with him once again would dispossess him of his "soul," thus returning him as Angelus, and this would also entail repeating her exposure to his violence (a position from which she firmly distances herself in a later episode – *Beauty and the Beasts,* 3004). Buffy is not a romantic heroine willing to abandon herself to him. And though she subsequently leaves Sunnydale and assumes another name, she soon reclaims herself, both in name and body, replying to her demon captor – where the required response is "I am no one" – with "I am Buffy the Vampire Slayer" (*Anne,* 3001).

But Buffy does not give up on her quest to retrieve Angel, and with his return in season 3, Buffy's struggle resumes, repeating the dismay and distress of the latter part of season 2. In a crucial episode, *Lovers' Walk,* 3008, Spike forces Buffy and Angel to confront the impossibility of their relationship:

> The last time I looked in on you two, you were fighting each other to the death. Now you're back making googly eyes at each other like nothing ever happened – makes me want to heave. You're not friends, you'll never be friends, you'll be in love 'til it kills you both. You'll fight and you'll shag and you'll hate each other 'til it makes you quiver but you'll never be friends. Love isn't brains, children, it's blood, blood screaming inside you to work its will. I may be love's bitch but at least I'm man enough to admit it.

Angel and Buffy's intractable dilemma is reiterated in *Amends* (3010), and her quest to recover intimacy with Angel is pursued through to the end of the season.

Indeed, in the last episode she insists that Angel drink from her neck (to save his life) declaring: "It is never over. I won't let you die" (*Graduation Day Part 2,* 3022). Here she appears to come close to self-abandonment, but this is again a gesture of commitment to and intimacy with Angel.[8] Because it is a substitution for the penetrative sex that would deprive him of his soul, she does not risk the return of Angelus – the main threat to her own survival. In some respects her action is "nurturant" (Busse, 2002: 214) but it is also an act of physically intense exchange, forcefully initiated by Buffy, thus confirming her agency and strength (though Xander is inclined to construe it otherwise). Of course, though she succeeds in saving Angel's life, she does not succeed in her quest to retrieve full sexual intimacy with him. At the end of the episode, Angel leaves. And Buffy does not follow.

The distress is revisited yet again in *Angel* (Season 1)*, I Will Remember You* (1008), during season 4 of *Buffy*. Neale's (1986) perspective on melodrama suggests the pleasure that might be found in seeing yet again the impossible "fulfilment" both displayed and denied: a "wish unfulfilled…can be preserved and re-stated rather than abandoned altogether" (Neale, 1986: 21). But whatever the form of our pleasures, it is not surprising that Angel's successor, Riley, was perhaps at best tolerated by some viewers (see Agarwal, 2001). In terms of the overarching construction of sexuality as fraught, difficult, and dangerous and of "people" as ambiguous and somewhat unpredictable, Riley is relatively incongruous and unchallenging. His efforts to mix with vampires, in season 5, are belated and unconvincing. For Buffy, for whom sex, like everything else, is a challenge, it is easy to see why her unambiguously sexual relationship with Riley, her fit but dull soldier boy, should turn out to be less than compelling (cf. Burr, 2003a, 2003b). Sex with Riley gives her nothing to do. Angel, on the other hand, is exactly the complicated and dangerous figure required to challenge her heroism and to force her to work through and confront what becoming sexual means in such unsettled times.

Blood Ties (5013)

Blood Ties is an emotionally powerful episode, almost a "tear-jerker." But it is not about sexual desire and the failure of its fulfillment. So why is it so upsetting? As I have argued, repeatedly in *Buffy the Vampire Slayer* affective relations are constructed between figures inhabiting "ordinary" and "supernatural" domains, and desire is blocked by the separation of those domains. The characters discover, in adolescence, that they do not know quite what they are, or what they can be, and thus also with whom they can be sexual, intimate, or whom they can trust. At fifteen Buffy is told she is a vampire slayer and, again and again, she questions and challenges the implications of not being "ordinary," carrying an identity not chosen but ascribed. At fourteen, in *Blood Ties,* her sister Dawn discovers that she is not really a person at all but rather a kind of ancient "key." She is thus, in her relationship with her mother, and more centrally with her sister, faced with a radical disauthenticity.

Introduced only in season 5, Dawn initially appeared awkwardly contrived to revive a show perhaps foundering in the preceding season. Gradually, however, the comprehensive allocation of false memories to Buffy and her mother and to all those who encounter Dawn becomes a puzzle central to the overall plotting of the season. Everyone knows Dawn and has known her for years, ever since the Summers family came to Sunnydale from Los Angeles. But, as an audience, we know, along with Buffy, that she's not really a person at all, long before with Spike's inadvertent help, she finds out what she is. We know, in short, that Dawn's desires are beset by extraordinary vicissitudes. Her anxieties about how others relate to her are read thus as both adolescent self-obsession and as incomplete clues to how profoundly "inhuman" she will turn out to be. As in a very early episode, *Out of Mind, Out of Sight* (1011), where a high school student who is ignored becomes invisible, the logic of this scenario is to translate a "feeling" attributed to adolescence into an ontological fact. If it is a characteristic of adolescence to feel that adults and older teenagers don't treat you as a person, or look at you as if you're not really a member of the world to which they belong, then *Blood Ties* explores this through the literal revelation of nonpersonhood and nonbelonging.

If intimacy is an issue crucial to beings unsure of their ontological, relational, and sexual status, what can intimacy with "a blob of energy…a fourteen year old hormone bomb" (Spike's comment on Dawn) be and how can it be achieved? One kind of answer to this is offered at the end of the episode. Other answers are explored, but implicitly undermined, in earlier exchanges between Buffy and her sister. It is Buffy's twentieth birthday, and Dawn gives her a photograph of herself, with Buffy, "that summer we visited dad in San Diego"; the frame is set with shells, "we picked them off the beach." Buffy responds "I remember" – which has to be read as a lie by both the audience and the friends gathered for the occasion. Dawn, misreading the silence, comments: "Well jeez don't get all movie of the week, I was just too cheap to buy you a real present," thus clinching the failed intimacy of the gift.

Once Dawn knows that she is a "key" transposed into human form, she enacts a further intense variant of "adolescent" turbulence and self-doubt. She appears behind Buffy, seen first by Tara (and Willow) holding the typically excessive kitchen knife found in slasher movies. She has cut open her arm – as if to investigate and display her own "being" – and speaks the following flat, distraught monologue:

> "Is this blood?
> This is blood isn't it?
> It can't be me…
> I'm not a key, a thing…
> What am I? Am I real?
> Am I anything?"

The force of this lies in its inversion of the generic order of reality in which such a scene of self-mutilation might "normally" be enacted. In such an order, a teenage girl might have nightmares about her own existence or might slip into psychosis. The progress of such a realist, familial drama might be toward the elimination of the delusional state, whatever its origin. But here the reality allows no such resolution. And there are no words to make it better – the fantastic truth of her ontology renders them banal:

> "Why didn't you tell me?"
> "We thought it would be better if we waited until you were older."

Again, the effect is to give a phenomenological credibility to feelings attributed to adolescents as symptoms of their "pre-adult" irrationality. Buffy, struggling with the implications, tells her mother, with considerable understatement:

> It's not that simple, we're not going to be able to fix this with a hug and a kiss and a bowl of soup.

Much of the drama of Dawn's traumatic discovery is played out in her bedroom. It is cluttered with the familiar debris of childhood and of teenage life. Posters are displayed on the walls and her shelves are thick with toys and memorabilia. Overhearing just the wrong words from Buffy's conversation with her mother, when she tries to explain to Joyce what it must feel like to be Dawn – "She's not real, we're not her family, we don't even know what she is" – Dawn strips her room bare and burns her diaries (dating back seven years). Here, as a teenager, Dawn effectively destroys all that she has and all that secures her as belonging to that household. Once the fire is set, she leaves.[9]

There is no escape from Dawn's predicament. She wanders and eventually returns to the hospital, where her mother has been treated, apparently successfully, for a brain tumor. Recognized as nonhuman by the demented inmates of the psychiatric ward, she takes refuge with Ben, a doctor, but also the vehicle for Glory, a voluptuous god in pursuit of her "key" (Dawn). The ensuing confrontation between a god and a teenager, ironically staged in the X-ray room (Glory cannot see what Dawn is), culminates in a provisional "recovery" of intimacy. Wounded in the battle with Glory, Buffy presses her blood soaked palm against Dawn's, mingling their blood: "You are my sister, there's no way you could annoy me so much if you weren't." So if, on the one hand, the grounds of this sisterly intimacy are antagonism, on the other, the intimacy is underpinned by a gesture suggesting, in the "post-AIDS" era, a possibly fatal exchange. It may be the same blood, "Summers' blood," but the meaning of Buffy's action also invokes a rhetoric of intensified intimacy predicated upon a willingness to share the risk of death.

Is this melodrama? Neale suggests that "spectators" viewing a melodrama want the key characters to be loved to fulfill their wish for the "union of the couple" and he argues that such a wish lies in "a nostalgic fantasy of childhood characterised by union with the mother: a state of total love, satisfaction, and dyadic fusion" (1986: 17). The episode does end with a restoration of sorts. Buffy and Dawn walk out together, commenting on the fire in her bedroom and "their" mother's willingness to forgive. Dawn asks:

> "Do you think she'd raise my allowance?"
> "Don't push it."

Of course, for Dawn there never was "union with the mother," no "dyadic fusion," and such a "fantasy" is not there to be recovered. But there are some precedents. In *Buffy the Vampire Slayer*, some kind of union is achieved and is (almost) sustained even where the answers to that recurring question "What are we?" differ radically between partners: Willow and her werewolf boyfriend Oz, Xander and his demon girlfriend Anya. There's a liberalism here, somewhat at odds with the rigidities on which much melodrama appears to depend. But it has its limits. For Buffy and Angel, vampire slayer and vampire, most obviously, a sustainable union remains a wish.

Can Buffy and Dawn *become* sisters? Crying, for both characters and viewers alike, may be "the vehicle of a wish – a fantasy – that satisfaction is possible, that the object can be restored, the loss eradicated" (Neale, 1986: 22). In Neale's terms, the "tears" in *Blood Ties* offer just enough of an acknowledgment of the wish that Buffy and Dawn could be proper sisters, in defiance of the knowledge that they aren't and can't be. But here Buffy's gestural exchange of blood goes further, implying both intense intimacy *and* the vampire ritual of "siring," thus asserting that it is in blood that their union can be constructed and secured (Busse, 2002: 213). Borrowing from vampirism, Buffy asserts that intimate relationships can be made in defiance of the apparently intractable fact of their difference. By securing Dawn as her sister, Buffy strives toward an optimism largely absent from her despairing efforts to establish sexual intimacy. In this moment, for Buffy, constructing a non-sexual commitment appears to be a more viable achievement – one which, at the season's end, she is prepared to die for.

Conclusion

In this chapter I have proposed a reading of *Buffy the Vampire Slayer* as addressing issues particular to the "post-AIDS" era and as re-exploring the anxieties attributed to adolescence with considerable emphasis on sexual relations as dangerous and uncertain. The significance of HIV/AIDS, and its possible contribution to a re-animation of vampire mythology in the past two decades, is not introduced here to contain and fix the meanings of *Buffy the Vampire Slayer*. But, in the absence of much discussion in the substantial published debate around the show, this relatively recent re-inflection of sexual relations deserves wider consideration. The meanings attributed to blood, as for example both threatening and facilitating intimacy, are surely impossible to determine without some acknowledgment of the impact of HIV/AIDS. Implicit in my argument is the view that the show's success lies partly at least in its capacity to engage with perhaps unacknowledged anxieties, especially among the "teen" and younger adult audiences to which it was initially addressed. In pursuing this concern it has been essential to work with the concept of "disavowal" (Moretti, 1988) and thus to explore how the show explores issues that it almost never identifies explicitly. Similarly, Neale's (1986) analysis of the structures of melodrama has provided at least a provisional guide to the more insistently painful dilemmas faced, in particular, by Buffy herself.

Buffy the Vampire Slayer engages with a multiplicity of anxieties about the body, both about its health and appearance and about its "legibility" to others. Such anxieties, here condensed in the show's specific preoccupation with youth and with "growing up," are both particular to "becoming sexual" and securing intimacy *and* a continuing locus of unsettled fascination for audiences supposedly well beyond such processes of change and uncertainty.

Chapter Five

Seeing Through the Skin: Whiteness in Two Novels by Francesca Lia Block

Introduction

This chapter offers a further discussion of Francesca Lia Block, a writer whose work, like that of Burgess and Haddon, illustrates significant trends in the expansion of young adult fiction. She began her writing career in the last years of the Reagan-Bush administrations and, continuing in their aftermath, she can also be read as making a variety of challenges to the moral rhetoric of neoconservatism and to Christian fundamentalism.[1] In this study of just two of her novels, my main concern is to consider in what sense her writing questions "whiteness."[2]

As I suggested in Chapter Two, there are problems in the class-bounded character of her fictional world and in the social circumscription of the audiences likely to engage with her novels and short stories. Reading her work requires some particular forms of cultural capital most likely to be available to those who have had a liberal Western middle-class childhood. If Block primarily addresses girls, clearly she addresses some girls more than others. It could be argued further that the "cultural capital" brought into play in reading Block's work is strongly associated with particular orientations to formal, "educated" literacy. The students I teach, many of whom are without such a particular "cultural capital," sometimes find her writing difficult and may struggle to represent their engagement with her novels in writing.[3]

Reading Block's Novels

Block's writing presents students with a variety of challenges. Perhaps most often her adoption of some of the strategies of magical realism can be problematic for some readers. As the Amazon customer reviews discussed in Chapter Two demonstrate, at the more negative end, some reject her writing with a mixture of exasperation and bewilderment. From among the students I have taught, I want to introduce, if briefly, three examples of their readings.

The first, a white woman in her twenties from upstate New York, was introduced to Block in a summer school at SUNY in 2003:

> Ever since reading *The Hanged Man,* I have been wondering about her past and how much of that was autobiographical and how much was fiction. That is why I went so crazy with surfing the web with information about Block. I was hoping that there would be some insight somewhere into her past traumas, but it was to no avail.

This is illustrative of quite a common reading strategy, centered on a conviction that Block's writing originates in her own life and perhaps in her particular misfortune or even pathology. One implication is that her representation of teenage girls is read more as an idiosyncratic and personal matter than more socially "typical." I have encountered many similar responses from students in London – speculating that she must have had "bad experiences with men." They too try to read through the fiction to the life of the author "behind" it. The search for such truths might also be seen as comparable to the generation of celebrity gossip around stars and other media figures. This could be construed as indicative of a lack of access to the kind of cultural capital that might allow a more detached "thematic" or "historical" reading and the pursuit of such claims to find the autobiographical truth behind the novels might usually result in a much lower grade than a response demonstrating a more distanced, analytical reading. However, such an academic devaluation of these responses might miss another point – the extent to which they assert the emotional credibility of a magical realist fiction.

Furthermore, such modes of engagement do not necessarily preclude a reading more attentive to formal structure or political context. In fact, the quote above is taken from a paper in which quite a sustained and detailed effort is made to map the complex symbolic structure of *The Hanged Man.* Though she could not find everything that she was looking for, Block's reflections on motherhood, published that year, would have served her argument that Block's imagery of whiteness and depletion can also be explained autobiographically (Block, 2003a).[4]

The second example (2004) comes from a black, Caribbean student critical of Block's "racial stereotypes" in *Cherokee Bat and the Goat Guys* (Block, 1992). She touches on a key theme in the analysis I want to elaborate later in this chapter:

> Valentine Jah-Love and Ping Chong are portrayed through typical characteristics of their race. Via the name, Valentine Jah-Love and without reading anything else about this person you know he is black. Block then goes on to describe him then you get the whole picture. The same explanation can be used for Ping Chong, Blocks description of these characters is clichéd. Weetzie is white and you get this image via

> her bleach blond hair… Cherokee's body is described as "powder pale" also…"She was whiter than ever." This almost conjures up images of her being ghostly, white to the point of where she looks ill. This representation of whiteness appears to be portraying white as being pure and superior. This notion is also linked to Richard Dyer's work. He goes on to say, "To be white is to have expunged all dirt, faecal or otherwise from oneself: to look white is to look clean" (Dyer, 1997). Block is creating Cherokee to be superior to the other characters. Cherokee is the central personality, she is the one who makes the drama within the story possible. She is the person who is the main thread to all events within the story.

In this case, the student appears to be pursuing a very familiar and broadly critical argument about "stereotyping." But within it the implication of whiteness in illness and death disrupts the more "superficial" case. It is possible to see her remarks as less contradictory than they might appear. If whiteness is somehow sickly, it is also a position of power enabling a kind of predatory consumption that is mobile and self-restorative. In her concluding paragraph she allows this more particular engagement with the text to underpin a more enthusiastic comment:

> The language is simple and flowing on the surface, but simmering underneath is a story that has a lot more to say than it shows at first glance.

From her standpoint, as a woman very nearly forty, it appears that an initially skeptical reading is, as she writes, progressively displaced, leading to quite a strong endorsement of Block's writing both for herself and for younger readers.

The final example is from an essay by a Theatre Studies student, a twenty-two-year-old white woman. Referring to *Weetzie Bat* (1989) she comments:

> The opening paragraph has a fast paced detail of the location of the novel that in my mind can appeal to both genders although the level of detail concerning everyday life could be considered a predominantly feminine trait…it is my opinion that the level of what I feel an average male reader would call superficial detail may well put a male reader off from continuing with the novel…Overall…I feel that the opening to this novel is more likely to draw a female readership through the level of detail of day to day events, the question of romance between Weetzie and Dirk, and the personalities of the characters themselves.

Though there is some uncertainty in this student's writing, the reading of Block as addressing women particularly through the detail of everyday life hints at significant debates around the priorities of women's lives. A habit of giving attention to people's manner, dress, and actions could be read as indicative of the need for self-protection. Of course, this might also be related to debates around the character of "post-feminism," in particular a concern with the attention to detail associated with shopping, with fashion, and with the wider habits of consumption. Such preoccupations are often derided (see Munford, 2007). Indeed, this student often refers to the shift into a feminine mode of address as a "lapse" and she does not explore why the "male reader" she invokes might not want to engage with the detail so frequently evident in Block's writing. But, however "diffident," her comment is an important one: she implies the need to look (not only to be looked at – see Berger, 1972), to pay attention, and, as I have suggested, these are the habits necessary to those positioned as "vulnerable."[5]

The Hanged Man and *Missing Angel Juan*

Block explores sexuality in "adolescence," mostly with reference to teenage girls but also, to some extent, young gay men. Vulnerability to the male gaze and to sexual violence is a central theme, and I will examine this, primarily, in *The Hanged Man.* The problem of vulnerability and of objectification by others is represented in that novel through images of translucence and intrusion. In *Missing Angel Juan,* though questions of vulnerability are also prominent, objectification of a male (and Mexican) character by the teenage girl, Witch Baby, is also at issue. In both novels, the central female protagonists' experiences of agency and desire are rendered as problematic. And in both novels, these themes are articulated through a racially inflected problematic in which "whiteness," rather than conferring superiority or security, is equated with objectification – either defensively as a means to block intrusion or as a possessive excess of desire. In both cases, whiteness is associated with deathliness. This association, as explored by Dyer (1997), is located in a logic of purity and of disembodiment in the construction of whiteness, culminating in absence, sterility, and depletion. Discussing *Blade Runner, Zombie,* and the *Alien* films, he identifies a "suspicion of nothingness and the death of whiteness," a feeling that "as far as white identity goes…we really do feel we're played out" (Dyer, 1997: 217). Such anxieties are apparent in Block's fiction but, rather than figuring as a central theme, whiteness is thus "marked," rendered visible and "raced" rather than positioned as the unmarked and taken-for-granted "norm" against which all else is "other."

The Hanged Man (1994) is a first person narrative from the vantage point of a seventeen-year-old white girl, Laurel, named after and living in Laurel Canyon, Los Angeles. As the narrative adopts aspects of the everyday language of middle-class white teenage girls, rather than pursuing the whimsical twists and neologisms characteristic of Block's Weetzie Bat novels, the "voice" appears more anchored in a recognizable teenage discourse.[6] But such a sense of "real world" reference is also simultaneously countered by the apparent solipsism of the narrative and the uncertain status of her experiences and even of the other characters with whom she appears to engage.

The novel is structured through a selective borrowing from the Rider-Waite Tarot Deck. There are ten chapters, each named after a card from the deck. The narrative moves from an establishment of both the physical setting (the "general environment at the time" I. The Moon) and Laurel's emotional crisis (mourning, recollection, and reflection in the immediate aftermath of her father's death) through a further elaboration of fear, distress, and risk to an ambiguous settling of emotional conflict and a renewed sense of agency (X. Strength). Thus, in common with perhaps a majority of those novels positioned as "young adult" in publishers' lists, on bookstore shelves, by Internet booksellers, and in libraries, this is a novel of emotional passage through disturbance to a relatively secure psychic state. In this respect it conforms to the models of "growth" and "progress" to adulthood emphasized in Trites' (2000) overview of young adult fiction.

But this is not a novel only about negotiating bereavement. Laurel's response to her father's death is specifically complicated by the history of her relationship with him, which included his repeated rape of her. It is also compounded by a wider sense of threat associated with sex – her lover Jack is constructed as mysterious, dangerous, almost menacing; an unidentified man is reported to be entering houses in the canyon, raping a number of women; AIDS figures as a more generalized risk of fatal contamination through sexual contact. Vulnerability to intrusion, invasion, and penetration is a central concern of the novel.

Laurel's skin, as a boundary between her self and the outer world, is a particular focus of distress:

> I used to just be afraid of getting pregnant and V.D. and getting hurt, of the way I'd feel transparent afterward as if my skin showed the man I was with everything underneath. That he could see my organs and my bones. Now they've started saying on the news how sex can kill you. (Block, 1994: 14)

Through recollections of a trip to Jamaica with her mother and father, this initial articulation of sexual vulnerability and objectification becomes, through her heightened self-consciousness of whiteness in a predominantly black social world, a more extended metaphor of insecurity (see Block, 1994: 39-41). Her own deck of Tarot cards becomes, in one respect, incongruous: "the people's skins – all of them – the High Priestess, Strength, the Star, the World – are white" (Block, 1994: 41).

In Block's emotional topography of the body, whiteness is equated with being thing-like – becoming an object in which the processes of living are arrested or disowned. Laurel will not eat and does not menstruate.

> Have you ever had the sensation of losing flesh? You begin to feel the bones of your skeleton under your flesh. Bones of the shoulders. Bones of the rib cage. Bones of the hips. It is like finding a new being, one free of desire, free of time, almost.
>
> At night, I lie awake thinking about the man who climbs in through windows and kills women. My eyes choke on the darkness and my stomach is like a live thing – a separate creature that I have imprisoned, that is under my power. It is a little painted demon howling inside me. I imagine that the reason I don't bleed anymore each month is because this demon, this lie-baby, is sucking up all the blood to feed itself, to keep itself alive. I hear horror stories about girls who don't eat – how their hair turns white and their gums bleed. But I feel beautiful, perfect. I am all pale bone and bone-pale flesh and pale hair and I am light, I am like some fairy thing. I dream about fairies dancing around the house with their rib cages showing like baskets under their flesh. (Block, 1994: 95–96)

Laurel, as Rose White, is incomplete, bloodless, closing down into bone, a skeletal fairy (see Purkiss, 2003).[7] But by taking Rose Red into her, she begins to reverse her movement toward death:

> It will be the three of us. I will be the mother, giving my breasts. I will be the lover, flexing my legs. The daughter, sucking milk flesh. I will be Rose White, breasts like the fleshy undersides of petals. Rose Red, unfolding red lipstick red blood red. I will be thorns. I will be the bear, massive and furred. I will be the mother, lover. I will be the daughter of the bear. (Block, 1994: 117)

Here assuming simultaneously these various, previously dispersed subject positions, Laurel moves beyond her objectification as sexual victim toward an affirmation of agency in desire. She subsequently confronts her mother with her complicity in her rape by her father. But with Jack's words ("Let go of it. Let go") she sheds the clutter of displaced emotion: "There are no broken plates, no white moths, no animals screaming – only us" (Block, 1994: 133).

Following a dream, releasing a tiger from a cage – "There is blood. He has Jack's eyes. I unlock the cage and watch him limp across the water" (Block, 1994: 134) – she finds a white rose on her bed and, at last, her blood flows. Again, Jack's *voice* is invoked ("I think the point was for them to blend together"). Jack's voice, introduced in the second paragraph of the novel – "his voice…cracks like ice when you pour the liquor over" (1994: 4), is thus, from the beginning, linked with cracking open what is frozen:

> I feel something moist and warm between my thighs. It is not like desire. It is something else, vaguely remembered. (Block, 1994: 135)

Her recovery of agency is further signaled by a desire to paint, rather than, as in the first chapter, be painted – when Laurel visits the Venice boardwalk and feels her "dreams being licked onto [her] face with paint" (1994: 19). For her, painting is "to make people feel their pulse." She resolves to paint her own deck of Tarot cards, representing her family, friends and lovers, and herself, but also that in her deck some people "will have brown skin" (1994: 137).

Thus, in the final paragraph of the novel, Block also reaffirms the positive counterpoint to the pallor of her anorexic, sexually victimized protagonist. This "visualisation" of brown skinned people, if slight, does recall much earlier literary precedents in which, according to Valerie Babb (1998), a challenge to such subordination is articulated through "identification":

> The repeated portrayals of white women as defenseless, dependent, incapable, and powerless defined white women as needing the protection of white men. Whiteness, then, effectively became a racial identity embodying gender values in which males were empowered and females disempowered. While representations of white women embodied race privilege, they did not embody gender equity. Challenges to this patriarchal tableau would be expressed in writings of the late eighteenth and nineteenth centuries through a variety of subversive literary techniques, among which is the repeated trope of white female identification with racially marginalized groups. (Babb, 1998: 74)[8]

A resistance to positioning as pure (white) and vulnerable, registered through such identification is, consistent with Dyer's (1997) argument, also evidence of a wider dissent from subordination within the monolithic power of whiteness. Reading *The Hanged Man*, not as just another "coming-of-age" novel but against the grain of the neoconservative racial and sexual politics of the late 1980s and since, brings into focus meanings otherwise rendered marginal to the narrative of emotional development (see also Meyer, 2005, 2006, 2007a, 2007b).[9]

In the same period – the first half of the 1990s, Block also wrote *Witch Baby* (1991), *Cherokee Bat and the Goat Guys* (1992), and *Missing Angel Juan* (1993). *Missing Angel Juan* is the fourth novel in the sequence known as the Weetzie Bat books, collected together under the title *Dangerous Angels* in 1998. Though *Witch Baby* is strongly focalized through the protagonist, *Missing Angel Juan* is the only one of these novels to adopt a first person narrative and thus to so consistently elaborate the subjectivity of a single character from the Weetzie Bat ensemble. Like *The Hanged Man*, the narrative follows a loss – for Laurel it is the death of her father, for Witch Baby the departure of her boyfriend for New York. In *The Hanged Man,* Laurel engages with Jack and with Claudia, persistently ambiguous figures corresponding loosely to the bear and to Rose Red in the Grimm's tale of Rose White and Rose Red. In *Missing Angel Juan* Witch Baby encounters and maintains an extended dialogue with Weetzie Bat's dead father, Charlie Bat, and, at several key moments, observes and finally accompanies Cake, an intensely white and mannequin-like figure. In both novels, the status of these apparent others is uncertain. Both can be read as if Jack and Claudia, and Charlie and Cake, are external others through whom the first person narrator negotiates a period of mourning. But both novels can also be read as more radically solipsistic, with these figures thus appearing as unsettling, troublesome, and sometimes dangerous aspects of the narrator's own subjectivity. For Laurel, Jack carries some of the characteristics of her own dead father, of the unidentified rapist and murderer, and of various animals. It is only gradually that Jack as a means to unite with Rose Red – with blood – and, ambiguously, as interlocutor and sexual partner is achieved.

Missing Angel Juan can be read apart from the sequence in which it is located. But the figure of Witch Baby is prominent in the preceding novels. A particularly important episode occurs in *Cherokee Bat and the Goat Guys* (1992), when Witch Baby strips naked and smears herself with mud, "clumped handfuls into her hair, stuffed it in her ears, up her nostrils and even ate some" (Block, 1992: 8). Taking refuge in the garden shed, she remains sealed off for several days only fully emerging when Angel Juan reappears from a long absence in Mexico, following the deportation of his family. In both *Witch Baby* and *Cherokee Bat and the Goat Guys*, she is troubled by her uncertain place in the wider family (as the child of a witch and Weetzie's once estranged partner) and by a preoccupation with images and stories of death and disaster. She is both a repository for pain and an observer of distress in the world that others, such as her mother, Vixanne, for example, ignore (Block, 1991: 108). Her self-enclosure in mud can be read as both a self-protective withdrawal and as an attempt to begin again, reseeding herself to enable a kind of autochthonous rebirth.

But Witch Baby moves between periods of retreat and ventures in which she wanders and investigates the outside world. Her use of photography is significant in that it enables her to reverse the prevailing male gaze, to look back and, in its refusal of objectification by others, to establish her agency.

But, it is also a means to witness suffering, to see beyond surfaces, and sometimes to see into the past lives of people: in *Missing Angel Juan*, she watches the earlier life of Charlie Bat and his family and, more fleetingly, that of a "lanka" couple and their child. Photography is both "self-protection" and "insight."[10]

The elaboration of Witch Baby's dilemmas becomes considerably more complex in *Missing Angel Juan.* Witch Baby travels to New York to find Angel Juan, who has left Witch Baby and the band to pursue his own music. But even before she leaves to follow him, she encounters a representation of her own feelings which she finds disconcerting. This is the first appearance of a figure whose presence implies the dominance of Witch Baby's desire to (re)possess Angel Juan. She visits her mother, Vixanne Wigg, and attempts to paint a picture of Angel Juan "As big as life. A boy that will never leave" (Block, 1993: 22). But what she sees in her painting is "a picture of a man with big teeth eating a cake that drips icing all over his face and hands" (1993: 23). The desire to possess is personified in the figure of Cake, an extraordinarily white figure ultimately revealed to be intent upon sealing up the living within plastic versions of themselves: idealized figures of youth but arrested in being "forever young."[11] In New York, Cake appears on several occasions before the main climax of the narrative. On each occasion, his presence is associated with Witch Baby's excitement at being close to repossessing Angel Juan.

First of all, there is the trip to a market where, looking into the window of a boutique, she sees:

> Boy and girl mannequins in black leather…kneeling around a man mannequin. He's wearing a white coat with the collar turned up and white gloves. He has white hair and pale no-color glass eyes and girl's lips.
>
> I feel so cold. I feel like one of those flowers in the salad bar frozen in ice. But I don't want to move away from the window. (Block, 1993: 60)

Next, Witch Baby, exploring Central Park, finds the treehouse where Angel Juan has been living and again the appearance of the white figure, looking up from below, makes her feel "frosty, stiff and naked like a winter branch" (Block, 1993: 71). At Coney Island, Witch Baby finds Angel Juan captured in three discarded photo-booth images, in each of which there is a "man's mouth and chisel chin and his white shirt – the rest of him is cut off" (1993: 79–80). A more elaborated encounter occurs at the Metropolitan Museum of Art, where Witch Baby "imagines" that she has been addressed by the statues on display. Still thinking of this she hears a voice asking her "Do you wish that you could turn him into stone? Make him a mummy? Keep his heart in a jar?," and feeling "cold like marble" she turns and recognizes the white coat of the man in Central Park (1993: 100).

The final encounter begins outside "a little fifties-style hot-dog-shaped stainless-steel diner-type place lit with tubes of buzzing red neon" (Block, 1993: 107), where, in the window, she finds Angel Juan but rendered in lifeless plastic:

> Then I hear something behind me and I turn around shivering like somebody just slid some ice inside my shirt down my spine. There's this guy standing there.
>
> He is tall and he has white hair and you can almost see the blood beating at his temples because his skin is so thin and white...He is probably the most gorgeous human being I have ever seen in real life and the most nasty-looking at the same time. (Block, 1993: 108)

Cake's "perfection" is a hypnotic and dangerous attraction drawing Witch Baby toward the ideal of immobility and ultimately death. Paradoxically, she is warned away, and partly saved, from Cake by a man who is in fact dead, appearing to her as a flickering ghost-like presence, thoroughly disembodied. But Charlie Bat profoundly regrets his spectral exclusion from the world of the living. For example, he excitedly persuades Witch Baby to eat well, savoring the smell of food he can no longer enjoy. Charlie presents a vision of a vibrant family life – as immigrant Polish Jews in Brooklyn – counterposed to Cake's obsessive and controlling activities. But of course Cake is a figure equated with Witch Baby's desire to possess and control, and Charlie Bat's warnings are thus not of any external threat but of the deathly logic of Witch Baby's quest to recover Angel Juan. Cake is, in this sense, a displacement of a fear internal to Witch Baby herself. A possessiveness intent upon enclosing the living within an unchanging version of their outer form is here rendered as a monstrous whiteness within. This is a disturbing moment and further exemplifies the argument cited in Chapter Four, that in the literature of terror the "protagonists brush against the awareness...that the perturbing element is *within them*: that it is they themselves that produce the monsters they fear" (Moretti, 1988: 102). Witch Baby eventually achieves a recognition of this ("Maybe Cake is me," Block, 1993: 123) but is also able to reduce Cake to "who he really is" (1993: 124), thus expelling him.

In part, her recognition of her own disavowal is accomplished through dialogue, most substantially with her dead quasi-grandfather. As in *The Hanged Man,* where Laurel engages in dialogue with Jack, such a relation to an other is crucial. Charlie not only persuades Witch Baby to eat, but also to seek out and become a participant in, for example, an intense and demanding African drumming session. Such experiences allow Witch Baby an experience of self-affirmation, though both in the drumming episode and in her earlier visit to Harlem, her whiteness is marked, initially registered as weakness and vulnerability:

> [Harlem:] I feel like the whitest white-thing around except for Charlie, and he's a vapor…I remember how I always wanted to slip inside of Angel Juan's brown skin…It seemed safer than mine. (Block, 1993: 52)

> [On the ninth floor of the apartment block] I go over to the head drummer – a tall man wearing full batik pants. His dreadlocks must be as old as he is, thick and wired with his power. I feel like a pale weasel baby staring up at him. (Block, 1993: 89)

Charlie facilitates Witch Baby's sense of connection with others – in Harlem, in drumming, in seeing the vision of Polish Jewish family life – and it is this sense of identification across "racial" boundaries that, as with Laurel's wish to paint brown skinned figures into the Tarot deck, signifies the achievement of a more secure sense of self.

In the earlier novel, *Witch Baby* (1991), there is an exchange between Witch Baby and Angel Juan prefiguring the concerns of *Missing Angel Juan* (1993). I need to quote this at some length:

> Witch Baby had seen sugar skulls and candelabras in the shapes of doves, angels and trees. She had seen white dresses embroidered with gardens, and she had seen paintings of a dark woman with parrots and flowers and blood and one eyebrow. She liked tortillas with butter melting in the fold almost as much as candy, and she liked hot days and hibiscus flowers, mariachi bands and especially, now, Angel Juan. (Block, 1991: 68)

This is Angel Juan's response:

> Where I'm from it's poor. Little kids sit on the street asking for change. Some of them sing songs and play guitars they've made themselves, or they sell rainbow wish bracelets. There are old ladies too – just sitting in the dirt. People come from your country with lots of money and fancy clothes. They go down to the bars, shoot tequila and go back up to buy things. It's crazy to see them leaving with their paper flowers and candles and blankets and stuff, like we have something they need, when most of us don't even have a place to sleep or food to eat. Maybe they just want to come see how we live to feel better about their lives, or maybe they're missing something else that we have. (Block, 1991: 68–69)

Witch Baby's desire to possess Angel Juan has to be understood not just as a generalized representation of possessiveness but also as an emotionally acquisitive relationship across the boundary between affluence and poverty, whiteness and its "other."[12] She is not a tourist but there are implications for their relationship in the comment that perhaps they lack "something else that we have." It is crucial therefore that, at the conclusion of *Missing Angel Juan*, Witch Baby has not repossessed Angel Juan and he does not travel back to Los Angeles with her. Her sense of self-worth is, precisely, not dependent on the recovery of her Mexican boy.

Conclusion

The reading of Block's work that I have suggested depends on a distinction between appropriation and participation. There is, throughout Block's writing, a kind of surface multiculturalism consisting largely in the consumption of diverse and exotic foods, of music and of styles of dress and self-presentation. This might be construed as similar to the cultural asset stripping identified by Skeggs (2004) and as, in effect, an exercise of power by those positioned as white and middle class. Such a liberal and consumerist multiculturalism is thus animated entirely by its own interests. But what I have offered here is an account attentive to some of the detail of these novels, showing how "racial" difference is not merely a component in a cosmopolitan lifestyle but necessary to a displacement of whiteness from its monolithic and unmarked normality. In the brief lines of speech attributed to Angel Juan, above, he looks back at white America. In *Missing Angel Juan*, early in the novel, he says to Witch Baby – "You're always taking pictures of me and writing songs for me but that's not me. That's who you make up" (Block, 1993: 3). Exotifying fantasies about the "other" are, if tentatively, undermined.

But difference and identifications across difference are also necessary to the unsettling of whiteness and, particularly, to the refusal of the sterility of ideals of white purity. If *The Hanged Man* is read as, in part, a response to the restoration of such ideals through the preceding years of neoconservative political rhetoric, it is possible to read it as a critique of a particular fantasy of female whiteness rather than in any way representing the position of actual, socially "white" young women. Block's trope of "whiteness" should not be understood, referentially, as implying greater vulnerability – to sexual abuse and male power – among those socially positioned as white. It is, rather, a challenge to the ethereal ideal of a whiteness beyond the reality and ambiguity of physical embodiment.[13] Such "whiteness as translucence" is, in *The Hanged Man,* overcome with the release of blood, and the restoration of blood to the flesh.

But given that such extraordinary whiteness is, additionally, a way of representing the anxiety of vulnerability, a metaphorical rendering of emotional crisis, it might also be understood as a trope not confined in its significance to those readers who are socially "white." Following the same logic, it is also possible to see how, in Block's elaboration of the processes of objectification,[14] and at this level of symbolic inversion, a darker skin can confer protection in the face of threat.

Chapter Six

Dead White People: Another Look at *Buffy the Vampire Slayer*

Introduction

This chapter returns to *Buffy the Vampire Slayer* and, following the discussion of Francesca Lia Block in the previous chapter, considers what meanings "whiteness" may have in the show. In some respects, it could be argued that *Buffy the Vampire Slayer* addresses an audience similar to that engaged by Block's novels. Lorna Jowett (2005), for example, argues that *Buffy*, in common with other "quality television," addresses "the white, affluent, urban middle-classes" (Jancovich and Lyons, 2003: 3, cited in Jowett, 2005: 9; see also Williamson, 2005: 77–91; Johnson, 2005: 107–121). She suggests that therefore

> Following this logic, it is hardly surprising if shows like *Buffy* are more preoccupied with issues such as gender and sexuality rather than race and class, since the former are of more significance in the lives of its consumers. (Jowett, 2005: 9)

She goes further, contrasting the prevailing whiteness of *Buffy the Vampire Slayer* with much else in American "quality" television:

> It has been noted that in the United States' history of representing itself, "being white became synonymous with being American" (Babb, 1998: 2), and *Buffy*'s white, middle-class, heterosexual "norm" is rarely named and remains largely invisible even as it influences constructions of identity and gender. As Richard Dyer points out, race is often a term "only applied to non-white peoples," and "as long as white people are not racially seen and named, they/we function as a human norm" (1997: 1). Some difference on *Buffy* is given a subject position and point of view (sexuality) but other differences are not (race and class). (Jowett, 2005: 13)

If "race" is understood to refer to nonwhite people and to the cultures of nonwhites, then this show has no sustained interest in "race" in that sense. There are black characters, and interesting narrative developments including them (Kendra in season 3, for example), but they are not, with any consistency, central to *Buffy the Vampire Slayer*. Its representation of southern

California is confined to the fictive Sunnydale, a suburban small town where even the town's young people are portrayed as curiously untouched by such pervasive contemporary "real world" phenomena as hip hop. White indie bands play at the characters' regular music venue, the Bronze, and black music and dress has no place.

However, the need to question the "racelessness" of whiteness has been suggested by various authors in the past twenty years (for example, hooks, 1992; Morrison, 1993; Fine, Weis, Powell, and Wong, 1997; Frankenberg, 1997; Babb, 1998). Some have drawn attention to the exhaustion of white hegemony.[1] The value of Richard Dyer's (1997) account, though not without significant precedents, lies in its detailed attention to visual media. His argument is that whiteness affords the power of subjectivity, the vantage point of those who observe, exercise surveillance over, and sometimes analyze, all those considered to be "other," objects of, rather than actors in, the social world. Processes of visual representation (photography, film, television), Dyer argues, are implicated in the pervasive "normalization" of whiteness. And yet, whiteness is also fundamentally contradictory and, in his final chapter, "White Death," he argues that its power is now in decline.[2] Though the "white race" perhaps still has an imaginary unity, it is increasingly characterized by its precarious, elusive, and insecure status. Other research, ethnographic rather than textual, has also suggested how incoherent whiteness may be in young people's lived experience (Perry, 2002).

Jowett's (2005) comments certainly indicate the difficulty that faces any attempt to explore questions of "race" in *Buffy the Vampire Slayer*, but her own study does make frequent reference to Dyer's influential case. At the risk of applying his categories too strictly, I want to take things a little further. After all, where whiteness is "unmarked," its status as "taken for granted" and as "normal" unquestioned, then some effort to render whiteness visible is necessary. The show does develop, across its seven seasons, as a story about young people, centrally young women, apparently requiring no further specification in "racial" terms. But it is possible to extend some aspects of Dyer's (1997) argument, and particularly his view of whiteness as implicated in sterility and death, to argue that in *Buffy the Vampire Slayer* whiteness is more a malaise than the secure ontological ground of identity. The preoccupation of the seven seasons as a whole with an embattled sense of insecurity and sterility is, arguably, a displaced anxiety arising from a loss of the unquestioned preeminence of white culture, if not of white material wealth and power, in the decades since the 1960s.[3] These are very broad assertions about *Buffy the Vampire Slayer* and, in the following discussion, I want to explore some of the particular arguments that might support the more general case.

There are analyses of *Buffy* focused on "race" (see Ono, 2000; Edwards, 2002; Money, 2002). One disturbing precedent is Neal King's discussion of what he calls *Buffy the Vampire Slayer*'s "nasty streak of racism." His article, "Brownskirts: Fascism, Christianity, and the Eternal Demon" (King, 2003: 199), offers a challenging indictment of the show's implicit politics. He pursues a reading of *Buffy the Vampire Slayer* as a "proto-fascist" allegory in which Buffy and friends figure as a fascist gang out to murder those they deem not to belong in their world. However, though the questions he raises and the doubts thus cast on the show's "liberal" politics are of critical importance, I do not intend to follow his allegorical account as such. In Chapter Four, I suggested that *Buffy the Vampire Slayer* could be read as "a highly illiberal fantasy of purification" but declined to pursue that reading, rejecting "allegory" and the search for "real" equivalents to the demons and vampires inhabiting Buffy's world. Much of King's argument depends on that strategy and, in his account, those routinely eliminated in every episode are in effect "racial" others to the core ensemble of young white Anglo Americans.

However, "racial" concerns can be identified in *Buffy the Vampire Slayer* without recourse either to allegorical reading or to a sole preoccupation with that minority of episodes where black actors appear. Of course, I am arguing that there is a kind of correspondence between the fictional world of *Buffy the Vampire Slayer* and the "racialised" social world of the United States in the later 1990s and beyond. However, the task of interpretation should not be a matter of resolving the show's ambiguities in favor of a direct correspondence between kinds of characters (vampires, slayers, demons, witches and so forth) and their "real" social referents. Correspondences arise in the narrative exploration of mythologies of identity which are far from solely internal to, or an invention of, the text. Such mythologies, the Christian discourse of the "body" and the "soul," for example, have a continuing and pervasive presence in many people's lives and are a vocabulary of explanation where questions of identity, ontology, reproduction, and death arise. If, as I suggested in Chapter Four, an animating question internal to *Buffy the Vampire Slayer* is that of what we are, of what constitutes us as human beings, in this chapter my preoccupation is with how such a question is posed from within particularly white cultural formations. First of all, there is the mythology of vampirism, in combination with the Christian dualist rhetoric of the soul and body, mostly located in a white European tradition. Second, there is a rather more recent secular mythology of hedonism and aspiration satirized, as I illustrate below, in the activities of Warren, Jonathan, and Andrew in season 6.

Buffy the Vampire Slayer and *Angel* are, despite their many secular elements relative to the older tradition of vampire fiction (see Forster, 2003), substantially preoccupied with the legacy of a white Christian mythology (Dyer, 1997: 15–18). The relationship between the body and the soul and its implications for the understanding of death, and of life, are central. In addition, heterosexual reproduction and its frustration, through sterility, fear or "bad" object choice are among the interrelated aspects of *Buffy the Vampire Slayer*'s white Christian problematic that I want to consider here (Dyer, 1997: 217). The "whiteness" which, in King's argument, is protected in the name of humanity by Buffy and her proto-fascist gang, is more internally contradictory, more insecure and more in crisis than he acknowledges. Most obviously, less than human ontologies are not attributed only to those external to the "gang" and frequently figure, if ambiguously, as internal to the core ensemble. Among its members (though membership is arguable) a majority are, between "human" and "other," ambiguously liminal: Angel and Spike (human/vampire); Dawn (ancient energy/human); Anya (demon/human); Willow (human/witch); Buffy (slayer/dead); and Oz (human/werewolf). Xander, Giles, and Tara are, almost unusually, perhaps just human. This is not an ensemble confidently projecting itself into an ontologically pure future.

The main focus of this chapter is first on three male figures, Angel, Spike, and Xander and, second, on the trio composed of Andrew, Jonathan, and Warren. In giving attention to these characters I am of course concerned with how the question of whiteness intersects with masculinity and perhaps more specifically the position of white heterosexual men in the reproduction of the "race." Though relatively marginal across the seven seasons as a whole, the trio's presence in season 6, variously referred to as "nerds" and "geeks," provides an interesting further representation of white masculinity. They are variously encumbered by lingering boyhood fantasies, are incapable of constructing sexual relationships with women (or each other?), and resort to manipulative scenarios with, ultimately, deadly consequences (*Dead Things*, 6013). At the end of that season, Warren is dead, tortured and flayed alive by Willow, and Andrew and Jonathan leave for Mexico.

Angel, Spike, and Xander

Here I want to examine each of the three main figures with reference to Dyer's categories: "dark white" (Angel), "extreme white" (Spike), and "ordinary white" (Xander). Angel, given Irish origin, with dark hair and a relatively "olive" skin tone is much less white than Buffy. As Dyer (1997: 28) suggests, men are typically represented as darker than the women with whom they have sexual relationships.[4] But Angel's coloring, and origin, in addition make him less than securely white. The Irish, Jews, and Latinos have been, and sometimes still are, positioned as less than white (Dyer, 1997: 12). As a vampire, the precariousness of Angel's whiteness is further compounded. These are Dyer's reflections on the whiteness of vampires:

> The horror of vampirism is expressed in colour: ghastly white, disgustingly cadaverous, without the blood of life that would give colour. The vampire's bite, so evidently a metaphor for sexuality, is debilitating unto death, just as white people fear sexuality if it is allowed to get out of control (out from under the will) – yet, like the vampire, they need it. The vampire is the white man or woman in the grip of a libidinal need s/he cannot master. In the act of vampirism, white society (the vampire) feeds off itself (his/her victims) and threatens to destroy itself. All of this is so menacing that it is often ascribed to those who are not mainstream whites – Jews, South East Europeans (Transylvania in *Dracula* and its derivatives), the denizens of New Orleans (Anne Rice's *Vampire Chronicles*). Horror films have their cake and eat it: they give us the horror of whiteness while at the same time ascribing it to those who are liminally white. The terror of whiteness, of being without life, of causing death, is both vividly conveyed and disowned. (Dyer, 1997: 210)

As the vampire Angelus, Angel embodies a rampant, voracious, and murderous sexuality (see Jowett, 2005: 154–156). This bodily "other" is suppressed, in specifically Christian terms, through the mechanism of the "soul." In this respect, Angel is thus closer to a full claim on whiteness than can be attained by those who, like Spike until season 7, lack such an animate resonance of divinity and are merely bodily.[5] As the name Angel also implies, he is, if with considerable irony, closer to God, a dark angel aspiring beyond his past immersion in flesh and blood. Of course the attainment of his aspiration through "romantic love" is blocked by the curse that, on its fulfillment, returns him to the murderous demands of his body. Given such a contradictory positioning, Angel's future redemption is among the core themes of the five-season "spin-off" *Angel*. But Angel is also a terminal figure in that, despite his association with sexual potency, he is sterile (see *Bad Eggs*, 2012). Though immortal, he cannot reproduce and, more specifically, cannot therefore contribute to the reproduction of the whiteness/humanity to which he both aspires and from which he is constantly threatened with exclusion. The "best" he can do is to attenuate, but never overcome, the various threats to human well-being proliferating in the dystopian Los Angeles constructed as the setting for his "own" show (*Angel*, seasons 1–5). So, with his intervention, some humans live a little longer, but Angel has, in his own immortality, the torment of virtual exclusion from the life that others, however briefly, can live as human.[6] Whatever the sexual power of his youthful "dark white" appearance (with hints of 1950s Brando and Elvis, perhaps), the extension of his televisual life in *Angel* season 5 is ultimately a story of decline into quasi-military rhetoric, with repeated exchanges focused on what it means to be a "hero" and a "champion" (see Jowett, 2005: 157–158). At the end of the final season of *Angel* he actually relinquishes any hope of becoming fully human. Indeed, alongside two vampires with souls and the ancient goddess Ilyria, the only genuinely mortal human left fighting is black (Gunn), someone with more "soul" perhaps (*Angel – Not fade away*, 5022).

Spike, uncomfortably phallic (see Wilcox, 2005), is constructed more out of punk than the fifties' legacy of brooding "antiheroes" from which Angel appears to derive (see Williamson, 2005: 72–75, commenting especially on his similarities to Billy Idol). In some respects, Spike is more securely white than Angel – English, not Irish, and with bleached white/blond hair and high cheekbones strongly Northern European in appearance.[7] His clothing, a long black leather coat and combat boots, invokes what Dyer calls extreme whiteness, though here signifiers recalling the Gestapo, transmuted through punk, are closer to an ironic evacuation of meaning than the perfection of white heroism (see Dick Hebdige, 1979: 116–117). The passage of signifiers of extreme whiteness through the prism of punk has to be acknowledged as a major complication in any discussion of Spike. Hebdige (1979) has argued for a reading of punk as formed in intimate exchange with black (reggae, dub) music.[8] He suggests that "punk includes reggae as a 'present absence' – a black hole around which punk composes itself" (Hebdige, 1979: 68). The "dead white face" of punk is the bearer of white ethnicity as a "hopeless condition" (Hebdige, 1979: 65–66), and in the title sequence of *Buffy the Vampire Slayer* this is repeatedly recalled in Spike's defiantly empty gesture (two fingers) "No future," indeed.[9]

Spike, for six seasons, is more "irredeemably" a vampire than Angel, as lacking a "soul" he cannot be what his white bodily appearance claims. Moreover, his hair is bleached in artificial contrast with the mundane brown characteristic of William, his "ordinary" human self. In this sense, the disparity is greater; Spike, with some of the characteristics of extreme whiteness, is nevertheless further from the attainment of "ordinary" whiteness. His "chip" is, like the high tech gimmickry employed by Buffy's boy-friend Riley Finn in seasons 4 and 5 or by the "nerds" in season 6, an inadequate and inauthentic substitute for the fully internally divided constitution, between spiritual and physical striving, of the white male (Dyer, 1997: 17). Buffy's relationship with and contempt for Spike in season 6 exemplifies the problem: her "intimacy" with him is predicated on her own death and the difficulty of being among the living, in the human world she now experiences as "hard and bright and violent" (*Afterlife*, 6003). Her desire for his body is confirmed, rather than contradicted, by her words – "You're a thing, an evil, disgusting thing" (*Smashed*, 6009) – because, in this construction of sexuality, "love" only arises between beings with souls, those internally divided against desires located "in the flesh." Perhaps there is also a lingering anxiety that her whiteness, confirmed in death, has too completely removed her from participation among the living, almost beyond feeling. She is positioned, like a vampire, as liminal, living but without feeling fully alive. Sex with Spike enables her to feel re-embodied, thus mitigating the effects of her own self-sacrifice. She initiates sex with Spike (*Smashed*, 6009) and continues to demonstrate a yearning for the re-embodiment it allows her.

In season 6, a lot of Spike's flesh is revealed – the long black leather coat comes off, along with everything else, again and again. In earlier seasons, Angel's body – as sexual but also as suffering torture – was on display and, given his soul, could be construed as confirming through pain a willingness to pursue redemption. Spike's body is perhaps more disconcertingly contradictory. What does Spike's body promise? Dyer's comments, first of all on the class-inflected meanings of white muscularity and second on the particular equation of bodybuilding with whiteness, provide a context in which to address this question. As William, Spike is ridiculed. As a vampire without a soul, he is always inferior to Angel. As an, approximately, English working-class punk, he is an outsider to the middle-class suburban milieu of southern California. Given all this, Spike's enjoyment of fighting (see Willis, 1977, Willis et al., 1990; Walkerdine, 1986), and of other opportunities to display his bodily strength, well illustrates Dyer's observation that:

> The possibility of white bodily inferiority falls heavily on the shoulders of those white men who are not at the top of the spirit pile, those for whom their body is their only capital. In the context particularly of white working-class or "underachieving" masculinity, an assertion of the value and even superiority of the white male body has especial resonance. (Dyer, 1997: 147)

Dyer's argument is also that the meanings of a built body arise from layers of connotations sedimented in a white cultural history. The display of Spike's body draws on these various connotations, but inconsistently:

> Bodybuilding in popular culture articulates white masculinity...First, bodybuilding makes reference to classical – that is, ancient Greek and Roman – art...second, bodybuilding now more often invokes a US, and *a fortiori* Californian, life style, with a characteristic emphasis on ideas of health, energy and naturalness...Third, bodybuilding has sometimes adopted the image of the barbarian, drawn principally

> from comic books... very often mobilis[ing] a sub-Nietzschian rhetoric of the Ubermensch that, however inaccurately, is strongly associated with Hitlerism and crypto-fascism. Finally, bodybuilding does also sometimes draw on Christian imagery. The activity itself involves pain, bodily suffering, and with it the idea of the value of pain. (1997: 148–150)

Spike, played by James Marsters, has a built body showing a clearly defined, hairless, developed, and implicitly hard musculature. Though not bulky, he is portrayed as extremely strong, sexually assured and, moreover, willing to suffer and able to endure considerable physical pain. In these respects he fulfills the image of the ideal "built" white body delineated by Dyer. But there are significant contradictions. He is indeed white but actually too white – whatever the condition of James Marsters' skin, there is logically enough, a suspicion that Spike must lack the tan that a properly white, living Californian male might be expected to display. Often Spike is lit very warmly – in the pre-title sequence to *Dead Things* (6013), for example. But somehow Spike, especially situated in various expressionistically lit subterranean settings, can also appear close to cadaverous. The implication may be that whiteness in itself is deathly and needs to be lit – from outside – to achieve the appearance of life, just as vampires need to ingest blood in order to achieve the appearance of being alive. Thus, as Dyer argues, the paradox of white bodily perfection is that it lurches into deathliness. The visible structure of his muscles seems almost to invite dissection, rather than admiration or desire. Whereas Angel's body is lit to appear rather less hard-edged in its musculature, Spike, even undressed, sustains hints of fascist extremity. Less ambiguously than Angel, he appears sterile, without a future. For someone for whom life has long been over, and without, until season 7, Angel's animating quest for redemption, his desire to achieve a "living" relationship with Buffy depends on her continuing need for a bodily "thing." As she regains a sense of purpose in living, and the need for sexual incarnation diminishes, the apparently terminal despair of his predicament is confirmed.

However, complicating the meanings of the numerous shots of Spike's naked body, there is also a sustained emphasis on facial close-ups, and thus nuances of expression significantly extending the resonance of the dialogue (see Symonds, 2005). By highlighting the relative complexity of James Marster's acting, and despite Buffy's most brutal rejection (in *Dead Things,* 6013 and subsequently), Spike's yearning is made as credible as that of Angel, Riley, or indeed Xander. His apparently bitter quest to return to his former state – ambiguously "pre-chip" or "pre-vampire" – at the conclusion of season 6, results in the re-embodiment of his "soul" so that, it seems, he can be lit from within and thus aspire to the spirit of whiteness.

Buffy glows – as Spike remarks, almost in awe (*Same Time, Same Place*, 7003: "Look at you, glowing…"). And so, apparently, did his beloved mother after he sired her: "You're glowing…" (*Lies My Parents Told Me*, 7017). Dyer reports a text from 1866 (*How to Be Beautiful*) where a "plain" girl finds that "the secret of how to be beautiful was to 'let Christ dwell in your heart'. The sign of this was the sense of glow, of something in but not of the body, something heavenly" (Dyer, 1997: 127). In the history of cinema in the twentieth century, the lighting of women repeats and extends the equation of light with purity and the spirit, "the woman is more fully in the light, the man posed so that he seems to intrude into, yearn towards it" (1997: 134). The visual contrast between Buffy and Angel and even between Buffy and Spike is, in these terms, entirely predictable: the light, glowing, blonde figure set against a somewhat darker, less illuminated male figure. But though the representation of sexuality seems therefore entirely consistent with long familiar conventions, in neither case are they the properly heterosexual reproductive couples thus implied. Desire is always compromised and ultimately blocked.

Spike returns in season 7, initially without the black leather coat, and apparently diminished in physical presence (in *Angel*, season 5, he can barely remain physically solid in the initial episodes at all). Previously distinguished through his physicality, Spike appears almost depleted by the presence of a soul, and by the chaotic feelings it brings. His appearance in the closing scene of *Beneath You* (7002), lit by a bluish white light and once more stripped to the waist, again returns him to the deathly pallor of the dead white body, despite his soul, and in agony on "the cross", his flesh burning, he embarks on the suffering for his own sin that, in Christ on the cross, is taken as emblematic of suffering on behalf of others. The trajectory of Spike's spiritual ascent thus borrows distinctive elements from the narrative of Christ's bodily torment, crucifixion, resurrection, and ascension. For Spike (and for Buffy) there is no more sex as such after season 6. The culmination of season 7 takes Spike to the limit of his spiritual ascent. Clad in his long black leather coat and fighting in the mouth of hell, wearing the amulet given to Buffy by Angel, he reflects light into the hordes of ubervamps. In so doing he becomes illuminated, lit from above and seemingly at last from within ("I can feel it Buffy, my soul, it's really there, it kind of stings"), his body is consumed in flames – the logic of Christian dualism, of construction of the soul/spirit as distinct from the body takes Spike of all people to martyrdom – the complete denial of the flesh.

Unlike Angel and Spike, Xander is alive in the usual sense. But for him, his "life" is less than fully lived. Xander, the most ordinary of white boys in

Buffy the Vampire Slayer, suffers a recurrent and corrosive level of self-doubt. Certainly he does "progress," and he has his triumphs, but there's a persistent sense of disappointment about Xander, that he can never be what he aspires to. Through the first four seasons there are repeated scenes of humiliation for Xander (*Teacher's Pet*, 1004; *Inca Mummy Girl*, 2004; *Reptile Boy*, 2005). At the opening of *The Zeppo* (3013) Xander calls for and fails to catch a ball thrown by a black student. Cordelia appears to compound his humiliation:

> It must be really hard when all of your friends have, like, superpowers, slayers, werewolves, witches, vampires and you're like this little nothing, you must feel like Jimmy Olson, the boy that had no cool...you're the useless part of the group, you're the Zeppo. Cool, look it up, it's something that a subliterate who's repeated twelfth grade three times has and you don't.

Though this episode plays out a fantasy of adolescent self-transformation from which Xander emerges quietly triumphant, his anxious lack of self-assurance is not eliminated, recurring often in later seasons. Notably, early in season 5, in *The Replacement* (5003), Xander is split into two polarized versions of himself, one confident and assertive and the other hopelessly diffident. Throughout, the voice of the "real" Xander appears to speak from the faltering self: "a demon has taken my life from me and he's living it better than I do," and, given the predominance of this Xander in previous seasons, it is difficult to accept his confident other half as equally credible.

In season 6, Xander and Anya appear to be a focus for hope. As Buffy says, early in *Hell's Bells* (6016), "You two have proved that there's light at the end of a very long, long nasty tunnel." But the episode actually brings to a disastrous climax all of Xander's horror of family and of reproduction – a demon out to ruin things for Anya persuades Xander to witness, and feel, his own future as a husband and father, fulfilling the nightmare of repeating his own family history. The bleak prediction is that "sometimes two people, all they bring each other is pain" – a comment that might also be applied retrospectively to Angel and Buffy, perhaps to Riley and Buffy and, concurrently, to Buffy and Spike. Xander, as the most ordinary of young white men, is split between desire and fear, between wanting Anya and the fear that nothing good will come of it. Xander's predicament is articulated not just in terms of a reasonable apprehension but is further compounded with the (repeated) conviction of his own lack of worth. Here Xander addresses Anya in the aftermath of Tara's death:

> "You think I'm the hero of this piece...I saw the gun before Warren raised it, I saw it and I couldn't move, he shot two of my friends before I could even...You want

> me to know how useless I am, that it's my fault, thanks, I already got the memo." (*Two to Go,* 6021)

Though Xander retrieves Willow from her bitterly destructive wave of anger in the final episode, this is a return to a friendship originating in kindergarten, one among several reaffirmed nonsexual relationships at the end of the season (Buffy and Dawn, Anya and Giles). At the beginning of season 7 Xander is, in his own words, a "dateless nerd." In the course of the season Xander is not just humiliated but, with one eye put out, partially symbolically castrated.

The Trio

The sixth season introduces its major external threat to the Buffy household in a relatively modest way. In *Flooded* (6004), the appearance of Jonathan, Andrew, and Warren, as the instigators of a demon attack on a bank, initiates a comic subplot largely focused on the fantasies and aspirations of teenage boys. However, over the full season, the consequences of the trio's actions become lethal. Though an intermittent and often apparently trivial threat, this narrative strand facilitates an extended and sharply satirical attack on a significant and enduring construction of masculinity.

Bill Osgerby's (2001) history of modern American masculinities documents the formation of a "hedonistic" masculinity and, in particular, its expansion in the 1950s and 1960s. He begins *Playboys in Paradise* with an account of a robbery:

> By any measure the robbery was audacious. In 1964, in the dead of a chill October night, thieves broke into the American Museum of National History in New York and made off with a small fortune in gems and precious stones – a haul that included the Star of India, the world's largest star sapphire. In itself the burglary was spectacularly newsworthy. Yet what was already one of the biggest news stories of the winter became a media frenzy when, several days later, FBI agents arrested three suspects in Miami. (Osgerby, 2001: 1)

In the opening scene (post titles) of *Smashed* (6009), Andrew, Jonathan, and Warren, equipped with various "gadgets," steal an exceptionally large diamond from a display case in the Sunnydale Museum. The robbery gains considerable media attention, not least because they "freeze" a guard in order to escape. Osgerby (2001: 1) cites Jack Roth, writing in *Esquire* (September 1965: 118):

> The crime was sexy, it was athletic, it was cool, way out, and as they say, not to be believed…the crooks had a kind of Man from U.N.C.L.E appeal…you can almost hear the beat of a souped-up musical score that might have been written for it by someone like John Barry (*Goldfinger*).

It is striking that the Sunnydale trio frequently refer to the popular "spy" genres of the 1960s. In the constant competitive banter between them they argue, for example, over Bond movies (*Life Serial,* 6005). There are, additionally, references to *Dr Who*, *Star Trek*, *Star Wars*, and *Superman* comics. Cumulatively, across the several episodes in which they appear, they are thus constructed as avid followers of "male fantasy" genres associated especially with the 1960s. Furthermore, their aspiration to be "super-villains" is animated by an investment in images of masculinity associated with a narcissistic and consumerist "playboy" lifestyle. The range and valence of cultural reference is confined to a particularly white, and "dated," repertoire. The resources for their imagined identities are not found, as might be expected in the later 1990s, in the imagery or language of gangsta rap nor do they lay claim to what Perry (2002: 110–111) calls the "putative" qualities of black urban culture – toughness, hard masculinity. The version of masculinity satirized in this narrative strand derives from past decades, from the genres of science and spy fiction. In this respect, the object of the satirical critique is entirely internal to white popular culture. Osgerby notes that

> Although seldom identified as such, white masculinity should also be considered as a cultural construction. As Richard Dyer (1997) argues, the power and authority of white culture has afforded "whiteness" a quality of virtual invisibility…From this perspective….the 1950s and 1960s masculine archetypes of the "footloose bachelor" and "vibrant youth" can be seen as specifically white cultural motifs…the "young man of action and acquisition" was an unmistakably white cultural phenomenon. (2001: 13)

If the "nerds" have a more contemporary repertoire, it is to be found in their preoccupation with new technologies. However, "gadgets," like the genres in which they are deployed, are also strongly associated with the 1960s:

> The obsession with push-button gadgetry might be seen, at least in part, as a desire for phallic accessories that could shore up a sense of masculine power. Yet, as Buxton (1990: 90) notes, the early 1960s craze for hi-tech gizmos also related to changing conceptualizations of technology. Breaking with traditional notions of machinery as bulky and cumbersome, the 1960s concept of the "gadget" conceived technology as a miniaturized and individualized consumer product – precise, functional and emblematic of stylish cool. And in the world of Playboy the aesthetic of the "gadget" reached its zenith in the "Playboy Bed." (Osgerby, 2001: 133–134)

Jonathan is small and appears vulnerable. Andrew appears constantly ill-at-ease physically, with a defensive and awkward manner. Warren, though bigger and considerably more aggressive, is both very hairy (a notable contrast with Angel and Spike) and, conventionally, somewhat ugly. Variously lacking the physical qualities and competences to achieve and live their imaginary identities, they attempt both to exercise masculine power and to be "cool" through technological ingenuity, with a multiplying array of intrusive and manipulative devices deployed in each of the episodes where they appear.

In seeking to "control" Sunnydale, and therefore to displace Buffy, they effectively intend to restore male power and significantly, sexual access to young women of their choice. Their objectives, announced repeatedly in *Flooded* (6004), include hypnotizing Buffy to make her a "willing sex bunny" (an allusion to Playboy's bunny girls, perhaps). At this point, comedy lies in the unsettling tensions between the boyish enthusiasm of Jonathan and Andrew ("I still can't believe it. We did it! We can do anything. We could stay up all night if we wanna") and Warren's menacing, and ultimately violently misogynistic, disposition (see Jowett, 2005: 112–115). A crucial episode in the trio's pursuit of "willing sex bunnies" is *Dead Things* (6013). With the successful completion of an "orb" (a "cerebral dampener") allowing them to exert hypnotic control over others, Warren identifies a young woman by whom he has been rejected in the past – Katrina. Intending to make her a "sex slave," they abduct her and take her to their den where, after a brief argument over who should have her first, Warren kisses her, orders her to her knees and, implicitly, is about to demand oral sex when the hypnotic state falters. She confronts them, asserting, "This is not some fantasy…it's rape." She attempts to leave, fighting off both Andrew and Jonathan, but is attacked from behind by Warren, who in his fury smashes a bottle over her head and kills her.

Though both Andrew and Jonathan are disconcerted by the accusation of rape and shocked by her murder, they collude with Warren in an attempt to transfer the responsibility for her death to Buffy. Andrew's comment on their apparent success – "We really got away with murder, that's kinda cool…" – is, however, met with a hesitant and troubled response from Jonathan – "Yeah…..cool." Clearly this episode abandons comedy as the primary mode in representing the three "nerds" and, as noted above, Warren is also subsequently responsible for the death of Tara. The anger leading him to his attempt to shoot Buffy (killing Tara "accidentally") arises from his failure to defeat her. But as with the "orb" in *Dead Things*, his power in *Seeing Red* (6019) is also located externally, in this case in two spheres kept in a pouch near his waist. To make the point explicit, Warren's "balls" are crushed by Buffy and his power instantly dissipates. "Gadgets" are vulnerable and, after so many have failed, he resorts to a gun. At his own death (*Villians,* 6020) following a misogynistic tirade against Willow ("You're really asking for it, you know that...and when I walk away from this you're going to beg to join your little girl-friend, you know that"), he is tortured with the slow penetration of a bullet into his chest, Willow remarking that being shot is not "like in the comics."

The scene stands out as exceptionally agonizing and protracted, but it is both the culmination of the misogynistic logic of his fantasies (the pursuit of "cool" masculinity) and a brutal dismissal of their source (male fantasy genres). Finally, Willow skins and burns him.

Conclusion

The complexity and scale of the question addressed in this chapter really deserves a more extended argument ranging across all the seasons of *Buffy the Vampire Slayer* in more detail and giving more attention to the very differently constructed urban world of Los Angeles in *Angel.* But in the context of this book, the argument that can be restated here is that this instance of "youth TV," which did no doubt successfully address teenagers, is also a kind of satirical excavation of layers of "youth culture" accumulated through the past fifty years and thus also attempts to engage an older (and probably predominantly white) audience. The visual prehistories of Angel and Spike and the backward looking fascination with arguably exhausted genres among the trio invite some recognition and pleasure but also a degree of critical distancing from those who may, in varying degrees, recall the decades in which these textual referents first appeared. For such an older audience, Xander may be the vehicle for a rather painful reflection on what it was like to be young. More broadly, as was argued in Chapter Four, *Buffy the Vampire Slayer* looks back at youth with regret, not that it passes, but that it is so difficult and that its vicissitudes persist into adult life. In this respect, it is a sustained challenge to the celebration of youth as emblematic of a hedonistic, and of course desirable, lifestyle. Because the range of backward looking generic reference is largely confined to white cultural forms, it is also possible to argue that this disengagement from "youth-as-hedonism" is an aspect of the slow decline of "whiteness" sketched in the last chapter of Dyer's (1997) study.

In Dyer's argument, the issue of reproduction and of sterility is central. In *Buffy the Vampire Slayer*, there is a problem of "regeneration." The problem is posed in part by the form of the show: each episode and each season plots the lives of the ensemble through a strongly conventionalized phase of life. Not only do the episodes follow each other chronologically, the core ensemble of young characters grow through the "stages" of later teenage life into adulthood. But these young white people seem unable to perform ordinary whiteness, and particularly unable to perform ordinary white heterosexuality. How then can this group of young white figures ensure its own future and its succession?

In her final meeting with Angel, in her "cookie-dough" speech, Buffy more or less dismisses "the guy thing" and subsequently formulates her plan to pass on, and thus establish succession, to "every girl in the world" who has the potential to be a slayer (*Chosen,* 7022). Only Willow has an apparently newly emergent sexual relationship in the seventh season – not a heterosexual one. It is partly through her agency, and a return to witchcraft, in communion with Buffy and her girlfriend Kennedy, that the solution to the problem of survival and succession is found. Of course this season is arguably a little more "racially" inclusive than any other in its recruitment of Principal Wood and of Asian and black potential slayers, but the imagery of light remains central. Willow, though Jewish, has a "nice white skin" (a compliment from the skin stripping demon in *Same Time, Same Place*, 7003) and, as she achieves the necessary broadening of the slayer prophecy, glows with an extremity of light, leaving her in a kind of post-orgasmic collapse (*Chosen,* 7022). Spike sacrifices himself, Anya dies fighting, Principal Wood is badly injured, and the ensemble gathered, and privileged, in the final shot is thus both human and white but also uncoupled (neither heterosexual nor homosexual) and unsettled. In the front row there is Dawn, with Buffy and Willow, and just behind them, Giles, Faith, and Xander. This ending seems to recall, but visually, an earlier refrain, "Where do we go from here?" from *Once More with Feeling* (6007). Looking into the distance, implicitly also into the future, the "we" composed here, marked as white, stand together but separately, not touching. It is liminal and uncertain, not triumphant and not conclusive.

Chapter Seven

Fictions of Identity: The Self in Narratives of Musical Identification

Introduction

In this chapter I want to focus on students' writing about the place of music in their lives. The writing was produced within an undergraduate module, Popular Music, Youth and Education, in part as material for assessment.[1] The students were invited to reflect on their own musical experience through short autobiographical sketches. In some respects, the autobiographies could be used to support the view that there is a strong correspondence between social positions and tastes in particular forms of music (Bourdieu, 1986). However, they also offer more complex evidence of efforts to construct and sustain a sense of self-identity (Richards, 1998b; 1999). Though "life-scripts" are more obviously available through narrative forms in film, television, and print, music is also a resource in a "fictional" elaboration of identities. In particular, music is construed as a powerfully affective medium and it is through musical reference that personal histories of "feelings," narratives of the emotional self, appear to be most easily articulated (Frith, 1987, 1996; Richards, 1998b; DeNora, 2000). Mark Slobin has argued that "people are often driven by a mixture of memory and desire in their choice of musics [sic], which swings closer to Barthes's passionate *jouisssance* than to any set of predictable strategies or methodical mapping" (Slobin, 1993: 76). The students who contributed the writing discussed in this chapter report and "re-present" their memories of affective self-construction.

Though the argument that tastes in music correspond to social positions remains a sociological common-sense in debates over the meaning of musical choices and affiliations, more unpredictable and perhaps idiosyncratic patterns of engagement have been acknowledged. Simon Frith, as a sociologist, argues that "tastes do correlate with class cultures and subcultures; musical styles are linked to specific age groups; we can take for granted the connections of ethnicity and sound" (Frith, 1996: 119–120) but he is equally insistent in suggesting that the question to pursue is "not what does popular music reveal about...people...but how does it create them as a people, as a web of identities?" (1996: 121). In an earlier article, he suggested that people engage with popular music to construct:

> a particular sort of self-definition, a particular place in society. The pleasure that pop music produces is a pleasure of identification – with the music we like, with the performers...with...other people who like it. And...the production of identity is also a production of non-identity...a process of inclusion and exclusion. (Frith, 1987: 140)

From Frith, the scope for agency amidst social determination emerges as a situated "production of identity."

Tia DeNora, interviewing women in both the United States and Britain, has also examined music as a "technology of the self" – music as a resource in her respondents' day-to-day emotional self-regulation:

> They drew upon elaborate repertoires of musical programming practice, and were sharply aware of how to mobilize music to arrive at, enhance and alter aspects of themselves and their self-concepts. This practical knowledge should be viewed as part of the (often tacit) practices in and through which respondents produced themselves as coherent social and socially disciplined beings. (DeNora, 2000: 49)

The demand for such work on the self is explained as characteristic of complex social worlds in which negotiation of multiple, differently constituted settings is essential. In addition to "tacit" knowledge, there is therefore a need to more deliberately choose and calculate the affective benefits of particular kinds of music:

> The self is called upon to be increasingly agile, to be able to manage perspectival and circumstantial incongruity, as happens, for example, when individuals move rapidly through numerous and often discrete worlds where personnel and values may clash. (DeNora, 2000: 52)

These everyday routines of emotional and "aesthetic reflexivity" are achieved over lengthy periods of time, with the accumulation of particular knowledge of music located in individual histories:

> Music's "effects" come from the ways in which individuals orient to it, how they interpret it and how they place it within their personal musical maps, within the semiotic web of music and extra-musical associations... (DeNora, 2000: 61)

Though DeNora's research has little to say about how access to particular forms of music might be governed by social position and how the music industry and the wider media shape the availability and relative prominence of particular forms of music, her approach can usefully inform a reading of the musical autobiographies. She suggests, for example, that music is used as "a technology for spinning the apparently continuous tale of who one is" (DeNora, 2000: 63) and that recollecting past experience through music "is making manifest within memory what may have been latent or even absent the first time through…The telling is part of the presentation of self to self and other(s)" (2000: 66). People talk, and write, "themselves" through musical recollection. Doing so appears to be experienced as constructive and may often be oriented toward the presentation of a cohesive sense of self. In DeNora's terms (Foucault is not cited), this is also obedient self-regulation. In writing, and as adults "looking back," the student contributors to this chapter could certainly be seen as especially concerned to demonstrate maturity and coherence.

It is important to emphasize that "coherence" is the product of particular kinds of self-presentation and is likely to be especially evident in writing produced within relatively formal, in fact specifically educational, contexts (Erben, 1998; Goodson and Sikes, 2001). The autobiographies I discuss below are one kind of account, and without doubt every one of these students would produce something different in other circumstances and in relation to other addressees (Bakhtin, 1994). By contrast, Maria Pini's (2001) study of informal dance scenes, *Club Cultures and Female Subjectivity*, is based on informal interviews and, in her account, the "maturity" and "responsibility" associated with adulthood are far less apparent. Her respondents' accounts enable her to argue, against Bradby's (1993) account of a "prolongation of youth," that what constitutes adult female identities has been recomposed:

> Bradby is right to point to the emergence of new and non-reproductive sexualities as these are suggested and played out within contemporary social dance cultures. But rather than viewing such an emergence as indicative of a general extension of youth, it is perhaps more correct to see this as evidencing the formation of new modes of adult femininity. (Pini, 2001: 16)

Whatever the validity of her argument that "adulthood" has changed for some women, the point I want to stress here is that across a variety of contexts and in speech or writing, people position themselves through their self-accounts without ever producing the fixed "truth" of who they are. Pini draws attention to the resources drawn into the talk of the women she got to know, referring to these as "the available fictions of femininity which circulate within a given culture at a given time" and their conversations as showing how "individual women negotiate a relationship with and make sense of these fictions" (Pini, 2001: 69–70). In reading the autobiographical sketches in this chapter, I want to make a similar case – that, in this case in writing, students position themselves through the "fictions of identity" made available in particular musical repertoires.

This questioning of "truth" need not imply that these identity constructions are somehow "unreal" or even necessarily ephemeral.[2] Stuart Hall, whose work directly informs these debates, comments:

> Identities are...constituted within, not outside representation...They arise from the narrativization of the self, but the necessarily fictional nature of this process in no way undermines its discursive, material or political effectivity, even if the belongingness, the "suturing into the story" through which identities arise is, partly, in the imaginary (as well as the symbolic) and therefore, always, partly constructed in fantasy, or at least within a fantasmatic field. (Hall, 1996: 4)

Don Slater (1997) also suggests that postmodern concepts of "neotribalism" and "lifestyle" tend to

> assume that we pick up and drop memberships and identities rapidly, easily and without commitment, and that these memberships and identities relate to unstable, image-based groupings with unpoliced borders and no relevant continuity over time. In fact, people continue to be part of communities with considerable longevity, which do demand commitment as well as the learning and observance of established norms. (Slater, 1997: 202–203)

"Established norms" may not be in Hall's theoretical vocabulary, but he is lending a similar weight to the persistence and strength of identifications. Hall highlights the dynamic of identification as always also an exclusion, identity requires "its constitutive outside" (Hall, 1996: 3). And, in reviewing the concept of "suture," he comments:

> The notion that an effective suturing of the subject to a subject-position requires, not only that the subject is "hailed," but that the subject invests in the position, means that suturing has to be thought of as an *articulation*, rather than a one-sided process, and that in turn places *identification*, if not identities, firmly on the theoretical agenda. (Hall, 1996: 6)

The metaphor of "investment" suggests the *effort* of continuing self-identification sustained often through many years.[3] Thus I want to argue both that music is a powerfully affective resource for narratives of identification allowing people to contradict the positioning force of discourses privileging social and cultural "belonging,"[4] and that such narratives continue across lengthy periods in people's lives.[5]

The Autobiographies

In reading these sketches, it is inevitable that they will be taken as *revealing* the lives of the writers, as "testaments of experience." Perhaps their authors would not wish them to be read in any other way. However, as I have suggested, these autobiographical writings are also performative self-constructions, drawing on music as a resource, and productive of particular identifications in a higher educational context. Coherence and ordered reflection are to be expected of writing in these circumstances.

Questions of ethnicity are especially prominent in many of the autobiographies I have collected (see also Nilan and Feixa, 2006). The shared physical space of London, from which almost all of these accounts arise, is construed differently by the various contributors. "Growing up" in this city, at least within the same decade, might produce some commonality of experience. But, as Bennett suggests:

> …by conceptualising the "local" not as a definite space but rather as a series of discourses, which involve ways of picturing the local and one's relation to it, it becomes possible to see the local as a contested space, as a place that is both real and, to use Chaney's (1993) terminology, *fictionalised*. (Bennett, 2000: 63)

The most apparent differences, and similarities, arise through histories of engagement with what Mark Slobin (1993) calls diasporic intercultures. The Black Atlantic diaspora (Gilroy, 1993) and the South Asian diaspora are both substantial presences in London. Choices between these resources inform significantly different personal histories.

These autobiographies, otherwise unpublished, have no visibility elsewhere. Somewhat in the spirit of the local publishing initiatives discussed in the introduction, I want to quote from the students' writing at some length. The oldest students here were born in 1967 and the youngest in 1985. Some focus on musical scenes in London in the late 1970s and early 1980s, others on the 1990s, and the youngest on such scenes in the first years of this century. They come from a range of ethnicities and class locations. It is inevitable that these are disparate narratives. Nevertheless, there are significant parallels between them, especially in their engagement with music as a powerfully affective medium.

Growing Up: From "Immersion" to "Maturity"

Some contributors sustain a continuing self-positioning in the musical scenes they entered as teenagers, but others claim a distance from past identifications. I want to begin with two examples of those who present themselves as having "moved on." Both present narratives of the self through a primary focus on periods of emotionally intense, but now past, musical involvement. Sean is white, male, and middle-class; Kassandra black, female, and from a Ghanaian family, perhaps located as working-class. Sean's account, written in January 2005 (born 1982), looks back to being seventeen and "creating a crew," playing "Garage" music:

> As more and more people heard of our "crew" the less and less I cared about what teachers were saying about my work. Boys that I hardly knew would come up to me and praise my lyrics; girls would introduce themselves to me out of nothing and ask when I was next going to play out at a party or club. I would get home and rather than try and do the 2 hours of homework that I would get everyday, I threw myself into writing new and fresh lyrics or listen to rappers and other "crews" on pirate stations in order to get fresh ideas or inspiration…
>
> The image of a Garage MC demanded that you were always as cool as anyone else and willing to try anything. Cocaine was rife in the scene and it was impossible to ignore it. You had promoters and older DJ's or MC's throwing the stuff at you as if it was nothing (again trying to seem cooler than us) and it was exciting. I started staying out later and later and my grades dropped lower and lower, which obviously strained my relationship with my parents, but I was still riding high (no pun, honest) on the popularity that this genre had provided me with…
>
> There was a point at which, as with most things, the sparkle and shine of that genre and the identity it offered began to fade, and the more important matter of my future became apparent to me. It may only be a coincidence, but as I began to focus on academic work my desire to listen to or create Garage music faded, to the point where I do not even like to hear it at all anymore, although it will always be part of my identity and memory.

In these extracts, Sean's narrative turns on the counterpoint between the "cool" and the "academic." The sense of possessing and being possessed by the music (Frith, 1987) is strongly anchored in the past and is contrasted with the subsequent achievement of autonomy: a "self-possession" somewhat independent of the "clubbing scene." Sean presents himself as making a decision to be "the kind of person that I wanted to become." It may seem that the narrative here is one of movement beyond the dynamic of identification (with garage) and exclusion (of all else). However, the marking of a boundary continues through to the concluding paragraph. But at the time of writing, the boundary lies between those like Sean who are mobile, uncontained, and unfixed by contrast with, implicitly, those who are stuck within one scene – the younger, fannish, those still caught within "the sparkle and shine."

Kassandra's narrative is, in some respects, similar. She begins with earlier childhood (born 1979):

> I grew up in Leytonstone, East London. I lived with my Mum and Dad, we was the only black family on the whole block for roughly ten years...I first began making my own music choices when I started secondary school. Up until that time, all of the friends I had were white. And the music we liked to listen to was pop music....
>
> [At high school]...I made a new friend. She was a black girl, and everything about her was different in comparison to me. She dressed differently, she talked differently, she used to do her hair in these funny hair styles and she listened to a type of music I had never heard before. Back then, we called it ragga, now they call it bashment...The artists would normally "chat" over the beat instead of sing. Popular artists at the time were Buju Banton, Shabba Ranks, Lady Saw and Beenie Man to name a few. The lyrical content of a lot of the songs were mainly about sex and homosexuality. Jamaica (where the music originates) was and still is very anti-gay, the lyrics of some of these songs would shock many people. But to us it was normal, it was cool to think this way....
>
> I learnt about sex and sexual positions from hearing this music too. The lyrical content of this music was certainly explicit to say the least. However, at the time I felt as though I was learning about a lot of taboo subjects that had not been addressed by my parents or by the teachers at school. The more I listened to it, the more my identity and my image began to change. With this music, came a new crowd. I no longer had white friends, my closest friend was now black. And we hung around the most popular black boys in school. And this was the first time boys began to take an interest in me, I loved the attention. I began to feel like more of black person because of the person I was closest to and the type of music I listened to.
>
> The way I wore my school uniform changed, with this music came a new image. I would wear a long black skirt and tie knots on each side and wear black leggings underneath. My shirt would be two sizes too big and would be left hanging out. My tie would be worn the unconventional way, with the short piece at the front and the long piece behind. My hair would be scraped up so tight into a ponytail with a long extension of false hair that dropped down into the middle of my back. And every morning it took me half an hour to gel down wavy patterns of hair onto my forehead. I pierced my nose and I wore excessively large gold earrings. This was a key look amongst female ragga listeners...
>
> By summer 1996 I had made a new best friend at college. We were so close, I went on holiday with her and her family to Barbados....
> A group of us went to a club in "town" called the "Pepper Pot." We went dressed in lycra hot pants and lycra tops with trainers or open toe shoes. I had really long single plaited hair extensions sitting neatly in a ponytail on top of my head...
>
> As we walked into the club the music hit me straight away, there was a soca song playing very loudly. And everyone was dancing, but the vibe in the club was one I

> had never felt before. Back home I was used to seeing people standing around, thinking they were too cool to dance. But here everyone was moving. The beat of soca is like no other. It is fast and hard, it is absolutely amazing…
>
> …in 2004…I discovered Amy Winehouse, I had heard her track "In My Bed" on Choice FM. I loved her voice so much, I went straight to HMV to buy her album. I was shocked to discover a white girl on the album cover and to later on discover that she was also British. Even though it did come as a shock, it felt good to break away from the norm. American, black, same image, same sound. Here was someone different, she was white and British, but she sounded just as good. Maybe even better than some.
>
> I find that the music I enjoy listening to now is a reflection of my personality. I love slow, sexy, smooth songs…I still like to listen to bashment and soca music, but now there is a time and place for that. Usually in a club or if I am getting ready to go out I might find a radio station playing either type of music. Sometimes, if I am feeling in a reminiscent mood I will dig out some old tapes and put them on. They remind me of when I [was] a teenager.

It may seem surprising to place this alongside the extract from Sean's writing on the grounds that they demonstrate similarities. Sean's account could be read as primarily a statement of cool masculinity, both in the past and in his educationally purposeful present. Kassandra's is apparently about becoming an object of heterosexual interest in dance settings distanced from the immaturity of "pop." However, the narratives share the trope of *immersion in particular musical scenes* and the subsequent distancing from such immersion, with its implication of containment, or fixing, within them.

For Kassandra, becoming black is experienced as achieved by no longer engaging with pop music, excluded as white. Particular musical scenes are strongly equated with racial categories, black on the one hand, white on the other, and a strong boundary is constructed between them. Locating herself as black is achieved, in part, by eliminating othered (pop) music from her experience. The rigidity of this division, and the need to fix identity within its structure, is, however, revealed as unsustainable. Listening to Amy Winehouse, assuming that she is black, ruptures her self-positioning within black music only, and Kassandra's present position is thus less invested in particular genres. Kassandra's shift, though not presented in terms of becoming "academic," is nevertheless a movement beyond strong and "racially" exclusive identifications toward a "maturity," itself anchored in the achievement of individuality, of "personality," by contrast with containment within particular scenes. Though less sharply framed in terms of educational self-positioning than Sean's account, Kassandra's narrative is also one of "progress" toward a greater mobility and eclecticism in relation to music.

Cumulative Histories

I want to introduce several further examples of narratives in which a self-identification through musical scenes is a central motif. However, in these, the division between a musical past and a more distanced present is not so evidently a feature of the accounts. First of all, as an immediate contrast to the two preceding narratives, this is a story both of belonging and of individualization by a young "East Asian" woman living, as a teenager, just to the north of London in an old and quite affluent town:

> …from the age of about eight I attended Theatre School…I was very shy and although I would sing in front of the mirror and prance around my bedroom, when it came to shows and performing at the theatre school, I would always feel too unconfident. A number of factors made me feel uncomfortable at the time. I remember having issues with my weight as I was relatively chubby and the majority of my friends at the time were slim. It often made me feel out of place when I couldn't fit into particular dress-up clothes and I always felt very self-conscious when we had to wear leotards and tight clothing…
>
> …towards the age of fifteen, I met some friends who were into rapping and UK-Garage music. It was a new type of music at the time hailing from the "streets" of London and I remember thinking the whole sound, image and culture of it was really "cool". I would idolise Craig David and his whole style. I met a boy at a local house party who became my first boyfriend and him and his friends used to MC and DJ at local parties around my area. This boyfriend actually looked quite a lot like Craig David, it was a bit mad and I remember feeling very much in "love" or "lust," whatever it may be. I'd listen to UK-Garage music all evening when I got in from school and make tapes to listen to on my walkman at break-times, it was a brilliant way of obtaining that sense of escapism from the boring daily life of school. One day, being very much into my poetry and song writing, I tried my luck at some rapping lyrics and put them on my mobile voicemail. My friends were amazed when they heard the voicemail and I remember as the news spread across our network of friends from other schools, people would ask for my phone number just to listen to my mcing. This boosted my confidence hugely as I pretty much went from a shy girl, who no one paid attention to, to some new phenomenal female mc who everyone in my area was talking about and it was a great feeling…Since then I've been involved in a number of professional music TV and radio projects, had songs out on major labels, presented my own radio show on London's Choice FM and have been nominated for "Best Newcomer" at the Underground Music Awards a number of times. I never would have thought I could have made a career out of music. I simply did it because it made me feel good about myself and it made me feel part of something where I actually fitted in. Now, aged twenty-one, I have substantially established myself as an artist in the UK-Garage music industry…

Though there is a narrative of progress here, from the shy and self-conscious child in the past to the "phenomenal female mc" in the present, the self-identification constructed through this account is one of strong and singular immersion within a particular music scene, where she "fitted in." No distance from her self-as-teenager is claimed and, to the contrary, self-discovery at fifteen is represented as continuous with her young adult self. Of course, this cannot be read as a definitive statement – at the time of writing Jennifer was twenty-one and has an assured sense of successful participation in UK-Garage.[6] But it is a self-positioning in a popular narrative of success in music; such narratives are variously circulated in, for example, TV pop talent shows but, in this case, it is inflected toward a black orientated genre, which she describes as "a blend of 'hip-hop,' 'reggae,' and 'dance'". As an "East Asian" girl (born 1985) in a predominantly white middle-class town, this inflection toward something other than mainstream pop (characterized by many as "white") also allows an affiliation powerfully countering her sense of marginality (see Buckingham and Sefton-Green, 1994: 60–83). In both respects, she is located in an ideal scenario from which she has no wish to disengage.[7]

Two further examples of substantial and enduring identifications within particular music scenes, recollected in both accounts as both social and individually self-defining, come from men now entering their forties. Jason[8] (born 1967) wrote a long account:

> In my new estate in the late 70s early 80s my first new friend was Terry. He was into punk and because he was a bit of a hero to me, so was I. He used to borrow me records that I would listen to on one of those record players in a wooden box…In about 81 I remember hearing a record by Grandmaster Flash called Adventures on the Wheels of Steel. I loved the eclectic feel of the track and became curious about the scratching…My mum meanwhile had a new boyfriend and a new job as a home help. After a while she was able to give me pocket money which I divided equally between comics and records. Because Flash was on the Sugar Hill label (and as I realised years later had a UK distribution deal) I started to buy anything on that label that Woolworth's in Dalston stocked. In those days they sold for 99p.
>
> In my final year of school the close friendship, that still exists today, between my friends Dave, Robert, Mark meant we would make rap tapes. I'd taught myself to mix and scratch and had a good record collection. Tim Westwood, then on a pirate station called LWR, had played our rap and scratch tapes. And, once we had left school and had been working for a year we were buying records together – legitimately – to play at parties. Sometimes I was the only white kid deejaying at the parties in Hoxton and Stokey and I got a buzz as some of the older party goers, there to hear the reggae deejays would stand around the decks to watch me do my thing.
>
> …a work friend who listened to my mix tapes decided to book a tiny studio in south London to try and make a track. This was the new breed of studio, drum machines, samplers, ¼ inch reel to reel, run by young people like us. My friend wanted me to

> scratch on a rhythm track he wanted to make. He booked the studio and paid but didn't turn up! This is how my music career started: chance, accident.
>
> The studio was run by two guys the same age as me Leigh and Michael...One was Jewish, the other Black. They became friends, like me and mine, through a love of hip hop. The Black kid was called Michael Menson (sadly, years later, he would be murdered in a high profile racist attack). He suggested, as the studio was paid for, that he engineer for me and see what I would come up with. Later that evening I left the studio with my first track! I had caught the studio bug and went back a few weeks later with Dave to cut our own track. We planned to get a dub-plate cut and play it at parties. As we went to the studio Acid music was starting to get played in the clubs. In typical Grandmaster Flash, post-modern style we sampled a sound from an acid track and replayed the bass line from Michael Jackson's Don't Stop 'Till You Get Enough over the top of a speeded up break beat and layered some rapping and scratching over the top. Tongue in cheek we called the track Acid Jackson and cut another version with more scratching and a different break which we called Rock the Discotheques after the Big Daddy Kane statement that I had scratched over the top.
>
> When we went to cut our dub plate at Jah Tubby's studio, Tubby himself suggested we do as the reggae acts did and press up some white labels to distribute in specialist stores. We did and, jokily again, called ourselves The Dynamic Guv'nors on the stamp that we used on the label. The first Saturday with the help of our pals, Dave and me hit the west end with 500 copies of our track. That night, while sitting up late and stamping the remainder of our stock (the 500 sold for cash like hot cakes) by pure coincidence I was listening to the show that came on after the rap show on Capital Radio when I heard our tune being played. As the weeks passed our record was reviewed in all of the magazines I used to buy, Blues and Soul, Echoes and Record Mirror.

The often close interconnections between white and black youth have been reported in a number of cultural studies monographs in the past thirty years (Hebdige, 1979; Hewitt, 1986; Jones, 1988; Back, 1996). Jason's autobiography adds a further example of how identities are formed across "boundaries." Jason's early teenage engagement with punk is defined through a friendship with Terry, five years his senior, but his more sustained interest is in black music, particularly hip hop.

Pamela Perry (2002), on the basis of research in two schools in California, has suggested that, at least where black students are in a small minority, white identifications with black music may well be with what she calls the "putative" qualities of blackness (an urban cool, a tough masculinity) rather than with black people. However, in the social world of many inner city London schools, white students have not been numerically dominant through the past three decades. Connections and identifications in such schools are unlikely to be solely with characteristics of the music but also with particular people, some of whom are "mixed race," some black. Jason's narrative includes no claim either to be "black" or to the qualities of "blackness" Perry finds attributed to rap.[9] But participation in scenes that are predominantly black does imply a degree of satisfaction in the cultural competence required to perform, both musically and socially, across boundaries. Black music for Kassandra (and other students not included in this chapter) provides a resource for becoming "black" in the terms of black youth culture. This is a matter of constructing a particular kind of black identity for someone already socially positioned as black and, with a very dark skin, not ever likely to be "read" as "mixed race." Jason is socially positioned as white and, similarly, is very unlikely to be read as "mixed race." So participation in black music scenes does not produce any shift in "racial" identifications, but it does require, and facilitate, a knowledge of, and competence in, the specific cultural practices of a hybrid, Black Atlantic, diaspora – a musical scene constituted through extended international links, migrations, and exchanges (an "interculture") and also expanded globally by the music industry (at the level of a "superculture").[10]

Jason concludes his autobiography with meeting the woman to whom he has been married since the early 1990s. In her own writing, contributed alongside Jason's, she defines herself as "mixed race" – her mother is English, her father is Ghanaian. Their relationship is constructed in both their accounts as the product and further confirmation of their participation in the London hip hop scene. His wife comments:

> On our first proper "date" I began talking about a rap artist called YZ, I was impressed that Jason not only knew who I was talking about, but also bought import records at the same shops that I visited and had a knowledge that matched my own with regards to hip hop. I think I was also impressed with this white guy who did not think he was "black"…

Jason's self-production is as a working-class white man living cultural hybridity not as a superficial fashion, or an ephemeral play with difference, but as the enduring core reality of friendship, marriage, musical production, and musical consumption. His punk friend Terry, by the way, as Jason reveals much later, was black.

The "constitutive outside" of Jason's self-identifications is perhaps quite closely comparable to that implied in Sean's refusal of immersion in a particular scene. Rigidity and closure are refused in both accounts, but for Jason the hip hop scene is eclectic and allows the mobility that, for Sean, seems possible only by moving on from his involvement in Garage. For Jason, the narrative dynamic here is toward confirmation and consolidation rather than separation from the past or distancing from participation in the mixed cultural space he describes. Moreover, the refusal to distance himself from this may also be a continuing assertion of working-classness in the midst of his late, and very successful, study at university for a degree. Unlike Sean, from a middle-class family, Jason's father was a jobbing electrician, and Jason was brought up in a council flat by his mother, left school in Islington (north London), and worked for many years, alongside his musical activities, as a plumber.[11] As a student he wrote often about issues very much embedded in his own working-class "lived experience." Graduating with a first class honors degree, he nevertheless sustained a degree of resistance to the implication that such educational success entails repositioning as middle-class (see Kuhn, 1995; Richards, 2005a).

One further example here of the strong continuity between earlier teenage identifications with music scenes and adult identities concludes this section. John (born 1967) was, like Jason, a late "mature" entrant to university. He too had a significant prior "career" in music, but as a black teenager in Hackney, a borough adjacent to Islington:

> As far back as I can remember music has been an integral part of my leisure time which has evolved into my business life, social life and beyond. From an early age I was influenced by my older brothers who all went through the traditional route into music at the time, via the sound system route then onto pirate radio stations. I recall the days when Hackney was "the centre of the raving world" during the late seventies and early eighties...
>
> From 1979 to 1984 I attended school in Upper Clapton...music was a part of the unwritten school ethos. This seemed to be understood by the teachers too, who would regularly allow the main hall to be used on Saturday evenings to hold reggae sound clashes...Listening to Saxon play against Sir Coxon, Volcano, Unity or Diamonds 'a girl's best friend'. Sound systems will forever remain some of the best moments of my life.
>
> It was at about the age of fourteen that I decided to make my own sound system which was originally called Earthquake, however we never managed to cause any seismic disturbance due to our lack of finances. After many different incarnations we finally established ourselves credibly as Twilight and the result was that we entered into an underground music scene that would take us eventually around the globe.
>
> ...with...three large Edwin Shirley 60 foot trailers laden two levels high with 50k of Turbo Sound equipment on each. Nothing can compare to the feeling of having control of thousands of partying people dancing into the early hours, after all of the static sound systems have been made to turn off their sets by the police. I felt like the Pied Piper as we meandered down the Portobello Road and past Westbourne Grove playing the latest soca tunes.

> One event took us to Trafalgar Square, providing a system for The Ten Thousand Man March, held by the Nation of Islam. This was a particularly uncomfortable hire as I didn't agree with their philosophy and was particularly aware that we were being filmed. However, most of the events that I have taken part in have been unique and memorable in their own respects, such as when I was paid to perform on stage in Tokyo for a six week period playing Hip Hop to fanatic Japanese clubbers. It was whilst in Japan that I realised how global [this] musical sub culture was; I was astounded to see how big reggae music was especially lover's rock, imagine the Japanese idolising Dennis Brown, Bob Marley, Carol Thomson and Sylvia Tella! I have also played music in clubs in New York, Paris and Amsterdam.
>
> Under the name of Tokyo J– I partnered The Jinks on Cool FM 94.5 on a Sunday morning from 11am till 2pm where I spoke to the callers on air whilst Jinksy played Jungle music with a touch of Jazz.
>
> My taste in music has evolved over the years and this fluidity of taste is reflected in my opening quote, "From RUN DMC to RAVEL." Run D.M.C.'s "My Addidas" was the first record I ever purchased and Ravel's Bolero was the most recent addition to my music collection.

Though some hints of distancing from his earlier identifications appear in the last paragraphs of his sketch, and these may be associated with his investment in studying English Literature alongside Education, there is an emphasis on a fluid continuity that, as for Jason, allows an identity to be constructed through *accumulation*. Layers of, sometimes disparate, musical forms are added without replacing or displacing earlier "tastes." Adult identity is thus made dense, an accretion of knowledge and experience, incorporating rather than separating from youth.

Religious Narratives

I want to turn now to several narratives which, though focused on music, frame both past and present self-identifications also in terms of religion. Religious belief, especially Christian and Muslim, but also occasionally Hindu and Buddhist, is very common if mainly most evident among "non-white" students. The first example here comes from Bertha (born 1977 and previously cited in Chapter Three). The extracts are taken from each of the three sections of her sketch entitled Infant Childhood, Teenage Years, and Young Woman:

> As an African child it would be impossible for me to have grown up without having heard music in some way or another. I grew up in a remote village called Nalergu in the Northern part of Ghana, a small tribal community with the majority of them be-

ing Muslims. I belong to a small tribal group called Mamprushi, the style of music and dress is distinctive in comparison to any other tribe in West Africa, for every tribe has its own individual sound....

My earliest memory of music began in our family home. We did not have possession of electric throughout the village only in the main hospital. Therefore my household did not have any electrical devices apart from a battery run radio, which was given to my grandfather. He loved his radio which was shiny, absolutely cherished by him. "It was not a toy to be played with," I remember being told, this meant that absolutely no one was allowed to touch it. The only time we got to see it was when he came out in the morning for breakfast. He listened to Dagbane station, this is a Muslim station, because my grandfather was a Muslim he only listened to that station. This station played a lot of Grunshi music, which my grandfather loved.

Garage music played an important role in my late teenage years. The style of clothes for example, brand names such as "kangaroo" were popular among youth. Myself and friends seemed to have conformed to the ways of garage music, by adopting a different style of dressing. Myself and friends had cheap imitations of Ralph Lauren jackets with "fruit of the loom" sweat tops to match. Image and popularity played a big part in this scene but to us we were more concerned with having a good time than anything else. It was all about the guys and the designer labels they had. The amount of girls they had on their arm and how much "Champagne" they drunk through out the night. We went out almost every week to every rave we knew of or heard about from other raves we attended previously. We were known in certain circles by MCs and DJs and bouncers who recognised us, this improved our popularity and we welcomed the attention.

The garage scene encouraged a lifestyle of drink and drugs, a "wanna be" lifestyle, as I like to call it, this was a core group of young people posing with rental cars and "dressed to kill" in "buy now pay later" designer labels.

All this came to an abrupt end in 2000 when I realised that I needed a change from this lifestyle. This led me to question what I wanted to do in my life and what significant contribution my lifestyle and music was making to my life...

My conversion to Christianity changed my focus on life and music. I first of all threw out all my secular music in order to start afresh with gospel music. This was a decision I did not find hard to make, in fact I was more than glad to make the move in changing my style of music. Socially I did not go out with the same people, musically I listened to a completely different kind of music. My identity belonged to a different social group and where music was concerned I now listened to people like Fred Hammond and Kirk Franklin, American gospel artists...This music was beneficial to me, I felt happy and enthusiastic about life...I began to consider myself a young woman with the responsibility of making life changing decisions. Gospel music...had this effect on me, as it allowed me to think critically about my self in relation to other people and God.

The sharpest contrast with those autobiographical sketches discussed so far is the emphasis on discontinuities in her experience and, particularly, the "expulsion" of prior musical resources. The maintenance of self-identity through strategies of biographical continuity is largely rejected. So too is any notion of self-identification through accumulation, allowing different sorts of music to be brought together over time. Instead, the categories are clear and bounded and cannot coexist. With the turn to gospel music, its "constitutive outside" (all secular music) is indeed literally "out." Such abjection is constitutive of a firmly bounded identity, producing, as Bernstein puts it, "a strong insulation between the sacred and the profane" (Bernstein, 1996: 78).[12] A further aspect of the shift from "teenager" to "young woman" is the disembedding of her musical taste from the social networks constituting the London garage scene, in favor of a network seemingly limited to the church of which she is a member. In this narrative of young adulthood, the whole of her "youth" appears completely excised.

However, there is a significant complication to this account of her "conversion." The music of Kirk Franklin, and even of Fred Hammond (from Detroit), demonstrates considerable continuities with soul and R&B and is not, except in their lyrical preoccupations, so very different from some of the music that constituted her "teenage years."[13] Some elements of rap are included in various albums by Kirk Franklin, for example. So Bertha's boundary and the direction of her "progress" is in many ways a familiar narrative within the history of African American music. The movement from mainly religious to secular then again to religious lyrical content, while maintaining some continuity in musical form, is a well-documented pattern in the lives of both performers and consumers of blues and soul. Perhaps what is most salient here, nevertheless, is the emotional vehemence of her account. It is the difference between gospel and garage that, for her, is critical to her repositioning.

Some further examples of religiously framed narratives of identification need to be considered, though these are not stories of "conversion" but of more gradual "focusing" within Islamic precepts. These extracts are selected from the autobiographical narratives offered by several "South Asian" women, some of whom present themselves as devoutly Muslim. Helena (born 1985), for example, presents her account as a quite rapid process of strengthening religious identification:

> ...in my teenage years I would argue with my mum over small things. I would try to avoid the problem by listening to slow songs as loud as possible to escape from my tensions...it would calm me down slowly but on the other hand certain songs taught

> me to stand up against my mum showing it is my life and let me live it how I want to.
>
> ...I now believe that music is the whispers of the Satan, calling me to his path and the path of wrongdoers...This is due to my spiritual journey to hajj in Saudi Arabia, which I undertook [for] two weeks without music. It was a miraculous feeling.
>
> ...music is a cause of Muslims wasting time in their lives as many children today waste their youth...listening to music, how many waste their free time...and how many ultimately waste their entire lives on such meaningless items.
>
> After understanding how music [is] defined in Islam, I begun to listen to nasheeds (Islamic song) that has become recognizable and popular in the Muslim community. It's a new way of understanding Islam, and spreading the message of Islam thru songs amongst the youths who tend to listen to non-Islamic song and view themselves as gangsters, or taking drugs which is not allowed in Islam. Also a message to non-Muslims to understand the purpose of Islam...as Muslims are shown negative in media and the west. The nasheeds are only voices and no music is used at the background.

From an opening description reminiscent of the accounts of emotional self-management identified by DeNora (2000), Helena shifts to the "miraculous" experience of doing without music. Initially, in her account, there is an absolute polarization between Islam and music, attributed to Satan and presumably therefore a route into evil. But this is not sustained. "Nasheeds," as a form of Islamic popular music, are introduced as both addressing wayward Muslim youth (implicitly male and preoccupied with gangsta rap) and non-Muslims.

There appear to be significant variations in what are nevertheless classed together as nasheeds (see http://www.muslimhiphop.com). Some nasheeds are entirely vocal, others accompanied by light percussion or other "background" music. The exclusion of music is one option, and sometimes various versions of the same song are available. Helena's references, unspecified, may be to a strictly vocal and traditional form, though the prominence of one figure, Sami Yusuf, seems implicit in her comment on the audiences addressed by these songs. Certainly, others refer explicitly to Sami Yusuf, and his popularity in the Muslim world, and perhaps especially among young women, is considerable.[14] Others represent their musical identifications in similar terms, with such figures as Sami Yusuf located in their own life histories as implicitly transitional in progress toward a more exclusively religious position. For example, Tehmeena (born 1982) writes:

> Another form of music I listen to is Nasheeds. I started listening to Islamic songs about 2 years ago...They are probably the most meaningful songs I have ever heard

> because they reflect on my religion, our Prophet Muhammad (peace be upon him) and God. Sami Yusuf is one of my favourite Nasheed artists. He is born here and sings Nasheeds beautifully. He has made 2 albums, both have two versions, with and without music. I must admit I like both. I have come to realise that that is my most important aim in this life, to concentrate on the hereafter. I am trying to wean myself off listening to music slowly. I think the month of Ramadan that has just passed has helped me as during that month I didn't listen to any music and I honestly thought I wouldn't survive without it but I did. The reason why I have decided to try to stop listening to music is because it emotionally weakens me. I have also been informed that certain instruments are not allowed in my religion. Sometimes music is a distraction. In a good and bad way. It plays on my emotions. In a way I can't see my life without music as I have grown up on it but I also believe my religion to be more important than anything else. I'm trying harder to refrain as I know I can stop but I just don't feel I can as yet. Bit by bit Inshallah (God willing).

Consistent with the wider attribution of affectivity to music, Tehmeena here identifies it as a powerful and distracting medium, a resource that is ultimately of use only to the wrong kind of self. In common with Helena, she situates her self-identity in a conflict between music and full devotion to Islam. In these terms, to give into music is a weakness and a kind of emotional depletion. Aliya (born 1984) is somewhat less preoccupied with a sense of conflict, instead subsuming music to religious purposes:

> ...religion plays a very significant role in my life, and by the ages of 19 and thereafter, I had gained a better understanding of my religion, and began shaping my identity around this. This meant that even in my spare time, the activities I chose to engage in were in one way or another related to religion, and this included music too. I would choose to listen to music with natural sounds of birds or water (favourite examples including ambient and oriental new age music) as not only did these put me in the correct mood for thinking about religion, but also allowed my mind to ponder and reflect on God and His creation. Furthermore I began listening to Islamic nasheeds (Islamic songs) by artists such as Sami Yusuf, which spoke specifically on subjects about God and how to be a good Muslim. I felt that these nasheeds were talking to me about certain important aspects of my religion and I found them easy to understand and relate to.

In each of these three examples, the narrative constructs "growing up" as a struggle to renounce secular music and, in the first two cases, ideally and eventually, all music. Emotionality, uncertainty and a lack of purpose are attributed to earlier musical experience. The "messiness" of secular music becomes the "constitutive outside" to the silence, order and purpose of self-positioning within Islam. Rather than the achieved self as discerning and autonomous amidst consumption, here the self is distanced from consumption, removed to a religious domain in which a constant and enduring affiliation is valued. However, it is important to stress that these are narratives written in the students' early twenties, invited to look back at their previous experience of school and adolescence, and thus representing a moment in a continuing process rather than a completed and entirely settled "maturity." It is not possible to know how these statements correspond to the lives these young women may lead. But they can be read as "ideal" narratives, "the available fictions of femininity which circulate within a given culture at a given time" (Pini, 2001: 70). Identification through religious duty and belonging is an aspiration for young women still in fact listening to music in a variety of forms. Nasheeds appear in their account as a liminal form, located biographically between the experience of Western popular music in the adolescent past and a potential future in which music of any kind may not figure at all. In terms of projected narratives, their movement is from relative variety in musical experience "inwards" to a more singular self-location within Muslim belief.

Growing "Older"

Another young "South Asian" woman (born 1975), though some ten years older, offers a contrasting history in which Western pop music figures as an emotional resource in negotiating and eventually separating from an arranged marriage. These extracts, from a lengthy account, represent a series of emotional thresholds through their correspondence to particular songs and the meanings they made available to her. The trope of strong identifications in the past, slowly giving way to a more eclectic range of engagements, reappears here and, in her own more analytical reflections, is represented as characteristic of a Western liberal self.[15] As in the accounts offered by Sean and Kassandra above, some mobility in taste, without any intense investment in any particular genre or performer, is claimed as characterizing her present self. However, in common with those who accumulate music, there is also some emphasis on the collection of music and therefore the continuing availability of past layers of "feeling" (Middleton and Edwards, 1990; DeNora, 2000):

> At the time of my marriage in 1993 I was seventeen and at Sixth Form College. The boy band era was passing and swing music seemed to be the kind of music that everyone was listening to. I however seemed to have a big thing for Suede with the track "Trash" defining how I felt about myself not feeling much worth for myself, much of this came from the knowledge that my parents were looking for prospective people for me to marry and the realisation that my youth and freedom would come to an end. The track made me want to get up and run away and assert some kind of self control over my life, but this never materialised and remained just a fantasy.

In Spring of 1993 I got married; the one song that still bears strong memories of how I felt on my wedding day is the song "Wide World" by Maxi priest. It was the last song I played in my room on my wedding day and it symbolized an acceptance and part defeat over what I saw as the end of my life. Me and my friends cried stupidly for a couple of hours until my mother came in and told us all to pull ourselves together as the guests had started arriving.

"Oh baby baby it's a wide world, I'll always remember you with a smile girl." (Wide World)

When listening to these words even to this date, it conjures up deep feelings of sorrow. Despite the song being about an ending relationship I believed that the words were a metaphor for the end of my relationship with my current and known life. I believed that even though I was going to be required to grow up and become mature overnight I could still look back on my past with a smile and that I would have my memories to see me through.

In 1996, George Michael released the "Older" album and the song title [of] the same name. I connected with this song as I had just had my second child and was going through a very rough patch in my marriage. It was a turning point and a realisation that I could no longer be living with the pretence of being in a loveless and abusive marriage; I had reached a state of recognition that I couldn't compromise my life for anyone else's expectations.

"Strange, don't you think I'm looking older? But something good has happened to me. Change is a stranger you have yet to know." (Older)

Although it took me another three years before I had the courage to get up and leave with the children, this song was something that I constantly played in my own space as means of building courage and reassuring myself that I was not in the wrong and there were others out there who understood the need for change and the need to move on for something more positive.

At the stage I am in now…I do not have any one artist that I follow, I find myself listening to all kinds of genres in music however music seems to now serve particular purposes…

…it is very difficult to summarise this autobiography without looking at how I have used music in the past…I have constructed my identity to be of a westernised and liberal individual whilst rejecting near enough everything about my ethnic culture. I hadn't really given much thought to how I even managed to establish this with the type of music I listened to, at the time it was just a series of music and artists that I admired and liked, it is only now that I have actually looked at my music collection and have come to realise that I do not possess any Asian music, which leads me to think that I have been living my life in somewhat denial of who I really am; a disturbing revelation that I am now having to come to terms with.

> In my opinion I haven't used music to rebel against my parents, even though the will to do so was very much there. I seem to have merely existed in fear of their expectations and any ramifications, which shows a very passive side to my character that I am beginning to abhor. I had always imagined myself to be quite headstrong and decisive, but it appears to be otherwise now that I have put pen to paper.
>
> It is also evident that I have and still use music to maintain or regulate my emotional states, at times I have thought this to be dangerous as music has the ability to bring to the surface real thoughts, emotions, regressing qualities and sometimes quite dark and dismal thoughts too. At times it is much easier to suppress such emotion, and brush issues aside rather than dealing with things as they occur. However, in relation to music, it just cannot be ignored and I am almost forced into accepting or dealing with situations, so maybe this is a good thing. (Aysha)

In some respects, like Sean and Kassandra, Aysha writes of music as something she can look back on reflectively and with some degree of control and even analytical poise. But, like Helena, Tehmeena, and Aliya, she tends to construct music as making emotional demands that she may prefer to avoid. To some extent music continues to figure in the present time of her account as, if engaged in more variety, also potentially troubling and emotionally dissonant. In addition to her construction of music as eliciting emotions located below the surface of everyday consciousness, she comments specifically of "classical" music that it

> ...has the power to almost push me off the edge; listening to classical music conjures up all kinds of unusual and manic thoughts; making me regress into periods of my life where I have been at a very low depressive state and where I felt like I couldn't go on; consequently I avoid listening to such music as it does nothing to help me keep a grip on things.

Her narrative includes no secure refuge – such as religion – from these disturbing feelings. The claims to a relatively stable and singular sense of self, evident in the others' fictions, are not sustained here as the secure outcome of a narrative of growth and development. With a history of intense identification with Madonna, interest in David Bowie, and a period of enthusiasm for boy bands, she also introduces an unresolved division between her continuing self-construction through Western pop music and her unsettling identification as Bengali. In this respect the power of discourses in which ethnicity is constructed as a natural foundation of identity, or as a point of origin and a "truth" about the self somewhat "covered over" and "falsely" denied, returns to further unsettle her account.

Earlier in her autobiographical piece, recollecting herself at the age of seven, she describes the music she rejected:

> Bengali Folk Music, by artists such as Abdul Alim, Abbas Uddin, Addul Jabbar and Ferdusi Rahman. Listening to this genre of music I felt like a prisoner, unable to escape. I had no choice but to listen as I had to help my mother in the kitchen, or I was by her side cutting the threads and neatening the dresses she was making in order to help meet her deadlines.
>
> In retrospect, I absolutely despised Bengali folk music. However, I find that if I am flicking through the radio stations or if I am shopping in Brick Lane and I come across this music, I am filled with a warm glow and memories of my childhood come to the surface.

Distance from the cultural world of her parents, actively constructed through more than two decades of "investment" in western popular music, achieved and substantial, is nevertheless tainted with loss (see Bourdieu et al., 1999). Her comments on Madonna suggest the early and continuing displacement of parental figures in favor of the ideal and mercurial other:

> I absolutely idolised Madonna...This was the person I had been waiting to emerge...I followed all of her songs and watched her transform and re-invent herself over and over. For me, she was the very person I wanted to be like, very much independent, feisty, attractive, and care free. Everything about Madonna reflected how I felt about wanting to be westernised and nonchalant...I took to Madonna as my mentor, adopting an imaginary character of myself in my head, I didn't like who I was, and I didn't like being in my skin so Madonna's music helped me to escape...the quality of being so driven and determined was something I wished I had possessed.

Here, she positions herself very explicitly as "other" to her own familial scene and to the rigidity of life as a young "South Asian" woman, characterized in her words, as "depressing," "oppressive," and "restricted." The "constitutive outside" of her identification thus lies firmly within her own immediate social world. "Her words" are not just her own, of course (Bakhtin, 1994). It might be argued that her self-positioning through the ideal of Madonna enables her to adopt a Eurocentric gaze, thus regarding the cultural world of her family as backward, full of "tales of oppression and poverty." "The person I had been waiting to emerge" is, ambiguously, either herself or Madonna or, significantly, both simultaneously. And in wishing to be in her skin, she appears to locate herself in "whiteness" as the precondition of modern female autonomy (independent, carefree, nonchalant, Westernized) at odds with her own physical appearance (see Dyer, 1997). Implicitly, she aligns herself with, broadly, a liberal white feminism that, along with other variants of second-wave feminism, has been subject to extensive critique (hooks, 1989, 1992, 1994b; Weedon, 2004). There is an unresolved tension in this account between her critical rejection of subordination within Bengali culture and an acknowledgment of her belonging to a Bengali migrant family. But, however dubious some aspects of the racial politics of Madonna might be, the meanings attributed to her in Aysha's account do suggest that she has been a resource in achieving agency and in making personal changes with, undoubtedly, wider social implications.[16] The narrative focus of this account is substantially upon a continuing effort to refuse hybridity and claim an entirely non-Bengali self-identity but, in producing this writing, a struggle with hybridity appears to interrupt and defer closure in the self-identity she is able to present. As Hall (1996) suggests, identity is not settled once and for all but is rather a continuing process of self-positioning amidst disparate and contradictory discourses.

Conclusion

This chapter has argued that music is represented as among the most powerfully affective forms engaged with by young people. Rather than being merely "background" music for each generation, it is a resource for the construction of the "self," of relations with others, and of both past and projected life histories. As such it is central to understanding the mobility and complexity of positions taken by young people in living through later "adolescence" and early adulthood. But, even across the limited range of examples presented here, there are differences in the way they represent their relation to music. Some represent themselves as carrying their youthful musical affiliations into their thirties and forties. Jason, John, and Aysha are the clearest examples of this. In keeping with Willis, Jones, Canaan, and Hurd's (1990) concept of the "symbolic mould," they appear to be formed through the music of their youth. However, few, if any, seem to lay claim to a lifestyle in continuity with their teenage years – Bertha, Sean, and Kassandra stress how differently they live their lives in the present. But Kassandra and Sean still represent music as integral to their self-formation. Those positioning themselves in explicitly religious terms are most emphatic in constructing a break between their present positions and those they locate in adolescence. But for several (Helena, Tehmeena, Aliya) this could be attributed to their proximity to "adolescence." At twenty or twenty-one, some degree of distancing from being a "teenager" has particular urgency for them, and they may wish to claim adulthood by marking a decisive step from one "stage" of life to another. Jennifer, by contrast, does not signal a break through any change in musical orientation. But she does claim a kind of transformation and a rapid movement beyond the shy anonymity of her earlier teenage years.

Placing these pieces of writing in the final chapter of this book, and perhaps implicitly privileging autobiographical writing, might suggest that after all the discussion of fictional representations of youth in the previous chapters, here, at last, is the real thing. These sketches do represent the intensity and significance of music in the lived realities of these students' lives. But, recalling Moss (1989), it is important to stress that these are "fictions" constructed out of popular modes of self-narration, replaying recollected experience through public "scripts" of life, making music an instrument of popular memory (Frith, 1987; Richards, 1998b). This does not "disauthenticate" their accounts, but it does recall the problems discussed in the introduction to this book and the need to question the adult wish to locate the authentic truth of youthful experience. "Youth" is variously inflected across their accounts, partly in accord with their actual ages, their religious orientations, their educational trajectories, and their familial responsibilities. But none of them write as "young" or as "teenagers." At whatever age, each invokes "youth" as a condition from which they now write at a distance and to which they look back with varying degrees of fascination, pleasure, and occasionally, dismay. And so, to conclude this chapter, reading their narratives does not allow an encounter with the authentic "voices of youth" that perhaps we wish they could be. These *are* autobiographies, but they are also fictions of the self, of identity, and of youth.

Postscript

Finishing this, I was left wondering if I had conveyed something like a sense of disappointment through the use of the word "fiction" – as if really I am saying it's all *just* fiction and, though we want it, there is no truth to be found and never will be any discursively uncontaminated experience to be recovered. If so, this seems unduly puritanical, as if telling stories is close to telling lies (see Le Guin, 1985: 39–45). Perhaps it is worth being more explicit. Fictional narratives are productive of versions of youthfulness that, in the midst of so many other competing representations ("factual" ones in the press and on the news, for example), contest the meanings attributed to the young. Some, Trites (2000), for example, may see the majority of these narratives as themselves confirming the prevailing construction of youth as a troublesome phase best brought to a settled conclusion as swiftly and as safely as possible. I know what she means. As a teenager, I would always avoid those novels in local libraries classified as JA/F (Junior Adult/Fiction), not wishing to be instructed and patronized or to be denied the mainly sexual knowledge hopefully to be found in the general Fiction section.[1] Amongst my out of school reading at fourteen and fifteen (1966–67), Kerouac was central; at sixteen in 1968 I had moved on to William Burroughs.

As a high school English teacher, I was never very interested in the sort of novels that looked, depressingly, as if they'd been written for school consumption. There were exceptions: Rosa Guy, Buchi Emecheta, S. E. Hinton, Ursula Le Guin, for example. But when I started reading Francesca Lia Block's novels, because my then eleven-year-old daughter Fay had started to read *Dangerous Angels* (in Seattle and Vancouver B.C. in the summer of 1998), I was drawn in, I felt, to something different and much more challenging than I had expected from "young adult" fiction. So I read more, both of Block's writing, and gradually, novels by Melvin Burgess, Judy Blume, Jacqueline Woodson, Laurie Halse Anderson, and so on. To some extent, I can share Burgess's perception that there wasn't much of real interest written *for* teenagers in the late 1960s (I'm just a couple of years older than he is), but that didn't matter to me very much because anything labeled in that way would have been passed over anyway. Reading Block, despite some initial misgivings over what I took to be pretentious whimsy (*Weetzie Bat*), suggested that youth was being represented here in "young adult" fiction in ways that sufficiently unsettled my expectations to consider putting together an undergraduate course with such writing at its center. However, I called the course Young Adult Fictions because I wanted to avoid too exclusive a concern with print and because I wanted "constructions of youth" to be a focus of debate. The course got started in 2003 as a three-week summer school in

Cortland, upstate New York, and I've been teaching it at London Metropolitan University ever since.

Another angle on this is represented in part by the previous chapter, on music-focused autobiographies. Rather than pursue a career as an academic writer on fiction, I have given most attention to how students engage with being taught about forms of popular culture that are already a part of their informal experience of the media. In my Ph.D., I concentrated mostly on what goes on in classroom settings where popular culture is the primary object of attention. Drawing on precedents in "ethnographic" educational research,[2] in discourse analysis and, more broadly, in the cultural study of youth, I looked at the specific dynamics of relations between teachers and students involved in the study of popular music. The thesis was conceived both as advocacy for teaching about forms strongly identified with "adolescent" experience and as analysis of the tensions and difficulties encountered in attempting to do so. But since completing that, I have researched and written several articles with a more biographical or life-historical emphasis, working from interviews conducted with teachers and students in the field of media education.

In the context of such enquiries, "fiction" may seem a remote and largely unconnected concern. However, both how people live their lives and how they represent them in talk and writing can be understood, in part, as somewhat narratively organized and, among the sources for such narratives, novels, films, and television – but also cultures of popular music – are significant. I suppose that, for example, my own lingering preoccupation with travel, in particular ways and particular regions, somewhat derived from reading "beat" novels in the mid 1960s, has both informed actual journeys that I have made and contributed to episodes of restlessness in relation to the routines and disciplines of regular employment.[3] Somehow, the feeling that the fixity and routine of work can't be the only or best way to live persists and, should anyone ask, might underscore any self-account I might offer. The wider point is that there is much more scope to examine how people both live and represent their lives in terms of the popular narratives with which they engage. Chapter Seven shows, however, that such narratives will also coexist with or be contradicted and perhaps displaced by other narratives privileged in either or both education and religion.

There are two main issues to make a little more explicit here. One is that fictional narratives allow a degree of agency both in their production and their reception: such narratives, somewhat unfettered from the discipline of "what really" happened, sometimes effectively contesting the closures enforced through the demand that we stick to the truth, are constitutive of "selves." Writers make this the central work of their lives; others carry it on more routinely and mostly without ever writing it down. When the occasion arises, personal narratives will weave together the strands of what really happened into the patterns to which, on the whole, in thinking our own lives, we have accustomed ourselves. But, and this is the second main point here, in doing so, we have and continue to construct our self-accounts from the resources, the "scripts," available to us and, in this major respect, we are situating ourselves through the repertoires of the "self" that, historically and culturally, figure in the social worlds we inhabit. Goodson and Sikes (2001), in a review of life history research, argue that

> When someone tells their story as part of a life history research project they are involved in a creative act, irrespective of how committed they are to telling the "truth," or telling it as it was. Rather than attempting to make unrealistic claims for representing "reality," life historians should simply acknowledge what they are able to do with the stories they use as data: namely, offer an interpretation through their writing and spell out the influences that may have coloured both the teller's story and their interpretation of it. (2001: 48)

Later, in elaborating further their distinction between life stories told by respondents and the researchers' work of elaborating these into life histories, they add:

> ...we are searching for...a way of locating our scrutiny of stories to show that the general forms, schemata, skeletons and ideologies, which we often employ in structuring the way we tell our individual tales, come from the wider culture. Hence, it is an illusion to think that we capture only the person's voice when we capture a personal story. What we capture is a mediation between the personal voice and wider cultural imperatives. In stressing the importance of contextualization, life history makes this mediation explicit. (Goodson and Sikes, 2001: 77)

The narratives of mobility, and perhaps of evasion, that might be seen as characteristic of novels by Kerouac, and that might also figure in some aspects of my own "personal" narratives, might then be subject to some critique in terms of their articulation with a mid/late twentieth-century "problematic of masculinity" (Ehrenreich, 1983; Osgerby, 2001).

Looking back over the chapters collected here, it is possible to speculate that the narratives generated in the production of the seven seasons of *Buffy the Vampire Slayer* may well have some lingering resonance in the lives of those who engaged with the show as fans or even perhaps as more casual viewers. Though television viewing, in particular, is often characterized as both superficial and ephemeral, there is a need to consider, and to investigate, how participation in particular cultures of viewing (and reading and listening) persists in people's lives. Has *Buffy the Vampire Slayer* contributed to a wider narrative of how to live "adolescence" and, indeed, how and what to be in "adulthood"? Or, similarly, has the enthusiastic reading and re-reading of *Dangerous Angels* (1998) informed, for *some* young women, a continuing negotiation of the "self"? The words of contributors to the Witch-baby list, discussed in Chapter Two, through the trace of fleeting exchanges, hint at possible directions for further investigation. Again, a central question, recalling Pini (2001), is that of whether or not these textual engagements are confined to a transition in "adolescence" or are the resources for the construction of more enduring, if also perceived as more youthful, modes of being adult. Is adulthood in this sense about sustaining as much of youthful identification as possible?

Following Bourdieu (1986), Bourdieu et al. (1999), Buchmann (1989), Skeggs (2004), and others, it is also important to consider how participation in some reading and viewing practices enables young people to project themselves into class differentiated adult identities. Through the consumption of texts distinguished as "cult" or "post-modern," readers and viewers both confirm their acquisition of the cultural capital enabling such consumption and extend their personal repertoires in ways that sustain their further social distinction. Such classed adult selves may require a long "youth" in which a facility with texts construed as ironic, reflexive, complex, and difficult is achieved. For example, having watched *Twin Peaks* (1990–1991) in the early 1990s might now be a desirable component of the viewing histories of new middle-class adults. Such adults do not "grow up" to texts endorsed by their elders as worthwhile but, on the contrary, carry their youthful textual engagements forward, forming "selves" anchored in one particular generational history but also characterized by a fluid, eclectic, and self-assured competence.

These are questions for a historical sociology of textual consumption and point well beyond the more limited focus of the chapters collected here. Nevertheless, the contribution of fictional narratives to the continuing process of recomposing adulthood is a significant focus for further research. Almost twenty years ago, Marlis Buchmann (1989) commented on the replacement of "traditions and customs" in the "structuring of the life course" by "an increasing range of biographical options…for searching for and experimenting with new forms of social relations and social identification and for testing new biographical models" (1989: 69). It is, as Chapter Seven has shown, of some interest to show how adult identities are produced out of both popular cultural resources and the more "traditional" scripts of life associated with family, education, and religion. In doing so, rather than only offer a proliferation of individual stories, it is essential to show also that there are similarities in people's tactics of self-positioning, in the resources most available, and in how those resources are incorporated into each personal narrative. Being "forever young" is an inescapable theme in the cultural imagery of "growth" and aging, identification and desire. It is negotiated individually but, as the examples collected in Chapter Seven illustrate, it is also engaged in ways differentially informed by the social and cultural positions in which individuals are located.

Notes

Introduction

1. For example, it is the title of a Canadian paper – *Forever Young: Canada's Leading Publication for Today's Fifty-Plus Lifestyle* (Metroland Media Group Ltd.) see foreveryoungnews.com. The copy I have has Sting on the cover, with grey designer stubble (Toronto Edition April 2007).

2. See Johnson, C. (2005) – she comments: "Over the 1990s, the quality teen drama series became increasingly visible in the network primetime schedules. Many of these series adopt characteristics of the quality television series, with ensemble casts, sophisticated writing and psychologically complex characters. These attributes are combined with a focus on adolescent issues which appeals to the teen audience but is not restricted to this demographic. Indeed, in contemporary Western society, 'youth' is not merely a demographic category, but also a sensibility that can extend (and be sold to) audiences outside the teen generation. In an era in which 'staying young' forms a central part of the drive of consumer culture, youth programming (particularly if it has the articulate, liberal, sophisticated edge of 'quality' television) has a valuable appeal to advertisers and broadcasters" (Johnson, 2005: 107).

3. *Skins*, a series produced for the British TV Channel 4 (E4), is an interesting example. See www.channel4.com.

4. See, for example, Richards, C. (1981/82) "Classroom Readings," *Screen Education* 40 Autumn/Winter, 67-79. The article was presented to the History Workshop conference, Brighton, Autumn 1980 and was informed by then recent work in Cultural Studies (McRobbie, 1978; Morley, 1980) and in Film Studies (Harvey, 1980). It examined how 13-14 year old school students had made sense of a short story (*Jealousy*) that I had presented to them. The story was written by Steve Drummond (when he was a student at Thomas Calton School) and first published in 1976 by the Inner London Education Authority's English Centre. The story examines jealousy and male rivalry and their violent consequences. A key focus for my discussion is a further story, *Brixton Alley*, written "in response" by a group of white girls in one of the several classes that I was teaching. *Jealousy* was originally published in a single ten-page volume. There is a slightly later edition, using *Jealousy* as the title story of a collection "all written by teenagers from two London comprehensive schools" Wasp, D. [ed.] (1978) *Jealousy and Other Stories,* Walton-on-Thames: Thomas Nelson and Sons.

5. See *Our Lives: Young People's Autobiographies* (1979), a collection published by the Inner London Education Authority's English Centre, edited by Paul Ashton and Michael Simons. It includes eleven contributions from Mohammed Elbaja, Zohra El Kssmi, Errol O'Connor, Marcia Chevers, Sabir Bandali, Mayank Patel, John Hawkridge, Anna Leitrim, Tang Hoi Lee, Joe Ackerman and Chelsea Herbert. The broader context of local publishing is examined in Morley, D. and Worpole, K. (1982) *The Republic of Letters: Working Class Writing and Local Publishing* London: Comedia.

6. Woodin (2005) notes that a key figure in *Centerprise* was "Glyn Thompson, an African-American draft dodger from the USA who, influenced by the civil rights movement, emphasized the role of culture in helping the oppressed to assert a subjectivity, to self-consciously use 'I'" (349).

7. For detailed discussions across a range of practices, see Sefton-Green, J. and Sinker, R. (eds.) (2000) *Evaluating Creativity: Making and learning by young people* London: Routledge

8. Some examples of other first novels/autobiographies: Anna Stothard (2003) *Isabel and Rocco* London: Arrow/Random House; J. T. Leroy (2000) *Sarah* London: Bloomsbury; Brett Easton Ellis (1985) *Less Than Zero* New York: Simon and Schuster; Susanna Kaysen (1993) *Girl, Interrupted* New York: Turtle Books/Random House.

Chapter One Young People Writing Online

1. www.voya.com (Accessed May 17 2007) "Owned by Scarecrow Press part of the Rowman and Littlefield Publishing Group, VOYA (*Voice of Youth Advocates*) is a bimonthly journal addressing librarians, educators, and other professionals who work with young adults."

2. www.ala.org/ala/yalsa - In addition to the various named awards, the division also publishes the following annual lists: Best Books for Young Adults; Great Graphic Novels for Teens; Outstanding Books for the College Bound; Popular Paperbacks for Young Adults; Quick Picks for Reluctant Young Adult Readers; Selected Audio Books for Young Adults; Selected DVDs and Videos for Young Adults.

3. http://alan-ya.org (Accessed June 26 2007)

4. www.davidbelbin.com (Accessed June 27 2007)

5. A mid-1970s single by The Undertones.

6. "Merlyn's Pen designs school programs that promote creativity, critical thinking about media, and self-acceptance. Its…New Library of Young Adult Writing…showcases compelling works of fiction and nonfiction authored by America's teens, grades 6-12." www.merlynspen.org (Accessed August 29 2007)

7. "Pomegranate Words was founded to address the lack of opportunities in schools for students interested in creative writing." www.pomegranatewords.com (Accessed July 11 2007)

8. "The Write Stuff is a writing club for young adult writers ages thirteen to twenty-three. We have been connecting teenagers who love writing from across the country (and the world) since 1996." www.geocities.com/writestuffclub (Accessed February 1 2008)

9. (Scarecrow Press, 2007) edited by Mary K. Chelton with Colleen Cool.

10. David Belbin defines young adult fiction as addressing readers "in their early to mid-teens, a time when research shows that half of the population stops reading fiction and never starts again. It provides a bridge to adult fiction, yet has its own very specific concerns, providing a vital place for reflection during adolescence, the most difficult phase of many people's lives." www.ntu.ac.uk/hum/school_news (Accessed May 20 2007)

11. "Young adult readers are a powerful market force in the book industry – teens spend $94.7 billion per year, increasing by $1 billion each year (Jupiter Research)." Cited by American Booksellers Association April 27 2004. (Accessed May 17 2007). And see "Young Adult: The New Black" – a session at the Algonquin, New York, May 31 2007 Backspace Writers Conference at www.backspacewritersconference.com (Accessed June 28 2007)

12. See Leander (2003); Nixon (2003); Stern (1999, 2002).

13. Writing Goals for 2007 (Elisabeth Wilhelm):

    1. Get book contract for my nonfiction how-to book for teen writers on proposal.
    2. Finish novel, edit it, and get representation for it.
    3. Write even when I don't want to.
    4. Turn AM nonprofit.
    5. Join a professional writers' association.
    6. Get published in a glossy magazine.

    (www.absynthemuse.com Accessed August 30 2007)

14. "Teenagers run every aspect of the publication and are assigned positions such as editor-in-chief, managing editor, photo editor, reporters, layout designers, administrators and technicians. Adult mentors, including journalism professionals from *The New York Times*, Black Entertainment Television, ABC News, *VIBE* magazine, *Time* magazine, and Bloomberg News guide them through the process…" www.harlemlive.org (Accessed July 10 2007)

15. "*YO!* Youth Outlook is an award-winning literary journal of youth life in the Bay Area. Featuring reporting pieces and first person essays, comic strips and poetry pages, *YO!* Is the communication outlet for youth who feel their voice and visions need to be seen and heard." www.youthoutlook.org (Accessed July 11 2007).

Chapter Two Online

1. Bibliography for Gay Teens – Gay, Lesbian, Bisexual and Transgendered Round Table – www.ala.org/ala/olos/outreachresource/gayteens21stcenturyaccessfuture.

2. "The Edwards Award recognizes Block's ground-breaking Weetzie Bat books, which enable teens to understand the world in which they live and their relationships with others and society. The Margaret A. Edwards Award is sponsored by School Library Journal and administered by the Young Adult Library Services Association (YALSA)."

3. One contributor, who dropped out of the exchanges after moving to Santa Fe, did respond with very carefully critical analyses of others' poetry – but always very politely and with some effort to be sympathetic and encouraging.

4. Jenkins (2006) discusses other approaches adopted by Christian groups including teaching "discernment" – see 198–205.

Chapter Three Writing for Young Adults

1. Arguably there are exceptions suggesting that this monolithic view is overstated – see Hinton (1970), Cormier (1974), and Blume (1975).

2. Monday April 28 2003, BBC TV Newsnight Review: *Doing It* .

3. Consider, for example, the *American Pie* films or the British Channel 4 (E4) TV series *Skins*.

4. For a detailed textual analysis of various examples, see McCallum, R. (1999) and also Trites, R. S. (2000).

5. May 27 2003, BBC TV Newsnight Review: *The Curious Incident of the Dog in the Night-Time*.

Chapter Four What Are We?

1. In the summer of 2001 Joss Whedon, the "originator" and executive producer of the show, commented, in a telephone interview, that *Buffy the Vampire Slayer* is "basically saying that the world's a scary, scary place and anybody who lives in it without becoming a dickweed is a hero" (Agarwal, 2001: 25).

2. The reading offered here was originally drafted during the BBC (UK) transmission of season 5, particularly during the second half of that season, after *Blood Ties,* late 2001, early 2002. The starting point for my analysis was an invitation from the (now defunct) Child Psychotherapy Trust (London) to contribute a chapter to a book on children, film, and therapy.

3. However, see Williamson (2005) for an extensive discussion of melodrama in relation to vampire fictions.

4. 3001 – Third season, episode one.

5. The earlier history of this equation between HIV/AIDS and the threat of monstrous invasion is sketched by Peter Redman (1997).

6. This is continued in Stephenie Meyer's (2005) novel *Twilight,* in the depiction of the high school vampire Edward Cullen.

7. The events of season 6 bestow considerable gravity on other couples: Xander–Anya, Willow–Tara.

8. Blood is central to vampire mythology. It is often described in detail in vampire literature or displayed in close-up (in film and television), making visible the fact of penetration – usually of teeth into necks. Like the "money shot" (the ejaculation of semen, not blood or tears) in hardcore pornography (Williams, 1990), here the appearance of blood seems to offer a compelling sense of bodily connection – and more powerfully so because the visible production of blood, unlike that of semen, does depend on some form of prior penetration. This scene suggests abandonment in orgasm (so intense she has to be rushed to hospital afterwards) and the close-up shot of blood welling around the wound in her neck is accompanied by the sounds of penetration and feeding (see DeKelb-Rittenhouse, 2002).

9. David Harvey has commented on the importance of such accumulations within domestic space for the construction of a sense of identity in the conditions of postmodernity:

   "Photographs, particular objects (like a piano, a clock, a chair), and events (the playing of a record of a piece of music, the singing of a song) become the focus of a contemplative memory, and hence a generator of a sense of self that lies outside the sensory overloading of consumerist culture and fashion. The home becomes a private museum to guard against the ravages of time-space compression." (Harvey, 1989: 292).

Chapter Five Seeing Through the Skin

1. Chris Hedges comments: "The dominionist movement, like all totalitarian movements, seeks to appropriate not only our religious and patriotic language but also our stories, to deny the validity of stories other than their own, to deny that there are other acceptable ways of living and being. There becomes, in their rhetoric, only one way to be a Christian and only one way to be an American." (Hedges, 2007: 11)

2. Skeggs (2004) is a particularly salient analysis in its attention to the complexities of simultaneously "racial" and classed strategies of "othering." To be a "cultural omnivore" (Skeggs, 2004: 144-145) can appear no more than living out a "progressive" liberal cosmopolitanism but, as Skeggs (among others) has argued, this is a position of some (mostly unacknowledged) privilege – the privilege of a white middle-class. In the opening pages of her book *Class, Self, Culture* (2004) she presents an argument made by Manthia Diawara (1998), elaborating the racial dynamics of what constitutes being "cool." She comments, "white characters that need to achieve 'cool' can move between black and white, attaching and detaching aspects of black culture and characteristics as and when appropriate…A particular version of racial inscription thus becomes a mobile

resource for some whilst being fixed and read onto some bodies as a limitation. The black male character appears not to be acting; he just *is*. Hence, black dispositions are culturally essentialized and made authentic. This is an example of a symbolic economy where the inscription and marking of characteristics onto certain bodies condenses a whole complex cultural history. Some bodies can be expanded rather than condensed. At the same time they become a resource for others." (Skeggs, 2004: 1)

3. It would be valuable to investigate students' reading histories and to explore in much more detail their encounters with novels by Block and others (see Richards, 2005a, b). There are precedents for such work in, for example, Sarland (1991), Cherland (1994), and Blackford (2004). More sociological reference points for the investigation of reading histories, particularly with reference to social class and cultural capital, can be found in the work of Skeggs (1997a, b, 2004) and Savage (2000).

4. Block's autobiographical *Guarding the Moon* (2003a) provides the kind of evidence these readers seek: "There was a time in my early twenties when I wanted to find the way to eat the least amount possible to sustain myself. Shredded wheat and nonfat milk for breakfast, a green apple for lunch, a tiny portion of tofu, rice, and vegetables for dinner. I ran around the track the moment I'd finished my meals. I got thinner and thinner. I felt a strange euphoria as I went below one hundred pounds. Down to ninety-five pounds. I had to drop out of school, leave my boyfriend, go through years of therapy. It took a long time to find a balance, but I still worried about my weight and would tend to get very thin when I needed to escape something in my life" (Block, 2003a: 76–77); "I want her to know her perfection always. None of the pain of fathers who stop seeing you when reach adolescence, of boys drawing cruel pictures, the pain that led me to drink myself into reeling blackness, get into careening cars, sleep with men who didn't love me, starve myself, imagine ways to cut myself open, trying to let out the hurt in my blood" (2003a: 87). It needs to be noted that such autobiographical "evidence" is itself a "re-creation" of the past "self" – see Usher (1998).

5. Though these are not the more overt fantasies of empowerment found in, for example, *Buffy the Vampire Slayer* (witchcraft, superhuman fighting skills, magically enhanced bodily strength, and endurance), they nevertheless occupy a related discursive field, centered on the problem of vulnerability, and located in texts arguably addressing young white women. See Richards, 1993, 1995.

6. For other variants, see "Wolf" in Block, Francesca Lia (2000b) *The Rose and the Beast: Fairy Tales Retold*, Joanna Cotler Books/Harper Collins.

7. Purkiss suggests that "A fairy is someone who appears at and governs one of the big crises of mortal life: birth, childhood and its transitions, adolescence, sexual awakening, pregnancy and childbirth, old age, death. She presides over the borders of our lives, the seams between one phase of life and another." (Purkiss, 2003: 4).

8. "Loss of sexual purity through intercourse with other races endangers visible race difference, a key driving force behind an ideology of whiteness that gives political, economic, and social advantages to those with the 'appropriate' racial lineage. That the white woman is made the locus of this race purity illustrates the sexual license patriarchy grants

white men by sanctioning white male sexuality and denying white female sexuality. This, along with portrayals of nonwhite sexuality as licentious, helps construct the myth of white sexual restraint." (Babb, 1998: 76)

9. For a very useful discussion of the politics of this period see Brewer, 2005, especially chapter 7 "The White Backlash: A Second U.S. Revolution."

10. Trites (2000) offers an interesting discussion of photography in young adult novels.

11. Stephenie Meyer's (2005, 2006, 2007a, 2007b) narrative of possession and of eternal youth offers a recent reworking of these themes.

12. Donna Haraway (1992) refers to a familiar and long standing tradition in Western constructions of the "other," suggesting that often what "we" lack is "found" elsewhere, in an exotic space. Haraway comments, in "The Bio-Politics of a Multicultural Field," that:"It has become clear to critics of anthropology how the observed and described peoples are turned into resources for the solution of other people's dilemmas (Fabian, 1983). Those studied are regularly found to have just those properties that the writer's culture lacks and needs or fears and rejects. It is this structure that defines the logical move that constructs what will count as 'primitive,' 'natural,' 'other'." (Haraway, 1992: 257)

13. Dyer comments on the white woman as angel (1997: 127).

14. There is scope here to reconsider the value attached to what Pamela Perry calls "the putative qualities of blackness" (Perry, 2002: 104–132).

Chapter Six Dead White People

1. For example, Greg Tate comments, if characteristically somewhat overstating the case:

> "Off the record (and off the cuff), a white critic once confessed his opinion that white men have nothing else to say in fiction...We hardly need an oracle to know that the fictions of the past 25 years already guaranteed future-classic status have been written by people of color, white feminists, and Latin American men. These writers have become bellwethers of the era's most progressive trends: the deflation of white male supremacy and the decolonization of the imaginations of the oppressed." (Tate, 1992: 220)

2. Dyer argues that claims to racial superiority are made through the division between the spirit and the body (1997: 44).

3. In horror, Dyer argues, it is possible for the association of whiteness with death to be explored (1997: 210).

4. Dyer suggests that sexual desire is projected onto darker skinned people by whites and thus disowned (1997: 28).

5. The fascination of Christianity lies in the mystery of the spirit which is in but not of the body (Dyer, 1997: 16–18).

6. There is no space to explore this here but of course Angel does have a son, Connor – frequently in the plotting of multiple twenty-two episode seasons "rules" get broken (another example is Principal Wood, the slayer's son, in season 7 of *Buffy the Vampire Slayer*).

7. Jowett (2005: 159) compares him to Roy Baty in *Blade Runner*.

8. "it was here, in the exclusiveness of Black West Indian style, in the virtual impossibility of authentic white identification, that reggae's attraction for the punks was strongest...Reggae's blackness was proscriptive. It was an alien essence, a foreign body which implicitly threatened mainstream British culture from within and as such it resonated with punk's adopted values – 'anarchy', 'surrender' and 'decline'...For the punks to find a positive meaning in such a blatant disavowal of Britishness amounted to a symbolic act of treason which complemented, indeed, completed, the sacrilegious programme undertaken in punk rock itself...the punk aesthetic can be read in part as a white 'translation' of black 'ethnicity'." (Hebdige, 1979: 64)

9. Extreme whiteness, in Dyer's argument, makes ordinary whiteness normal and unremarkable (Dyer, 1997: 222).

Chapter Seven Fictions of Identity

1. The full data set for this research is composed of writing in both autobiographical and diary form by 70 students ranging in age from 19 to 40. The data was collected over a period of three years, commencing in 2004.

2. See also C. Weedon (2004) *Identity and Culture: Narratives of Difference and Belonging* Maidenhead: Open University Press

3. See Paul Willis on "symbolic moulds" in P. Willis et al. (1990).

4. See my discussion of the white Essex blues band The Hamsters – Richards (2006).

5. This is an emphasis contrasting with the more situated and "contingent" status attributed to the writing discussed in Richards (1998b), chapter 7.

6. Jennifer (Lady Destiny) www.ladydestiny.com and www.myspace.com/ukladydestiny

7. She was not an Education Studies student, which might have implied a disruption or abandonment of this career trajectory. She graduated in Music and Media Management.

8. Jason's recording name is the Mad Doctor X – see, for example, Chillonometry MARCD006 Marble Bar Entertainment Ltd., 2001.

9. Frith suggests that identity is always "ideal," "fantastic" but also "real, enacted" (Frith, 1996: 123). His argument informs some aspects of Perry's (2002) analysis.

10. The "black Atlantic" refers to Paul Gilroy's (1993) highly influential account of black culture in the aftermath of slavery and of subsequent migrations. "Supercultures," "intercultures," "subcultures," and "affinity cultures" (etc.) are terms used by Mark Slobin (1993) – as flexible and provisional.

11. There are some similarities in the structure of his account to an interview I conducted with a fireman studying for a Film Studies degree – see Richards, 2005a. The assertion of some connection to his father – in Jason's case, an "inherited" eclectic taste in music, and the emphasis on "chance" and on the pleasure of unexpected public acknowledgment of his productivity, are significant points of comparison.

12. Basil Bernstein comments on fundamentalist identities: "This is a retrospective identity constructed from fundamentalist religious resources. It provides for an unambiguous, stable, intellectually impervious, collective identity. It consumes the self in all its manifestations and gives it a site outside current and future instabilities and ambiguities for judgement, relation and conduct. It produces a strong insulation between the sacred and the profane such that it is possible to enter the profane world without being either appropriated or colonized by it. In less metaphoric terms it produces a strong insulation between conduct and modernizing or postmodernizing influences. Thus Islamic fundamentalism enables the appropriation of western technologies without cultural penetration." (Bernstein, 1996: 78)

13. Some examples: Kirk Franklin The Nu Nation Project Audio CD (November 9 1998) Label: Interscope ASIN: B00000AFGN; Kirk Franklin Hero (May 29 2006) Label: Bmg ASIN: 000AOJ9XA; Kirk Franklin presents 1NC (One Nation Crew) (August 21 2000) Label: Gospo Centric ASIN: B00004C4QO. And Fred Hammond Somethin' 'bout Love (September 6 2004) Label: Verity ASIN: B00024I376; Fred Hammond Pages of Life (April 28 1998) Label: Authentic ASIN: B000005Z0Z; Fred Hammond Purpose by Design (no date) Label: Verity ASIN: B00004RCXZ.

14. See The Guardian (Unlimited) Muslim Superstar November 5 2007 at www.guardian.co.uk/g2 (accessed November 12 2007). Sami Yusuf My Ummah (July 1 2005) Label: Awakening Records ASIN: B000KZRLVG. See also MuslimHipHop.com and Sami Yusuf on YouTube.

15. Self-presentation as "complex" and as "introspective" is also consistent with educational aspiration in the liberal university setting and is likely to be "valued" more highly than the devotional narratives of those young women explicitly positioning themselves as more singularly Muslim (see Richards, 1998b: 145–174).

16. Weedon comments: "Second-wave feminism in Western countries in the late 1960s and 1970s was marked by a variety of forms of universalizing theory – liberal, radical feminist and Marxist – that claimed to represent the interests of all women. They shared a tendency, seldom made explicit, to assume that white Western norms and practices were the measure of all things. The often unconscious legacies of colonialism and of nine-

teenth-century scientific racism informed the ways in which women outside the West were perceived. Often this was as victims of traditional, highly patriarchal cultures and religions which, at best, had their roots outside Western modernity and were assumed to be static and unchanging. Powerful symbols and cultural practices such as the veil, arranged marriages and genital mutilation came to exemplify the plight of Third World women, who were assumed to lack the power and agency with which to bring about progressive social change." (Weedon, 2004: 57–58)

On Madonna see, among the many discussions, bell hooks (1992); Fouz-Hernandez and Jarman-Ivens (2004), especially Patricia Pisters, "Madonna's girls in the mix – Performance of femininity beyond the beautiful" and David Gauntlett, "Madonna's daughters – Girl power and the empowered girl-pop breakthrough."

Postscript

1. In the mid-1960s in the school that I attended, a novel called *The Passion-Flower Hotel* (Erskine, 1962) circulated among teenage boys, briefly, as a tantalizing opportunity to imagine what sex might be like. A much harsher example from the same period is Jan Cremer (1965) *I, Jan Cremer* London: Calder and Boyars.

2. On methodological issues, see J. Green and D. Bloome (1995) "Ethnography and Ethnographers of and in Education: A Situated Perspective."

3. Consider, for example, the life history of the West Coast poet Gary Snyder (born 1930). There is a chronology (611–614) in Gary Snyder (1999) *The Gary Snyder Reader: Prose, Poetry and Translations,* Washington D.C.: Counterpoint.

Bibliography

Agarwal, M. (2001) "Slay It Again" (Interview with Joss Whedon) *Time Out,* London, August 22-29, 2001, 25–26.

Ashton, P. and Simons, M. (Eds.). (1979) *Our Lives: Young People's Autobiographies*, London: ILEA English Centre.

Babb, V. (1998) *Whiteness Visible: The Meaning of Whiteness in American Literature and Culture*, New York: New York University Press.

Back, L. (1996) *New Ethnicities and Urban Culture: Racisms and Multiculture in Young Lives*, London: UCL Press.

Bakhtin, M. (1994) *Speech Genres and Other Late Essays*, Austin, TX: University of Texas Press.

Barker, M. and Petley, J. (2001) *Ill Effects – The Media/Violence Debate (second edition)*, London: Routledge.

Bennett, A. (2000) *Popular Music and Youth Culture: Music, Identity and Place*, Basingstoke: Palgrave.

Bennett, T. (1979) *Formalism and Marxism*, London: Methuen.

Berger, J. (1972) *Ways of Seeing*, Harmondsworth: Penguin.

Bernier, A., Chelton, M., Jenkins, C., and Pierce, J. (2007) "200 years of young adult library services history," *Voice of Youth Advocates,* (www.voya.com), Lanham, MD: Scarecrow Press.

Bernstein, B. (1996) *Pedagogy, Symbolic Control and Identity: Theory, Research, Critique*, London: Taylor and Francis.

Blackford, H. V. (2004) *Out of This World: Why Literature Matters to Girls*, New York: Teachers College Press.

Block, Francesca Lia (1989) *Weetzie Bat*, New York: A Charlotte Zolotow Book/Harper and Row Junior Books.

Block, Francesca Lia (1991) *Witch Baby*, New York: A Charlotte Zolotow Book/Harper Collins (First Harper Trophy edition 1992).

Block, Francesca Lia (1992) *Cherokee Bat and the Goat Guys*, New York: A Charlotte Zolotow Book/Harper Collins (First Harper Trophy edition 1993).

Block, Francesca Lia (1993/2004) *Ecstasia*, New York: Penguin/Firebird.

Block, Francesca Lia (1993) *Missing Angel Juan*, New York: Harper Collins (First Harper Trophy edition 1995).

Block, Francesca Lia (1994) *The Hanged Man*, New York: Harper Collins (First paperback edition 1999).

Block, Francesca Lia (1994/2004) *Primavera*, New York: Penguin/Firebird.

Block, Francesca Lia (1995) *Baby Be-Bop*, New York: Joanna Cotler Books/Harper Collins (First Harper Trophy edition 1997).

Block, Francesca Lia (1996) *Girl Goddess #9,* New York: Joanna Cotler Books/Harper Collins.

Block, Francesca Lia (1998a) *Dangerous Angels: The Weetzie Bat Books*, New York: Harper Collins.

Block, Francesca Lia (1998b) *I was a Teenage Fairy*, New York: Joanna Cotler Books/Harper Collins.

Block Francesca Lia (1999) *Violet and Claire*, New York: Joanna Cotler Books/Harper Collins.

Block, Francesca Lia (2000a) *Nymph*, Cambridge, MA: Circlet Press (First paperback edition 2003).

Block, Francesca Lia (2000b) *The Rose and the Beast: Fairy Tales Retold*, Joanna Cotler Books/Harper Collins.

Block, Francesca Lia (2001) *Echo*, Joanna Cotler Books/Harper Collins.

Block, Francesca Lia (2003a) *Guarding the Moon: A Mother's First Year*, New York: Harper Resource/Harper Collins.

Block, Francesca Lia (2003b) *Wasteland*, New York: Joanna Cotler Books/Harper Collins.

Block, Francesca Lia and Carlip, Hillary (1998) *Zine Scene: The Do It Yourself Guide to Zines*, Los Angeles: Girl Press.

Blume, Judy (1975) *Forever*, London: Gollancz.

Boethius, U. (1995) "Controlled Pleasures: Youth and Literary Texts" in Fornas, J. and Bolin, G. (Eds.), *Youth Culture in Late Modernity*, London: Sage.

Bourdieu, P. (1986) *Distinction: a Social Critique of the Judgement of Taste*, London: Routledge.

Bourdieu, P. (1993) *Sociology in Question*, London: Sage.

Bourdieu, P., et al. (1999) *The Weight of the World: Social Suffering in Contemporary Society*, Cambridge: Polity.

Bradby, B. (1993) "Sampling Sexuality: Gender, Technology and the Body in Dance Music," *Popular Music,* Vol 12 No 2, May, 155–176.

Bragg, S. (2000) *Media Violence and Education: A Study of Youth Audiences and the Horror Genre*, Unpublished PhD dissertation, University of London.

Bragg, S. (2001) "Just what the doctors ordered? – Media regulation, education and the 'problem' of media violence" in Barker, M. and Petley J. (Eds.), *Ill Effects: The Media/Violence Debate*, London and New York: Routledge.

Bragg, S. (2002) "Wrestling in Woolly Gloves: Not Just Being 'Critically' Media Literate" *Journal of Popular Film and Television*, Vol 30 No 1 (Heldref Publications) 42–52.

Brewer, M. (2005) *Staging Whiteness*, Middletown, CT: Wesleyan University Press.

Brooker, P. and Humm, P. (Eds.) (1989) *Dialogue and Difference: English into the Nineties*, London: Routledge.

Buchmann, M. (1989) *The Script of Life in Modern Society: Entry into Adulthood in a Changing World*, Chicago: University of Chicago Press.

Buckingham, D. (1990) *Watching Media Learning: Making Sense of Media Education*, London: Falmer Press.

Buckingham, D. (1993a) *Changing Literacies: Media Education and Modern Culture*, Institute of Education/Tufnell Press.

Buckingham, D. (Ed.) (1993b) *Reading Audiences: Young People and the Media*, Manchester: Manchester University Press.

Buckingham, D. (1996) *Moving Images: Understanding Children's Emotional Responses to Television*, Manchester: Manchester University Press.

Buckingham, D. (Ed.) (1998) *Teaching Popular Culture: Beyond Radical Pedagogy*, London: UCL Press.

Buckingham, D. (2000) *After the Death of Childhood: Growing up in the Age of Electronic Media*, Cambridge: Polity.

Buckingham, D. (2001) *The Making of Citizens: Young People, News and Politics*, London: Routledge.

Buckingham, D. (2003) *Media Education: Literacy, Learning and Contemporary Culture*, Cambridge: Polity Press.

Buckingham, D., Davies, H., Jones, K., and Kelley, P. (1999) *Children's Television in Britain: History, Discourse and Policy*, London: British Film Institute.

Buckingham, D., Grahame, J., and Sefton-Green, J. (1995) *Making Media: Practical Production in Media Education*, London: The English and Media Centre.

Buckingham, D. and Scanlon, M. (2003) *Education, Entertainment and Learning in the Home*, Buckingham: Open University Press.

Buckingham, D. and Sefton-Green, J. (1994) *Cultural Studies Goes to School*, London: Taylor and Francis.

Burgess, Melvin (1996) *Junk*, London: Andersen Press.

Burgess, Melvin (1999) *Smack*, New York: Avon Books Inc.

Burgess, Melvin (2000a) "Teenage Fiction Comes of Age," *The Bookseller,* August 11 (http://web.onetel.net.uk/~melvinburgess/).

Burgess, Melvin (2000b) "Ban Sex and Drugs? Not in My Book," *Times Educational Supplement,* ("Rethinking Literacy" at http://web.onetel.net.uk/~melvinburgess/).

Burgess, Melvin (2001) *Lady: My Life as a Bitch*, London: Andersen Press.

Burgess, Melvin (2003) *Doing It*, London: Andersen Press.

Burgess, Melvin (2004) "Sympathy for the Devil," in *Children's Literature in Education*, Vol 35 No 4, December 289–300.

Burn, A. and Parker, D. (2003) *Analysing Media Texts*, London: Continuum.

Burr, V. (2003a) "Ambiguity and Sexuality in the Buffyverse: A Sartrean Analysis," *Sexualities*, 6: 343–360.

Burr, V. (2003b) "*Buffy* vs. the BBC: Moral Questions and How to Avoid Them," *Slayage: The online journal of Buffy studies*, No 8.

Busse, K. (2002) "Crossing the Final Taboo: Family, Sexuality, and Incest in *Buffyverse Fan Fiction*" in Wilcox, R. and Lavery, D. (Eds.), *Fighting the Forces: What's at Stake in* Buffy the Vampire Slayer, Lanham, MD: Rowman and Littlefield.

Buxton, D. (1990) *From The Avengers to Miami Vice: Form and Ideology in Television Series*, Manchester: Manchester University Press.

Cabot, Meg (2002) *The Guy Next Door*, New York: Avon/HarperCollins.

Carroll, Jim (1978) *The Basketball Diaries*, New York: Tombouctou Books.

Chaney, D. (1993) *Fictions of Collective Life: Public Drama in Late Modern Culture*, London: Routledge.

Cherland, M. R. (1994) *Private Practices: Girls Reading Fiction and Constructing Identity*, London: Taylor and Francis.

Cormier, R. (1974) *The Chocolate War*, New York: Pantheon.

Cremer, Jan (1965) *I, Jan Cremer*, London: Calder and Boyars (Translated by R. E. Wyngaard and Alexander Trocchi).

Danesi, M. (1994) *Cool: The Signs and Meanings of Adolescence*, Toronto: University of Toronto Press.

Davis, G. and Dickinson, K. (2004) *Teen TV: Genre, Consumption and Identity*, London: British Film Institute.

Davis, M. (1990) *City of Quartz: Excavating the Future in Los Angeles*, London: Verso.

DeKelb-Rittenhouse, D. (2002) "Sex and the Single Vampire: The Evolution of the Vampire Lothario and Its Representation in *Buffy*" in Wilcox, R. and Lavery, D. (Eds.), *Fighting the Forces: What's at Stake in* Buffy the Vampire Slayer, Lanham, MD: Rowman and Littlefield.

DeNora, T. (2000) *Music in Everyday Life*, Cambridge: Cambridge University Press.

Diawara, M. (1998) "Homeboy cosmopolitan: Manthia Diawara interviewed by Silvia Kolbowski," *October*, 83 (Winter): 51–70.

Donald, J. (1992) *Sentimental Education: Schooling, Popular Culture and the Regulation of Liberty*, London: Verso.

Drummond, S. (1976) *Jealousy*, London: Thomas Calton – ILEA English Centre.

Dyer, R. (1997) *White*, London: Routledge.

Edwards, L. (2002) "Slaying in Black and White: Kendra as Tragic Mulatta in *Buffy*" in Wilcox, R. and Lavery, D. (Eds.), *Fighting the Forces: What's at Stake in* Buffy the Vampire Slayer, Lanham, MD: Rowman and Littlefield.

Ehrenreich, B. (1983) *The Hearts of Men: American Dreams and the Flight from Commitment*, New York: Anchor Books/Random House.

Ellis, Brett Easton (1985) *Less Than Zero*, New York: Simon and Schuster.

Erben, M. (1998) *Biography and Education: A Reader*, London: Falmer Press.

Erskine, Rosalind (1962) *The Passion-Flower Hotel*, London: Jonathan Cape.

Fabian, J. (1983) *Time and the Other: How Anthropology Makes Its Object*, New York: Columbia University Press.

Fine, Anne (1996) *The Tulip Touch*, London: Puffin.

Fine, Anne (2003) "Filth whichever way you look at it" (Review of *Doing It*), *The Guardian,* March 29 (http://books.guardian.co.uk/review/story/0,12084,923907,00.html#article_continue).

Fine, M., Weis, L., Powell, L. C., and Wong, L. M. (Eds.) (1997) *Off White: Readings on Race, Power and Society*, New York: Routledge.

Fornas, J. and Bolin, G. (1995) *Youth Culture in Late Modernity*, London: Sage.

Forster, G. (2003) "Faith and Plato: 'You're Nothing! Disgusting, Murderous Bitch!'" in South, J. (Ed.), Buffy the Vampire Slayer *and Philosophy: Fear and Trembling in Sunnydale*, Chicago and La Salle, Illinois: Open Court.

Fouz-Hernandez, S. and Jarman-Ivens, F. (Eds.) (2004) *Madonna's Drowned Worlds: New Approaches to Her Cultural Transformations, 1983-2003*, Burlington, VT: Ashgate.

Frankenberg, R. (Ed.) (1997) *Displacing Whiteness: Essays in Social and Cultural Criticism*, Durham NC and London: Duke University Press.

Frith, S. (1987) "Towards an aesthetic of popular music" in Leppert, R. and McClary, S. (Eds.), *Music and Society – The Politics of Composition, Performance and Reception*, Cambridge: Cambridge University Press.

Frith, S. (1996) "Music and Identity" in Hall, S. and du Gay, P. (Eds.), *Questions of Cultural Identity*, London: Sage.

Gauntlett, D. and Hill, A. (1999) *TV Living: Television, Culture and Everyday Life*, London: Routledge.

Giddens, A. (1991) *Modernity and Self-Identity: Self and Society in the Late Modern Age*, Cambridge: Polity Press.

Gillespie, M. (1995) *Television, Ethnicity and Cultural Change*, London: Routledge.

Gilroy, P. (1993) *The Black Atlantic: Modernity and Double Consciousness*, London: Verso.

Gilroy, P. (2004) *Between Camps: Nations, Cultures and the Allure of Race,* London: Routledge.

Giroux, Henry A. (1998) "Teenage Sexuality, Body Politics, and the Pedagogy of Display" in Epstein, J. (Ed.), (1998) *Youth Culture: Identity in a Postmodern World,* Malden, MA: Blackwell.

Goodson, I. and Sikes, P. (Eds.) (2001) *Life History Research in Educational Settings: Learning from Lives*, Buckingham: Open University Press.

Graff, H. J. (1997) *Conflicting Paths: Growing Up in America,* Cambridge, MA: Harvard University Press.

Gray, A. (1992) *Video Playtime: The Gendering of a Leisure Technology*, London: Routledge.

Green, J. and Bloome, D. (1995) "Ethnography and Ethnographers of and in Education: A Situated Perspective" in Flood, J., Heath, S. B., and Lapp, D. (Eds.), *Handbook of Research on Teaching Literacy through the Communicative and Visual Arts*, New York: Macmillan.

Griffin, C. (1993) *Representations of Youth: The Study of Youth in Britain and America*, Cambridge: Polity.

Haddon, Mark (2003) *The Curious Incident of the Dog in the Night-Time*, London: Cape.

Hall, S. (1996) "Introduction: Who needs 'Identity?'" in Hall, S. and Du Gay, P. (Eds.), *Questions of Cultural Identity*, London: Sage.

Haraway, D. (1992) *Primate Visions: Gender, Race, and Nature in the World of Modern Science*, London and New York: Verso.

Harvey, D. (1989) *The Condition of Postmodernity: An Enquiry into the Origins of Cultural Change*, Oxford: Blackwell.

Harvey, S. (1980) *May '68 and Film Culture*, London: British Film Institute.

Hebdige, D. (1979) *Subculture – The Meaning of Style*, London: Methuen.

Hedges, C. (2007) *American Fascists: The Christian Right and the War on America*, London: Jonathan Cape.

Herald, D. and Monnier, D. (2007) "The Beasts Have Arrived: The Blooming of Youth Participation in the Young Adult Library Services Association," *Voice of Youth Advocates*, June, 116-119. Lanham, MD: Scarecrow Press.

Hermes, J. (1995) *Reading Women's Magazines*, Cambridge: Polity.

Hewitt, R. (1986) *White Talk Black Talk: Inter-racial Friendship and Communication Amongst Adolescents*, Cambridge: Cambridge University Press.

Hey, V. (1997) *The Company She Keeps: An Ethnography of Girls' Friendship*, Buckingham: Open University Press.

Hills, M. (2002) *Fan Cultures*, London: Routledge.

Hinton, S. E. (1970) *The Outsiders*, London: Gollancz.

Hinton, S. E. (1972/1988) *The Outsiders*, London: Collins/Lions Teen Tracks.

Hinton, S. E. (2003) *The Outsiders*, London: Puffin Modern Classics.

Hinton, S. E. (2006) *The Outsiders*, New York: Penguin Classics.

Holland, J., Ramazanoglu, C., Sharpe, S., and Thomson, R. (1998) *The Male in the Head: Young People, Heterosexuality and Power*, London: the Tufnell Press.

hooks, b. (1989) *Talking Back: Thinking Feminist, Thinking Black*, Boston: South End Press.

hooks, b. (1992) *Black Looks: Race and Representation*, Boston: South End Press.

hooks, b. (1994a) *Teaching to Transgress: Education as the Practice of Freedom*, New York: Routledge.

hooks, b. (1994b) *Outlaw Culture: Resisting Representations*, London: Routledge.

Hotaling, D. J. (1999) "The Scribe of Shangri-La: She Just Gets It. Novelist Francesca Lia Block Captures the Magic and Mood Swings of Growing Up in L.A." *Los Angeles Times*, Los Angeles, California, November 14, p. 26.

Howell, A. (2004) "'If we hear any inspirational power chords…': Rock Music, Rock Culture on *Buffy the Vampire Slayer*" *Continuum: Journal of Media and Cultural Studies,* Vol 18 No 3, 406–422.

Jameson, F. (1974) *The Prison-House of Language: A Critical Account of Structuralism and Russian Formalism*, Princeton: Princeton University Press.

Jancovich, M. and Lyons, J. (Eds.) (2003) *Quality Popular Television: Cult TV, the Industry and Fans*, London: British Film Institute.

Jarvis, C. (2001) "School is Hell: Gendered Fears in Teenage Horror" *Educational Studies,* Vol 27 No 3, 257–267.

Jenkins, H. (2006) *Convergence Culture: Where Old and New Media Collide*, New York: New York University Press.

Johnson, C. (2005) *Telefantasy*, London: British Film Institute.

Jones, K. (Ed.), (1992) *English and the National Curriculum: Cox's Revolution?* London: Kogan Page and the University of London Institute of Education.

Jones, K. (2003) *Education in Britain: 1944 to the Present*, Cambridge: Polity.

Jones, S. (1988) *Black Culture, White Youth: The Reggae Tradition from JA to UK*, London: Macmillan.

Jowett, L. (2005) *Sex and the Slayer: A Gender Studies Primer for the Buffy Fan*, Middletown, CT: Wesleyan University Press.

Kaveney, R. (Ed.) (2001) *Reading the Vampire Slayer: An Unofficial Critical Companion to Buffy and Angel*, London: Tauris Parke.

Kaysen, Susanna (1993) *Girl, Interrupted*, New York: Turtle Books/Random House.

Kearney, M. C. (1998) "'Don't Need You': Rethinking Identity Politics and Separatism from a Grrrl Perspective" in Epstein, J. (Ed.), *Youth Culture: Identity in a Postmodern World*, Malden, MA: Blackwell.

Kearney, M. C. (2006) *Girls Make Media*, New York: Routledge.

Kellaway, K. (2003) "Autistic Differences" *The Observer* Review, April 27.

Kenway, J. and Bullen, E. (2001) *Consuming Children: Education-Entertainment-Advertising*, Buckingham: Open University Press.

King, N. (2003) "Brownskirts: Fascism, Christianity and the Eternal Demon" in South, J. (Ed.), Buffy the Vampire Slayer *and Philosophy: Fear and Trembling in Sunnydale*, Chicago and La Salle, Illinois: Open Court.

Kress, G. (2003) *Literacy in the New Media Age*, London: Routledge.

Kress, G. and van Leeuwen, T. (1996) *Reading Images*, London: Routledge.

Kress, G. and van Leeuwen, T. (2001) *Multimodal Discourse*, London: Arnold.

Krimmer, E. and Raval, S. (2002) "Digging the Undead: Death and Desire in *Buffy*" in Wilcox, R. and Lavery, D. (Eds.), *Fighting the Forces: What's at Stake in* Buffy the Vampire Slayer, Lanham, MD: Rowman and Littlefield.

Krzywinska, T. (2002) "Hubble-Bubble, Herbs, and Grimoires: Magic, Manichaeanism, and Witchcraft in *Buffy*" in Wilcox, R. and Lavery, D. (Eds.), *Fighting the Forces: What's at Stake in* Buffy the Vampire Slayer, Lanham, MD: Rowman and Littlefield.

Kuhn, A. (1995) *Family Secrets: Acts of Memory and Imagination*, London: Verso.

Leander, K. (2003) "'Writing travelers' tales on New Literacyscapes," *Reading Research Quarterly* Vol 38 No 3, 392–397.

Le Guin, Ursula K. (1985) *The Language of the Night: Essays on Fantasy and Science Fiction*, New York: Berkley Books.

Leroy, J. T. (2000) *Sarah*, London: Bloomsbury.

Lesko, N. (1996) "Denaturalizing Adolescence: The Politics of Contemporary Representations," *Youth and Society,* Vol 28 No 2, December, 139–161.

Lesko, N. (2001) *Act Your Age! A Cultural Construction of Adolescence*, London: Routledge.

Lindley, R. (1989) 'Teenagers and Other Children', in Scarre, G. (Ed.), *Children, Parents and Politics*, Cambridge: Cambridge University Press.

Livingstone, S. (1998) *Making Sense of Television: The Psychology of Audience Interpretation*, London: Routledge.

Livingstone, S. (2002) *Young People and New Media: Childhood and the Changing Media Environment*, London: Sage.

McCallum, R. (1999) *Ideologies of Identity in Adolescent Fiction: The Dialogic Construction of Subjectivity*, New York: Garland Publishing Inc.

McDonell, Nick (2002) *Twelve*, New York: Grove/Atlantic.

McRobbie, A. (1978) "Working-Class Girls and the Culture of Femininity" in Women's Studies Group (Eds.), *Women Take Issue*, Birmingham and London: CCCS/Hutchinson.

McRobbie, A. (2005) *The Uses of Cultural Studies: A Textbook*, London: Sage.

Meyer, Stephenie (2005) *Twilight*, New York: Little, Brown and Company.

Meyer, Stephenie (2006) *New Moon*, New York: Little, Brown and Company.

Meyer, Stephenie (2007a) *New Moon,* London: Atom

Meyer, Stephenie (2007b) *Eclipse*, New York: Little, Brown and Company.

Middleton, D. and Edwards, D. (Eds.) (1990) *Collective Remembering*, London: Sage.

Money, M. A. (2002) "The Undemonization of Supporting Characters in *Buffy*" in Wilcox, R. and Lavery, D. (Eds.), *Fighting the Forces: What's at Stake in* Buffy the Vampire Slayer, Lanham, MD: Rowman and Littlefield.

Moretti, F. (1988) "Dialectic of Fear" in *Signs Taken for Wonders: Essays in the Sociology of Literary Forms*, London: Verso.

Morley, D. (1980) *The "Nationwide" Audience*, London: British Film Institute.

Morley, D. (1992) *Television, Audiences and Cultural Studies*, London: Routledge.

Morley, D. (2000) *Home Territories: Media, Mobility and Identity*, London: Routledge.

Morley, D. and Worpole, K (1982) *The Republic of Letters: Working Class Writing and Local Publishing*, London: Comedia.

Morrison, T. (1993) *Playing in the Dark: Whiteness and the Literary Imagination,* New York: Vintage Books.

Moss, G. (1989) *Un/Popular Fictions*, London: Virago.

Munford, B. (2007) "It's buy, buy to women. Now the girlies rule" *Times Higher*, March 9, 16–17.

National Council of Teachers of English (NCTE), (1994) "How to Write a Rationale" (http://www.ncte.org/about/issues/censorship/resources/115785.htm).

Neale, S. (1986) "Melodrama and Tears," *Screen*, Vol 27 No 6, 6-22.

Nilan, P. and Feixa, C. (2006) *Global Youth? Hybrid Identities, Plural Worlds*, London: Routledge.

Nixon, H. (2003) "New Research Literacies for Contemporary Research into Literacy and New Media?" *Reading Research Quarterly,* Vol 38 No 3, 407–413.

Ono, K. A. (2000) "To Be a Vampire on *Buffy the Vampire Slayer*: Race and ('Other') Socially Marginalizing Positions on Horror TV" in Helford, E. R. (Ed.), *Fantasy Girls: Gender in the New Universe of Science Fiction and Fantasy Television*, Lanham, MD: Rowman and Littlefield.

Osgerby, B. (1998) *Youth in Britain since 1945*, Oxford: Blackwell.

Osgerby, B. (2001) *Playboys in Paradise: Masculinity, Youth and Leisure-style in Modern America*, Oxford: Berg.

Osgerby, B. (2004) *Youth Media*, London: Routledge.

Perry, P. (2002) *Shades of White: White Kids and Racial Identities in High School*, Durham, NC: Duke University Press.

Pini, M. (2001) *Club Cultures and Female Subjectivity: The Move from Home to House*, Basingstoke: Palgrave.

Postman, N. (1994) *The Disappearance of Childhood*, New York: Vintage Books.

Purkiss, D. (2003) *At the Bottom of the Garden: A Dark History of Fairies, Hobgoblins, and Other Troublesome Things*, New York: New York University Press.

Quart, A. (2003) *Branded: The Buying and Selling of Teenagers*, London: Arrow.

Radway, J. (1984) *Reading the Romance: Women, Patriarchy and Popular Literature*, Chapel Hill and London: University of North Carolina Press.

Rampton, B. (2006) *Language in Late Modernity: Interaction in an Urban School*, Cambridge: Cambridge University Press.

Redman, P. (1997) "Invasion of the Monstrous Others: Heterosexual Masculinities, the 'AIDS Carrier' and the Horror Genre" in Steinberg, D., Epstein, D., and Johnson, R. (Eds.), *Border Patrols: Policing the Boundaries of Heterosexuality*, London: Cassell.

Reid, S. and Hutchinson, B. (1994) "Lanky Lizards! Francesca Lia Block Is Fun To Read But…Reading Multicultural Literature in Public Schools," *The Alan Review,* Vol 21, No 3, Spring (ALAN – Assembly on Literature for Adolescents at the National Council of Teachers of English) 60–65.

Richards, C. (1981/82) "Classroom Readings," *Screen Education,* 40 Autumn/Winter, 67-79.

Richards, C. (1990) "Intervening in Popular Pleasures: Media Studies and the Politics of Subjectivity" in Buckingham, D. (Ed.), *Watching Media Learning: Making Sense of Media Education*, London: Falmer Press.

Richards, C. (1992) "Teaching Popular Culture" in Jones, K. (Ed.), *English and the National Curriculum: Cox's Revolution?* London: Kogan Page and the University of London Institute of Education.

Richards, C. (1993) "Taking Sides? What Young Girls Do with Television" in Buckingham, D. (Ed.), *Reading Audiences: Young People and the Media*, Manchester: University of Manchester Press.

Richards, C. (1995) "Room to Dance" in Bazalgette, C. and Buckingham, D. (Eds.), *In Front of the Children: Screen Entertainment and Young Audiences*, London: British Film Institute.

Richards, C. (1998a) "Beyond Classroom Culture" in Buckingham, D. (Ed.), *Teaching Popular Culture: Beyond Radical Pedagogy*, London: UCL Press.

Richards, C. (1998b) *Teen Spirits: Music and Identity in Media Education*, London: UCL Press.

Richards, C. (1999) "Live Through This: Music, Adolescence and Autobiography" in McCarthy, C., et al. (Eds.), *Sound Identities: Popular Music and the Cultural Politics of Education*, New York: Peter Lang.

Richards, C. (2004) "What are we? Adolescence, Sex and Intimacy in *Buffy the Vampire Slayer,*" *Continuum: Journal of Media and Cultural Studies,* Vol 18 No 1, 121–137.

Richards, C. (2005a) "Translations: Encounters with Popular Film and Academic Discourse," *European Journal of Cultural Studies,* Vol 8 No 1, February 23–43.

Richards, C. (2005b) "Securing the Self: Risk and Aspiration in the Post-16 Curriculum," *British Journal of the Sociology of Education,* Vol 26 No 5, November. 613–625.

Richards, C. (2006) "In the wake of Hendrix: reflections on a life after death" in Homan, S. (Ed.), *Access All Eras: Tribute Bands and Global Pop Cultures*, Milton Keynes: Open University Press.

Richards, C. (2007) "Addressing 'Young Adults'? The Case of Francesca Lia Block" in Matthews, N. and Moody, N. (Eds.), *Judging a Book by Its Cover: Fans, Publishers, Designers, and the Marketing of Fiction*, Aldershot and Burlington, VT: Ashgate.

Rose, J. (1984) *The Case of Peter Pan or The Impossibility of Children's Fiction*, London: Macmillan.

Rosen, M. (1997) "*Junk* and Other Realities: The Tough World of Children's Literature," *The English and Media Magazine,* Vol 37 Autumn, 4–6.

Sarland, C. (1991) *Young People Reading: Culture and Response*, Milton Keynes: Open University Press.

Savage, M. (2000) *Class Analysis and Social Transformation*, Buckingham: Open University Press.

Searle, C. (Ed.) (1971) *Stepney Words*, London: Centerprise.

Searle, C. (Ed.) (1977) *The World in a Classroom*, London: Writers and Readers Publishing Cooperative.

Sefton-Green, J. (Ed.) (1998) *Digital Diversions: Youth Culture in the Age of Multimedia*, London: UCL Press.

Sefton-Green, J. and Sinker, R. (Eds.) (2000) *Evaluating Creativity: Making and Learning by Young People*, London: Routledge.

Shank, B. (1994) *Dissonant Identities: The Rock'n'Roll Scene in Austin, Texas*, Hanover, N.H.: Wesleyan University Press.

Skeggs, B. (1997a) *Formations of Class and Gender: Becoming Respectable*, London: Sage.

Skeggs, B. (1997b) "Classifying Practices: Representations, Capitals and Recognitions" in Mahony, P. and Zmroczek, C. (Eds.), *Class Matters: "Working-Class" Women's Perspectives on Social Class*, London: Taylor and Francis.

Skeggs, B. (2004) *Class, Self, Culture*, London: Routledge.

Slater, D. (1997) *Consumer Culture and Modernity*, Cambridge: Polity.

Slobin, M. (1993) *Subcultural Sounds: Micromusics of the West*, Hanover, NH: Wesleyan University Press.

Smith, D. (2005) "Writing Frankly, Young-Adult Author Pushes Limits," *The New York Times,* February 23.

Snyder, Gary (1999) *The Gary Snyder Reader: Prose, Poetry and Translations*, Washington D.C.: Counterpoint.

Snyder, I. (Ed.) (2002) *Silicon Literacies: Communication, Innovation and Education in the Electronic Age*, London: Routledge.

South, J. (Ed.) (2003) Buffy the Vampire Slayer *and Philosophy: Fear and Trembling in Sunnydale*, Chicago, IL: Open Court.

Stebbins, R. A. (2007) *Serious Leisure: A Perspective for Our Time*, New Brunswick, NJ: Transaction Publishers.

Stern, S. (1999) "Adolescent Girls' Expression on Web Home Pages: Spirited, Sombre and Self-Conscious Sites," *Convergence: The International Journal of Research into New Media Technologies,* Vol 5 No 4, Winter, 22–41.

Stern, S. (2002) "Virtually Speaking: Girls' Self-Disclosure on the WWW," *Women's Studies in Communication,* Vol 25 No 2, 223–231.

Stoehr, Shelley (1991; 2003) *Crosses*, Lincoln, NE: iUniverse, Inc.

Stoker, Bram (1995) *Dracula*, Koln: Konemann (Originally published 1897).

Stothard, Anna (2003) *Isabel and Rocco*, London: Arrow/Random House.

Susina, J. (2002) "The Rebirth of the Postmodern Flaneur: Notes on the Postmodern Landscape of Francesca Lia Block's *Weetzie Bat*," *Marvels and Tales: Journal of Fairy-Tale Studies*, Vol 16 No 2, 188-200. Detroit: Wayne State University Press.

Symonds, G. (2005) "A Little More Soul Than is Written: James Marsters' Performance of Spike and the Ambiguity of Evil in Sunnydale," *Slayage: Online Journal of Buffy Studies,* No 16.

Tate, G. (1992) "White Magic: Don De Lillo's Intelligence Networks," in *Flyboy in the Buttermilk: Essays on Contemporary America*, New York: Fireside/Simon and Schuster.

Thornton, S. (1995) *Club Cultures - Music, Media and Subcultural Capital*, Cambridge: Polity Press.

Tonkin, B. (2001) "Entropy as Demon: Buffy in Southern California" in Kaveney, R. (Ed.), *Reading the Vampire Slayer: An Unofficial Critical Companion to* Buffy *and* Angel, London and New York: Tauris Parke.

Trites, R. S. (2000) *Disturbing the Universe: Power and Repression in Adolescent Literature*, Iowa City: University of Iowa Press.

Turnbull, S. (2003) "Teaching *Buffy*: the Curriculum and the Text in Media Studies," *Continuum: Journal of Media and Cultural Studies,* Vol 17 No 1, 19–31.

Usher, R. (1998) "The Story of the Self: Education, Experience and Autobiography" in Erben, M. (Ed.), *Biography and Education: A Reader*, London: Falmer Press.

Vonnegut, K. (1973/1975) *Breakfast of Champions*, St.Albans: Panther.

Walkerdine, V. (1986) "Video Replay: Families, Films and Fantasy" in Burgin, V., Donald, J., and Kaplan, C. (Eds.), *Formations of Fantasy*, London: Routledge and Kegan Paul.

Wasp, D. (Ed.) (1978) *Jealousy and Other Stories*, Walton-on-Thames: Thomas Nelson and Sons.

Weedon, C. (2004) *Identity and Culture: Narratives of Difference and Belonging*, Maidenhead: Open University Press.

Weeks, J. (1995) *Invented Moralities: Sexual Values in an Age of Uncertainty*, Cambridge: Polity.

Wilcox, R. (2005) *Why Buffy Matters: The Art of Buffy the Vampire Slayer*, New York: I.B.Tauris.

Wilcox, R. and Lavery, D. (Eds.) (2002) *Fighting the Forces: What's at Stake in* Buffy the Vampire Slayer, Lanham, MD: Rowman and Littlefield.

Wilhelm, E. (2006) "Saving the World, One Mouseclick at a Time: A Report from the World Summit on the Information Society," *Voice of Youth Advocates,* April, 20-23. Lanham: MD: Scarecrow Press.

Williams, L. (1990) *Hard Core: Power, Pleasure, and the "Frenzy of the Visible,"* London: Pandora Press.

Williamson, M. (2005) *The Lure of the Vampire: Gender, Fiction and Fandom from Bram Stoker to Buffy*, London: Wallflower Press.

Willis, P. (1977) *Learning to Labour: How Working-Class Kids Get Working-Class Jobs*, London: Saxon House.

Willis, Paul (2000) *The Ethnographic Imagination*, Cambridge: Polity.

Willis, P., with Jones, S., Canaan, J., and Hurd, G. (1990) *Common Culture: Symbolic Work at Play in the Everyday Cultures of the Young*, Buckingham: Open University Press.

Wolff, Tobias (1990) *This Boy's Life*, New York: Harper Collins.

Wolff, Tobias, (1999) *This Boy's Life*, London: Bloomsbury.

Woodin, T. (2005) "Building Culture from the Bottom up: The Educational Origins of the Federation of Worker Writers and Community Publishers," *History of Education,* Vol 34 No 4, July, 345–363.

Zipes, J. (1983) *Fairy Tales and the Art of Subversion*, Heinemann Educational Books.

Zipes, J. (2001) *Sticks and Stones: The Troublesome Success of Children's Literature from Slovenly Peter to Harry Potter*, New York: Routledge.

Television

Angel USA WB 1999-2004

Episodes cited:

Season 1: *I Will Remember You* Episode 8 Written by David Greenwalt and Rennine Renshaw, Diected by David Grossman

Season 5: *Not Fade Away* Episode 22 Written by Jeffrey Bell and Joss Whedon, Directed by Jeffrey Bell

Buffy the Vampire Slayer USA, WB (1997-2001), UPN (2001-2003) Executive Producer Joss Whedon

Episodes cited:

Season 1

Teacher's Pet Episode 4 Written by David Greenwalt, Directed by Bruce Seth Green
Never Kill a Boy on the First Date, Episode 5 Written by Rob Des Hotel and Dean Batali, Directed by David Semel
Angel Episode 7 Written by David Greenwalt, Directed by Scott Brazil
Out of Mind, Out of Sight Episode 11 Teleplay by Ashley Gable and Thomas A. Swyden, Story by Joss Whedon, Directed by Reza Badiyi
Prophecy Girl Episode 12 Written and Directed by Joss Whedon

Season 2

Inca Mummy Girl Episode 4 Written by Matt Kiene and John Reinkemeyer, Directed by Ellen S. Pressman
Reptile Boy Episode 5 Written and Directed by David Greenwalt
Lie to Me Episode 7 Written and Directed by Joss Whedon

What's My Line? Part 1 Episode 9 Written by Howard Gordon and Marti Noxon, Directed by David Solomon
What's My Line? Part 2 Episode 10 Written by Marti Noxon, Directed by David Semel
Ted Episode 11 Written by David Greenwalt and Joss Whedon, Directed by Bruce Seth Green
Bad Eggs, Episode 12 Written by Marti Noxon, Directed by David Greenwalt
Becoming Part 2 Episode 22 Written and Directed by Joss Whedon

Season 3

Anne Episode 1 Written and Directed by Joss Whedon
Beauty and the Beasts Episode 4 Written by Marti Noxon, Directed by James Whitmore Jnr.
Lover's Walk Episode 8 Written by Dan Vebber, Directed by David Semel
Amends Episode 10 Written and Directed by Joss Whedon
Gingerbread Episode 11 Teleplay by Jane Espenson, Story by Thania St. John and Jane Espenson, Directed by James Whitmore Jnr.
The Zeppo Episode 13 Written by Dan Vebber, Directed by James Whitmore Jnr.
Graduation Day Part 2 Episode 22 Written and Directed by Joss Whedon

Season 4

The Harsh Light of Day Episode 3 Written by Jane Espenson, Directed by James A. Contner

Season 5

The Replacement Episode 3 Written by Jane Espenson, Directed by James A. Contner
Blood Ties Episode 13 Written by Steven S. DeKnight, Directed by Michael Gershman

Season 6

After Life Episode 3 Written by Jane Espenson, Directed by David Solomon
Flooded Episode 4 Written by Douglas Petrie and Jane Espenson, Directed by Douglas Petrie
Life Serial Episode 5 Written by David Fury and Jane Espenson, Directed by Nick Marck
Once More, with Feeling Episode 7 Written and Directed by Joss Whedon
Smashed Episode 9 Written by Drew Z. Greenberg, Directed by Turi Meyer
Dead Things Episode 13 Written by Steven S. DeKnight, Directed by James A. Contner
Hell's Bells Episode 16 Written by Rebecca Rand Kirshner, Directed by David Solomon
Seeing Red Episode 19 Written by Steven S. DeKnight, Directed by Michael Gershman
Villians Episode 20 Written by Marti Noxon, Directed by David Solomon
Two to Go Episode 21 Written by Douglas Petrie, Directed by Bill Norton

Season 7

Beneath You Episode 2 Written by Douglas Petrie, Directed by Nick Marck
Same Time, Same Place Episode 3 Written by Jane Espenson, Directed by James A. Contner
Lies My Parents Told Me Episode 17 Written by David Fury and Drew Goddard, Directed by David Fury
Chosen Episode 22 Written and Directed by Joss Whedon

The Lost Boys (1987) DVD Warner Bros. Entertainment Inc. 2004

Index